THE
DBT
SKILLS
WORKBOOK
FOR TEENS

3 BOOKS IN 1

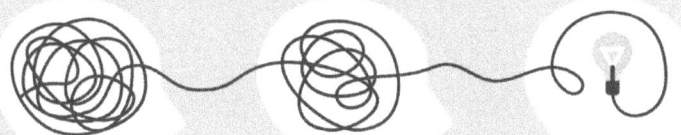

A Complete Guide For Helping Teens With
Anger Management, Developing Mindfulness, Coping
with Anxiety, and Building Self-Regulation Skills

M.A. MARTINE

DISCLAIMER NOTICE

Please note the information contained within this document is for educational and entertainment purposes only. All effort has been executed to present accurate, up to date, reliable, complete information. No warranties of any kind are declared or implied. Readers acknowledge that the author is not engaged in the rendering of legal, financial, medical or professional advice. The content within this book has been derived from various sources. Please consult a licensed professional before attempting any techniques outlined in this book.

By reading this document, the reader agrees that under no circumstances is the author responsible for any losses, direct or indirect, that are incurred as a result of the use of the information contained within this document, including, but not limited to, errors, omissions, or inaccuracies.

GET THIS EXCLUSIVE

5-minute Audio Guided Meditation

*To help safely **MANAGE YOUR TEEN'S** sudden emotional meltdown.*

and more mindfulness resources...

JOURNALS & SELF-CARE PLANERS

COLORING BOOKS

SCAN QR CODE TO GET YOUR COPY

TABLE OF CONTENTS

BOOK 1 -
ANGER MANAGEMENT & MINDFULNESS

TABLE OF CONTENTS

TABLE OF CONTENTS

TABLE OF CONTENTS

TABLE OF CONTENTS

BOOK 2 - ANXIETY RECOVERY

TABLE OF CONTENTS

TABLE OF CONTENTS

TABLE OF CONTENTS

TABLE OF CONTENTS

BOOK 3 -
ADHD

TABLE OF CONTENTS

TABLE OF CONTENTS

THE DBT SKILLS WORKBOOK FOR TEENS

ANGER MANAGEMENT

Essential coping skills to manage angry outbursts and gain self control through effective self-regulation

M.A. MARTINE

INTRODUCTION

I t started like any other day, but it ended excitingly uncomfortable after taking a vastly more disruptive turn. I found myself on the precipice of transformation. It was the day when it all came tumbling down like a ton of bricks. All the slammed doors and the splinters of broken glasses or mugs—whatever were the closest that moment when my anger became so intolerable, I knew throwing something was the only way to decompress—that left a trail of destruction from my teenage years, right up to my early 20s.

While it was evident that my anger was getting out of control long before I turned 16, the most memories I have of my behavior being erratic and fueled with rage is from the year I was that age. I think what made it even worse that year was the idea of it being my "sweet 16," and I couldn't identify anything sweet to the age or me being that age.

I hated school, I hated my family, and I had no friends and hated that too. But, then again, I wasn't that fond of people either, so heaven knows why I hated not having friends. Even then, that wasn't the worst part of my life. I could remove myself from all those things—escape them as I often did, sitting, simmering in my own misery behind closed doors in my room. What I couldn't run from, which made me probably hate it even more, was myself. I remember looking in the mirror, and I couldn't see anything about myself that I liked no matter how I searched. Mom would say, "You have such beautiful hair," or, "Your skin is so healthy," but it meant absolutely nothing to me. I couldn't see it, and it felt like she pitied me. I just knew that I hated my appearance, thought my skills were useless, and couldn't even stand hearing my voice.

Let's just say that much hating happened during my teenage years. For the longest time, I thought I was a harsh & intolerable person with no emotion to express other than anger.

It was only much later that I learned that anger is often nothing other than a blanket used to cover an immense pain rooted so deep inside that it seems impossible to reach. A pain without cause or reason &, therefore, so much harder to ease. I remember thinking—no, knowing—that someone would hurt me, disappoint me, or—the worst—reject me. But I refused to allow that to happen to me, so I turned to anger. See, if you reject them first, they cannot reject you.

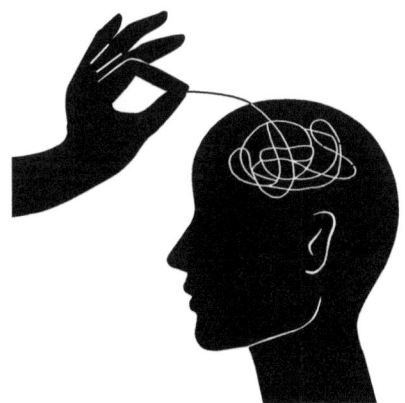

STANDING ON THE PRECIPICE OF TRANSFORMATION

I remember that day well when I couldn't do it anymore. See, when you allow a raging fire of anger to burn inside you for too long, it ravishes all that keeps you upright and offers stability, and then one day, you collapse. I am unsure whether, on the day I collapsed, the debris of my being also extinguished the raging fire within or if perhaps there was nothing more left to burn. So, I started to seek a way out of the ash and smoke of my smoldering existence.

It all happened by chance. I had to escape, and I walked out of my apartment, out of another relationship, another dream to die on its own as I wandered the streets of my neighborhood. It was cold, so I grabbed a coffee from the local vendor. We were familiar with each other as regular clients sometimes turn into friends, and he introduced me to his friend chatting at his stand. She was pretty, but I found her kindness uncomfortable and didn't know what to say. It didn't matter, she started talking, and strangely enough, she didn't stop until she got me hooked on a thing called dialectical behavior therapy (DBT). When I walked away from her—finally—I couldn't forget our conversation. I wanted to know more. She was a starry-eyed student in her field, and her passion for her subject was so contagious that even miserable me caught on. For the first time in my life, it felt like maybe things could be different.

Now, almost a decade later, I know that day was my crossroad day. It was the day when a stranger saved me from myself. I've never seen her again, not even bumped into her by accident. But what she did for me was introduce me to a therapy that changed my life. Her passion for helping others attracted my interest to the point where I was keen to learn more. I studied everything I could find about emotional intelligence, anger management, and how mindfulness can transform your life. I've read more than 100 books on the topic in 1 year and devoured every video I could find to watch.

Each time I completed working through another bit of information, I would diligently apply the skills and techniques I'd learned. I wouldn't stop until I could fix every cognitive distortion overshadowing my life—yep, eventually, I became familiar with terms to describe the challenges I was facing more elegantly. DBT became more than my lifeline with which I could pull myself out of the misery I referred to as my "life." It also turned into my life purpose, my passion.

MEET ME AT THE CROSSROAD

Today, I am helping many other teens discover their anger's underlying causes. These teenagers have so much in common with the teenage version of me, a person who was in so much pain, even though there was no apparent reason for me to be angry. It was also a version of me who was destructive & hurtful with my words and actions.

My journey required intensive reading and self-study. I am grateful that I was introduced to this type of therapy by a random stranger in a random act, putting a stop to my familiar routine of discarding all that was precious before it was time to let go of it. I will never be able to make it up to the coffee-stand girl who scooped me up emotionally when I was at my lowest, but I can—and I did—commit myself to formulating all the snippets of information into a unity that is easy to understand. It is this unity of knowledge, a collection of practical skills and steps, that I am presenting to you. As you progress through the pages, you'll notice subtle changes. You'll become aware of how the anger dissipates to make room for other emotions. Once you acknowledge these emotions, you can finally process them and let go of the burden they lay upon you.

However, if you know someone, a teenager engulfed in unidentified emotions that they reflect as anger, this book will also bring you the necessary tools you seek to help them. Over the past 12 years, I've been diligently working towards finding the most practical approach to present the knowledge I know will make a difference to your life, as it did to mine and the lives of the many patients I've seen as a clinical psychologist. I started to have conversations with therapists working with teenagers, and the ideas we shared inspired me to present the information so that this book can also be a helpful tool to the therapist who's agonizing over the lack of progress they are making in their sessions too.

There is one thing I regret, though: losing so much time wandering without purpose and being angry without a cause. Most of my teenage years are trapped in one dark and dreary blur.

Time is precious and limited, and we never know when the last day for you or a dear loved one will come. I know now that I would hate it if time had run out on me before I could gain control over my emotions and, subsequently, my life.

I don't know where you are on your journey in life, whether you are ready to let go of your anger and improve how you manage your emotions. I don't know if you seek a solution and the process found this book. Nor do I know if this book randomly landed in your field of interest, like I unknowingly stumbled into the answers I've been seeking entirely randomly. You need to determine whether you are ready to make that change, let go of your anger, and free yourself from the hurt. It doesn't require any significant changes in your life. But, through consistent minor changes, you will gradually start to experience a shift of epic proportions as you steadily begin to levitate toward a life of contentment, joy, satisfaction, hope, & anticipation over the future.

Are you at your crossroad? Is now a good time to unfold the possibilities of your future? Let's take the first step to exiting the familiar emotional turmoil.

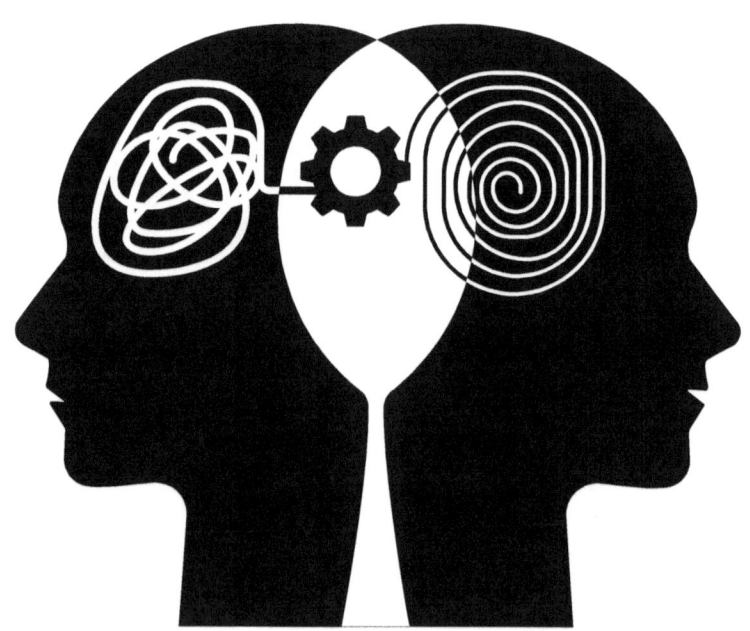

CHAPTER 1: ANGER AND YOU

> 66 Where there is anger, there is always pain underneath. 99
> — Eckhart Tolle

Do you sometimes feel guilty for being angry so often? The emotion of anger is often vilified by the wider population. It almost comes across as perfectly normal to feel any other emotion—and you may even be encouraged to be more in tune with these emotions—as long as it is not anger, for being angry is "bad." That is not the case at all. Anger is just another emotion like sadness, joy, excitement, or jealousy—the latter which doesn't even have as bad a reputation as anger. This tendency is often explained that anger has a bad reputation due to how angry people behave while in this state. Of course, this is a questionable statement too, for have you ever seen how erratic someone overcome with jealousy can be?

But let's stop tripling around the emotion's reputation & jump right in to explore what anger is.

DEFINING ANGER

After consulting a few expert definitions of anger, it is safe to attach the following attributes to the emotion.

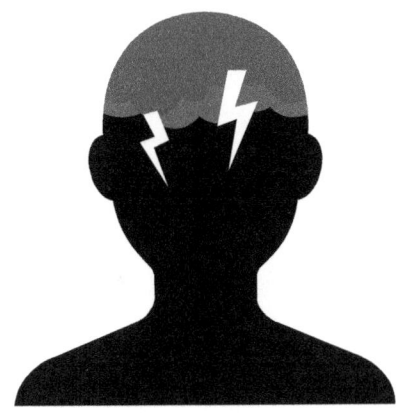

Anger is an intense human emotion, often causing a great sense of animosity towards someone or something. It is often accompanied by irritation, frustration, annoyance, hostility, and an increased level of stress. It is an emotion everyone feels at some time in their lives—some more often than others.

Anger is often triggered by emotional pain but can also result from being disturbed, interrupted, or threatened. Anger can present itself in various degrees of severity.

Up to this point, these attributes are still aligned with the characteristics of most other negative emotions.

The difference comes in the last characteristic of anger that I need to highlight: If anger is not managed well, it can lead to erratic behavior, stepping over the boundaries of what is socially acceptable to the point where you are making yourself guilty of criminality.

DANNY'S STORY

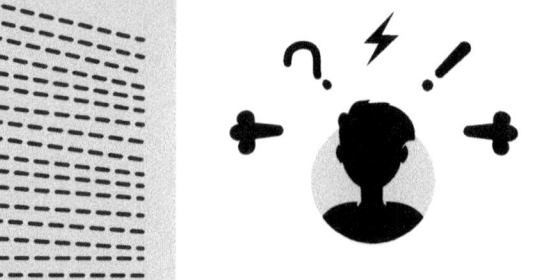

Danny's entire team has already left the changing rooms and is probably almost home, but he is still sitting on the bench stuck in his gear.

Football is his life. It was the one thing his dad taught him before he got sick. It is the only reason he comes to school and works hard on his subjects to get good grades, just to stay on the team.

His phone beeping distracts his thoughts. He realizes how late it is and that he needs to get home. Now, he has to tell his mother and younger brother what a failure he is. Danny gets up, and as he does, his anger breaks loose while he remains incapable of taking control. The janitor walked in on the mess; every mirror in the changing room was shattered on the floor. It is also where he finds Danny huddling over his broken hand. The pain that shuddered through every single bone from the impact when his hand made a dent in his locker door brought the destruction to an end.

> an also have another outcome.

His phone beeping distracts his thoughts. He realizes how late it is and that he needs to get home. Now, he has to tell his mother and younger brother he isn't playing on Saturday. As he takes his gear off, his mind is consumed, searching for solutions to his problem. He'll check in with Coach about why he isn't playing and ask him for extra exercises to improve his game. He'll just have to practice more, work harder, and make Coach see that the team needs him. That will make his dad proud. That is what he'll tell his mother and little bro.

The two versions of Danny's story teach us one more valuable lesson about anger: We have the choice to use our rage destructively or constructively. The outcome you choose will depend on how well you can manage your anger as well as your capability to recognize the underlying causes of why you are responding in this manner.

WHAT IS YOUR ANGER TYPE?

For some, the topic of the number of ways how anger manifests is still a lively debate. While some experts state the correct number is 8, others distinguish 12 types of anger. I prefer to highlight the following 10 types, and I encourage you to explore each type discerningly to determine with which you identify the most vividly.

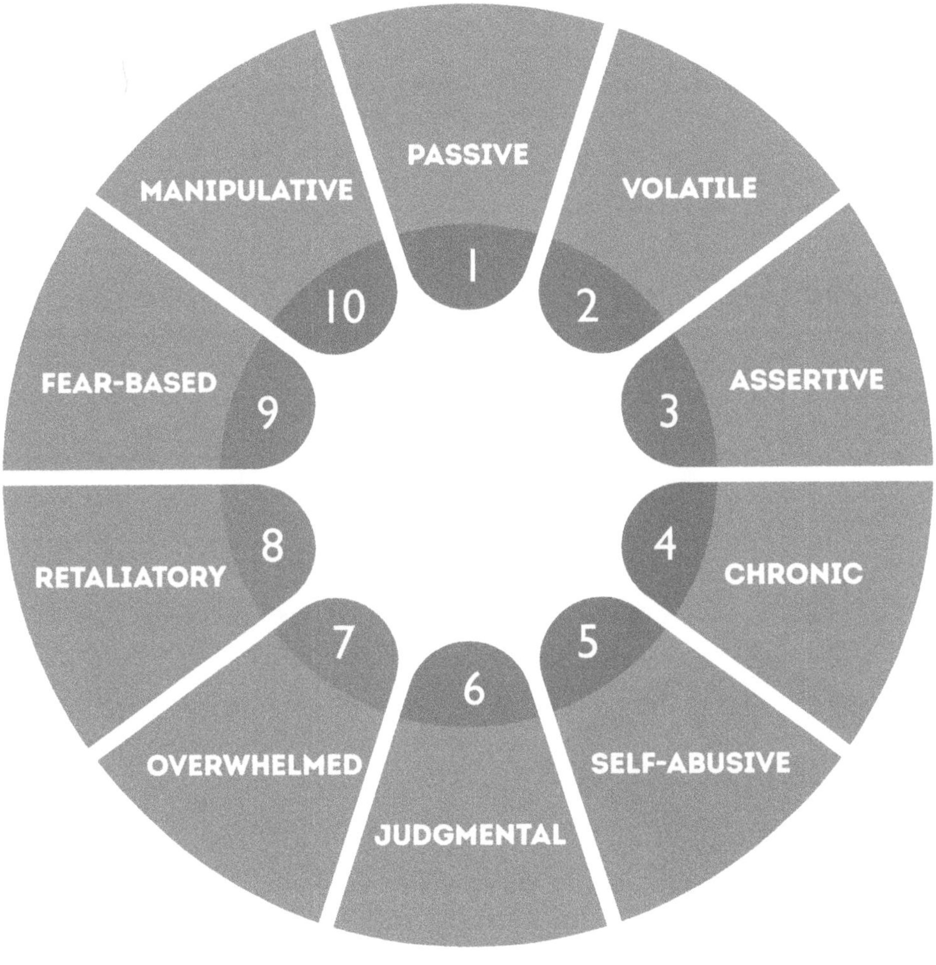

PASSIVE
1

VOLATILE
2

MANIPULATIVE
10

ASSERTIVE
3

FEAR-BASED
9

CHRONIC
4

RETALIATORY
8

SELF-ABUSIVE
5

OVERWHELMED
7

JUDGMENTAL
6

1. PASSIVE

Passive anger can be hard to distinguish as it doesn't manifest similarly to most other forms of aggression. It is not accompanied by a significant outburst of emotions, but it can be extremely hostile. The person who is passively angry reverts to sarcasm, being purposefully forgetful, dragging their feet to get things done, or may revert to a range of other ways to express their anger without being upfront about it. This type of anger is often internalized and can therefore be highly toxic to the angry person. Typical behaviors identified with this type of anger include binge eating, excessive drinking, panic attacks, and even self-harm. It is the opposite of the following kind of anger—volatile anger. In volatile anger, the angry person takes out their rage externally, but for the passive-aggressive person, the rage occurs internally.

2. VOLATILE

Typically, this person would make it clear to all that they are angry, and they do this by portraying explosive behavior. We find this type of anger right on the other end of the spectrum from passive anger, as here, the angry person isn't internalizing any rage at the moment they explode. Still, these explosions can be caused by prolonged suppression of their emotions. Like a volcano, they will be brewing underneath the surface for quite some time and then explode entirely unpredictably. This explosion can be triggered by something insignificant; typically, they cool down rapidly after letting off their steam. Danny's volatile and destructive explosion in the changing rooms has a lot resembling this type of anger outburst.

3. ASSERTIVE

Assertive anger is widely considered to be the most constructive form of anger. The feelings that immerse during this type of anger are usually applied constructively to bring about change to the situation, causing frustration, irritation, or any other negative emotion. We seldom witness confrontations, physical outbursts, or even internalization of this anger, as the angered person applies the energy of their anger constructively. Danny's portrayal of rage in the second version of his story can be classified as assertive anger.

4. CHRONIC

Many parents of teenagers would claim they are dealing with this type of anger in their homes. It is the type of anger that seems persistently present and can manifest as irritation and frustration with others and yourself. Rather than witnessing severe and abrupt outbursts, the person with chronic anger appears to be constantly in a bad mood, giving even those who are merely innocent bystanders in their life a piece of their mind. While no anger ever positively impacts your overall well-being, it is particularly bad as it keeps the angered individual in this state for a prolonged period.

5. SELF-ABUSIVE

We find guilt and shame at the core of this type of anger. Together with low self-esteem, the circle of negativity continues to expand, becoming more profound and affecting more parts of the person's life and, eventually, their health and well-being. At times, the angry person may react and have an outburst, increasing the isolation and guilt already burdening them. Other ways the angry person may express their internal anger are through self-harm, negative self-talk, or eating disorders.

6. JUDGMENTAL

Considering themselves in a morally superior position, those suffering from judgmental anger perceive their anger as righteous. They will blast you with verbal criticism if you are the victim of their rage. They would consider you to be the one at fault for being or behaving unjustly, according to their moral compass.

While this is a harsh and often highly distorted form of anger, it can be applied constructively to bring about change in toxic situations. However, when you portray this kind of anger, your actions and approach towards others would likely serve as a tool to isolate you from others, causing you to lack social interaction and support. This type of anger is also closely linked to Asperger's syndrome and is a pretty common way for those on this spectrum to express their anger (Bajori, 2019).

7. OVERWHELMED

Depending on your outlook on life, it can be easy to agree that life is challenging at the best of times. If you are the kind of person who would rather see the cup half empty than half full, you would be more prone to experience this kind of anger. It is likely to reach a peak when you persistently feel overwhelmed and overstressed and when life is generally pressing down on you. Do you often think that life is just too demanding and that you don't have the energy to continue?

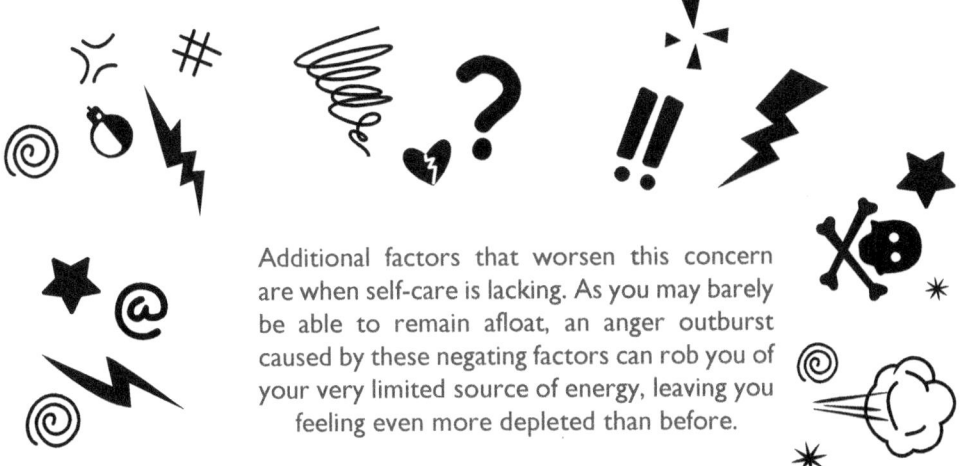

Additional factors that worsen this concern are when self-care is lacking. As you may barely be able to remain afloat, an anger outburst caused by these negating factors can rob you of your very limited source of energy, leaving you feeling even more depleted than before.

8. MANIPULATIVE

Anger can be used to get others to do what you want. You can come across as threatening when your angry outburst is highly volatile. Due to the fear you instill in those around you, they may be intimidated by you and comply with your demands only because they want to defuse the situation. Evidently, this is not a healthy situation to be in, as your relationships are somewhat toxic. The person using anger in their favor in this manner is always aware of the impact of their outbursts on others. However, they may not realize that people, even your loved ones, can only take so much before walking away from you, leaving you rejected by others due to how you utilize your anger to their detriment.

9. FEAR-BASED

While this specific type of anger is connected to fear alone, the mechanics of this kind of anger is very much the same for many other emotions that may leave you vulnerable. The choice you are making is, rather, to express your feelings in the form of fear, as it hurts less than acknowledging that you are scared, hurt, lonely, or any other negative emotion that you are concerned may cause you to come across as weak. Examples of this kind of anger are when you see how a younger sibling runs across the road and is almost hit by a car; instead of expressing gratitude for making it across fine, you shout at them for being stupid. Or, when you are feeling hurt by a friend for blowing you off on the plans you were looking forward to, you become mean towards the friend and may even be a little passive-aggressive not to admit that you are feeling hurt by what they did.

10. RETALIATORY

This kind of anger is based on the principle of an eye for an eye. You've made me angry by hurting me or taking something I treasure away from me, and now I'll get you back and take something from you. At the core of this kind of anger, we find the need to revenge for something that we perceive as dreadful that has happened. It can often present itself in purposeful actions as you try to get back at someone else. It is seldom that this kind of anger presents itself as an outburst. No, it is much more aligned with a subtle approach that may stretch over days, weeks, or even months as you plot your plan to get back at someone else.

Which of these 10 types of anger can you identify with in your life? You may experience a combination of different types of anger. But then again, it is also possible that you find yourself in a position where admitting to being guilty of any of these types is simply too hard to do right now. Openly admitting that you have an anger problem can be challenging. After all, it is one thing to be painfully aware that your anger is out of control when you are alone, but admitting it to others is entirely different. If you aren't ready yet to share this with anyone else, then do so in the privacy of your mind, just as long as you take the first and vital step of admitting the challenge you are facing as it is where your healing journey starts.

THE MOST COMMON TRIGGERS OF ANGER

 Anger triggers are no different than any other type of emotional trigger. These triggers can be insignificant, sparking an emotional response in the person.

Triggers can also take on various forms: from scents or aromas; to music or sounds; images; experiences; or anything else that awakens a memory of a bad experience or reminds you of someone, causing a deep and intense emotional experience. In the case of anger triggers, the particular emotion is always anger.

By understanding that these triggers exist and have a negative effect on you and by identifying your unique triggers, you can start to address them more constructively. While some may prefer to avoid exposure to these triggers at all costs—and it may be helpful to a certain degree—it is not necessarily the most wholesome approach to the matter. Effectively, you are not resolving anything and are merely limiting your life, as it may happen that you rather avoid certain situations and rob yourself of experiences.

A much more effective approach is to determine the roots of these triggers and the underlying causes of concern, so that you can address these matters and disempower the trigger from the hold it has on your life.

Some of the most common examples of anger triggers are witnessing or experiencing any of the following:

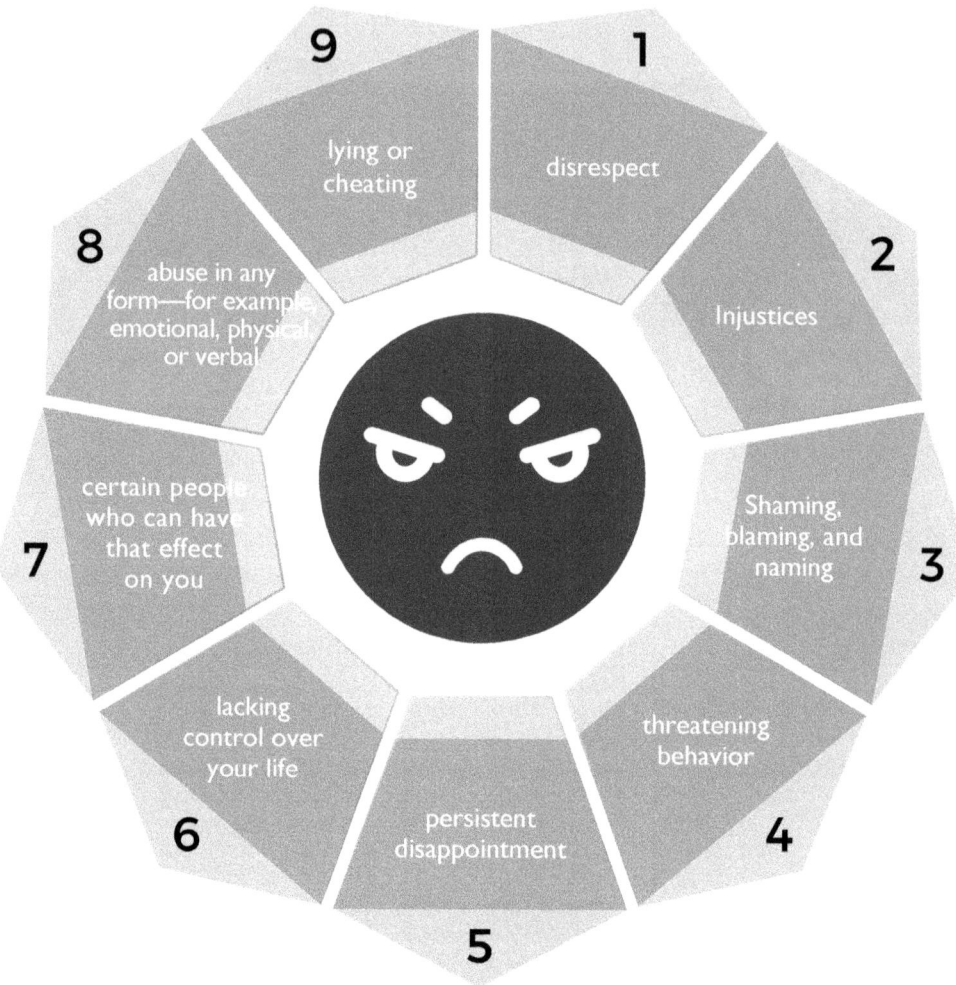

These triggers can originate in events that took place during our childhood years; past events; life experiences; our values & belief systems; or even from believing stories we are told.

An effective way to identify your triggers is by keeping a journal where you can record the anger outburst that you have had and by capturing the details of the events preceding your outburst. Once you've collected the details surrounding these events over a period, you'll be able to notice certain patterns; these will guide you to determine the common factors that were present before the event, usually identifying your triggers.

UNDERSTANDING THE ANGER CYCLE

When we are angry or even witness someone who is, it feels like anger is just one pool of steaming hot and melted emotions. It can be easy to be so overwhelmed at that moment that we struggle to see that anger is not one single event but a series of events or stages. The anger cycle is an umbrella term referring to this series of events or stages.

Once we can dissect the cycle into greater detail and learn how to identify in which stage we or those near to us are, we can change our approach and have a positive impact on the outcome. As we delve a little deeper into the mechanics of this cycle and how it all fits together, I want you to observe how every stage follows the previous in a very natural order, but also to be aware of the fact that during any of these stages, you can step in, change the course you are on, or impact the angered person in such a manner that the outcome can be completely different.

STAGE 1-TRIGGERED

The number of variables that serve as triggers is limitless. A trigger can be an event, a specific treatment, a reminder, or anything from various factors that trigger your anger. It is the initial phase where it all starts. As this is the primary stage of the anger cycle, it is also the most desired stage to put an end to it.

However, there is a saying that nobody notices when you are being provoked, only when you respond or react. It is most likely the most frustrating part of the entire anger cycle.

You are feeling provoked, often by the repeated comments or actions of another, and while you are being offended or treated unfairly, nobody comes to save you. They don't even notice what is happening to you and what you must endure. However, the moment you react, you have the entire room's attention.

One of the most common places where I've seen the frustration of not being noticed boil over into a hot mess, only to be seen once the person being provoked reacts, is in schools.

A bully can torment a child for a long time, and the bully's victim may take one knock on the chin after another, holding their composure. As they are only human, one day, they snap. That is the day when all chaos breaks loose, and instantly, the victim is made out to be the perpetrator while the bullied is considered the wronged one onto whom everyone rains their empathy.

STAGE 2-BUILDUP

This stage is trapped between the moment of being triggered and the response. It is a time when the anger escalates. Your thoughts become more negative. It is an emotional response that manifests physically too, as your eyes widen, eyebrows twist, muscles tense, and your tone of voice may go up a pitch or two. You can feel your heart beating faster, maybe there is a slight shiver in your hands, and your breathing becomes rapid. Remember that anger, like any other emotion, presents itself on all levels of your being.

This stage can last only for a few seconds or, in the case of the school bully tormenting you day after day for several weeks, it can have a much more gradual buildup. In the latter case, you may feel how anger rises in your physical being every time you walk into your school but manage to control these emotions. However, due to failing efforts to resolve the cause of your anger, the buildup only increases as time passes.

STAGE 3-EXPLOSION

When you arrive at this stage of the anger cycle, there is little chance of turning back—your mind and body are prepared to fight. As a matter of fact, fighting may seem the only solution to shake the tension that has your entire being in a grip.

The desire to seek relief that will restore your internal calm is so strong that all reason and rationality dissipate from the situation. You strike out, and the pressure is gone.

STAGE 4-RECOVERY

It's over. You've said what you had to say. You did what was necessary to relieve the buildup inside. Physically, your entire state returns to normal.

Adrenaline levels, heart rate, and blood pressure all return to normal, and as the biological equilibrium is restored, rationality and reason return, taking you to the next and final stage of the anger cycle: regret.

STAGE 5–REGRET

This is the stage where you come back to your senses. As you analyze the situation and determine what has just happened, why you were so out of control and blindly infuriated, it dawns on you with absolute clarity that there were different ways you could've resolved the matter. Regret is always too late. Now, you realize that you should've addressed the concern when you initially identified the trigger or realized that you were being provoked. You should've reported your bully to the school administration, discussed the matter with a school counselor, or addressed your concerns with your parents. While you believed you were strong enough to overcome the challenges of being triggered, you now know you were wrong.

One of the two most predominant mistakes we make regarding anger is to confuse it with aggression. In contrast with aggression, anger is a healthy emotion to experience if we manage it effectively. The second is that we underestimate how intense anger can be and to what extent it will override our rationale, principles, values, and beliefs if we don't manage it effectively.

Stage 1 remains the most desired and possibly effective time to take action and change your direction. This is true not only for your anger but also for stepping in and changing the outcome of someone else's anger.

DIGGING DEEPER

The secret to any successful relationship is having a fair balance between giving and taking. The success of this book is built on the same principle. There will be many times when I give of myself; my knowledge and experiences; and my recollections. But there will be times when you will need to give too. You need to do this by getting yourself a DBT diary. This can be an online document or an old-school journal to capture your thoughts. I promise to never ask you to start an entry in this journal with the old clichéd words, "Dear Diary...," but you need to promise to complete the writing assignments I do give, as there went a lot of thought into each of these to ensure you reap optimal benefits from reading this book. I want you to see concrete changes in your life and be able to effectively manage your anger when we go our separate ways.

In your DBT journal, reflect on an instance where you've been unforgiving in expressing your anger. Don't summarize the event; rather, expand on the details of what happened before you were triggered, what the trigger was, what thoughts went through your mind, how you blew off steam, the collateral damage you've caused, and that sinking feeling of regret you've felt afterward. Sit with your anger for a while. Nobody has ever conquered anything by running away from it, and now is the time to face your anger.

But I want you to go deeper too. While you are capturing your story, I want you to constantly ask yourself why you act in this manner and respond as you did. I want you to delve into the underlying emotions that surfaced as anger. By dissecting your anger, you'll get familiar with it, and this familiarity is the starting point of our journey. Enjoy the process.

CHAPTER 2: INTRODUCING MINDFULNESS

> 66
> Mindfully recognizing being overwhelmed already reduces the feeling of being overwhelmed
> 99
>
> — *Lilian Cheung*

So, what is DBT, or dialectical behavior therapy? Maybe you've already made the connection between the word dialectical and talking. If this is the case, you likely assume that the therapy has something to do with using speech to change behavior. If so, then you are almost spot on. DBT is a type of talk therapy to help ease the intensity with which you experience emotions. While it has initially been used as a type of therapy to address several major psychological concerns—like post-traumatic stress disorder (PTSD), borderline personality disorder (BPD), suicidal behavior, self-harm, and even depression and anxiety—the benefit of this type of therapy quickly became evident to address other concerns too.

We can say that DBT is a leg of another type of therapy: cognitive behavioral therapy (CBT). CBT specifically focuses on providing those who are experiencing intense emotions with a way to better identify what they are feeling, accept these feelings even when it is tough to do so, learn how to manage these emotions effectively, and then also teach the skills needed to make changes that will benefit your overall well-being.

What sets DBT apart from CBT is that in CBT, you'll learn how to change your current habits and beliefs, or, simply put, your known ways to improve how you think and consequently behave. DBT takes this one step further, a step many consider contradictory. DBT does all the above mentioned as part of CBT, but it also teaches the necessary skills to accept yourself for who you are. So, here you'll learn both acceptance of the self and the skills to change the self to become more of the person you want to be. This is vital, so let's pause for a moment. I hear you ask how I accept myself as I am and change myself simultaneously, and your question is entirely valid.

Whether you are cooking a meal from a recipe or solving a problem as part of a math or science assignment, you first need to understand and grasp the content you are working with before you can make any improvements. Similarly, you first need to understand yourself—something that truly only happens once you've gained an appreciation for who you are—to be able to make any changes.

Let's make this more practical and assume you need to be more carefree. You sometimes find yourself looking at your peers and thinking, How can they laugh so freely? Why don't they feel as pressured as I do? Why are they so confident in who they are? Why does everyone else seem to have a load of fun all the time, and I just don't? Then, the desire to be more carefree begins to rise within. Now, you want to be carefree and may even pretend to be more like the others. Yet, it is not authentic, for you only hold up a front. See, there are times when we can fake it until we make it, but this is not one of those times. To experience the same emotional freedom and joyous contentment you observe in others, you first need to understand why you are not naturally leaning in that direction. You have to understand and accept yourself first. Once you comprehend why you are the way you are, you can work effectively to create the desired outcome. That is, why you must accept yourself comes first, and then learning the tools to be more like you want comes easier.

What will DBT expect of you? Even though it doesn't feel that way, you are the master pulling the puppet strings of your life. You are the only one with the power to change who you are. Based on that knowledge, DBT, or any other type of therapy, will only be as effective in helping you if you are committed to change. Thus, DBT works best if you are amped to change for the positive by applying yourself without reservation to therapy and homework assignments and by shifting your focus from the past to the present moment and future. You'll also benefit from attending group sessions where you can connect with others experiencing similar challenges.

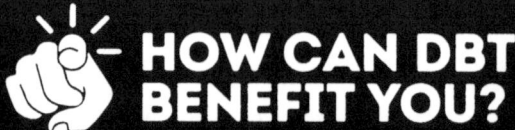

HOW CAN DBT BENEFIT YOU?

Maybe we live in a skeptical world, or maybe we don't, but I've also been an angry teenager not too long ago. I know that skepticism easily becomes the tool we use to keep ourselves from getting pulled into matters demanding stepping outside our comfort zones. So, I want you to be skeptical, for once you've got the answers you are looking for, your level of commitment to DBT will be much higher.

The best place to start is to explore what DBT looks like. At the core of DBT and what sets it apart from other forms of therapy is that it focuses on methods to find a balance between accepting oneself and changing who you are. This is achieved by teaching skills, making both desired treatment outcomes possible.

DBT can be presented as individual therapy sessions, group sessions, consultations, phone coaching, or skills training classes. While your journey with DBT doesn't have to include all these alleys toward success, it will likely consist of more than one route to achieving your desired success.

As DBT has already early on shown immensely positive results as a medium to resolve several concerns teenagers are dealing with, it has been adapted to address particular concerns surfacing during this developmental stage of life. The most noticeable difference between DBT for adults and teenagers is that the adapted version for teenagers focuses on including parents or other caregivers—even family sessions aren't uncommon in this approach. Soon, professionals in the field realized that through the involvement of caregivers, the results achieved by the form of therapy turned out to be much more effective.

Now that you have a better idea of how DBT is presented, we can move on to exploring the techniques used. The type of therapy mainly centers around several methods:

Validation: It teaches how to validate feelings. I would describe this as the basis of DBT, as it is essential to learning the skills needed to understand and validate your feelings and those of others. Even when you are wrapped in conflict, it remains vital to honor the emotions, thoughts, and actions you bring to the conversation and those of the other person, regardless of who they are.

Behavioral change: Once validation takes place, it is easier to change behavior. However, it is not only a case of behavior that needs to change. These changes should also take place in such a manner that it is sustainable. Change without sustainability is futile.

Conversation: Another component of validation is that it requires a conversation that flows from both opposing sides. It means you must verbally express your thoughts and feelings and offer the other person the opportunity to do the same.

Acceptance: This becomes much easier when you accept yourself for who you are. This is where mindfulness comes in as a critical component of the process, as greater self-awareness is achieved through mindfulness.

Mindfulness: The term mindfulness is often confusing to those who have never been introduced to the concept. Mindfulness doesn't come naturally in the world we are living in, as we are mostly surrounded by a busy environment aiming to attract our attention. When we allow any other force to consume our minds, we lose focus on what we are feeling, hearing, experiencing, or even seeing in the present moment. Social media and the constant influx of information through excessive online time are some of the most known forces distracting our attention. Yet, it also happens while walking in the streets of our neighborhoods, cities, or even in the passages at school where there is an overstimulation of the senses. We live in an age where there are so many outside forces for which sustainability depends on how well it can attract our attention and get our buy-in to what it offers. It steals our focus, robs our time, and prevents living and experiencing the present moment.

How does all of this happen? Let me give you a practical example of how these forces rob you of the opportunity to be mindful. Think back to when you were having a snack or meal at your computer or browsing on your phone. Whether interacting on social media or chats, or watching a movie, a favored series, or just clips, your mind was consumed with what was happening on the screen.

Were you able to taste the food you were eating? You may have finished a plate without ever noticing the texture of the food. It is when we can go through an entire bag of chips without ever taking notice of the flavor, the crunch between our teeth, or the salty taste it has. When it happens, you know that you were robbed of being mindful.

Mindfulness demands that you slow down, shift your focus to the present moment, and simply experience every stimulus from your current environment. It means that when you eat, you notice the flavors and colors of your food and the texture it has in your mouth. When you are walking to school, feel the wind on your cheeks and notice the new green growth on the trees marking the start of a different season. Or, when you shower, feel the warm sensation of the water on your skin or the smooth, soapy lather of your shampoo or soap.

When you've accomplished a greater proficiency in all these skills and techniques, you'll be able to find the golden midway. Wandering on the middle path means seeing both sides of the story. It helps you change your behavior to encourage a mutually beneficial outcome during conflict situations instead of showing destructive anger. This is how you develop your personal skills to validate your feelings and emphasize those of another.

When this happens, you essentially overcome your anger and take control of your thoughts, behavior, and, consequently, your life. It is when you become capable of putting yourself in someone else's shoes without feeling that you are giving up some of yourself in the process; when you can grow a greater understanding of why your parents or school have specific rules in place, keeping you from doing certain things; also, when you can allow others to have a particular opinion that differs from yours without feeling the need to convince them otherwise with the force of your anger. Walking on the middle path also gives you the insight to forgive others for hurting you. This forgiveness is not saying that it is okay and that they can just get away with what they did; rather, it is okay as your feelings are validated, and you choose to no longer carry the burden of anger and resentment they caused you to feel. Walking the middle path is the journey to much greater emotional freedom and more effective management of your emotions.

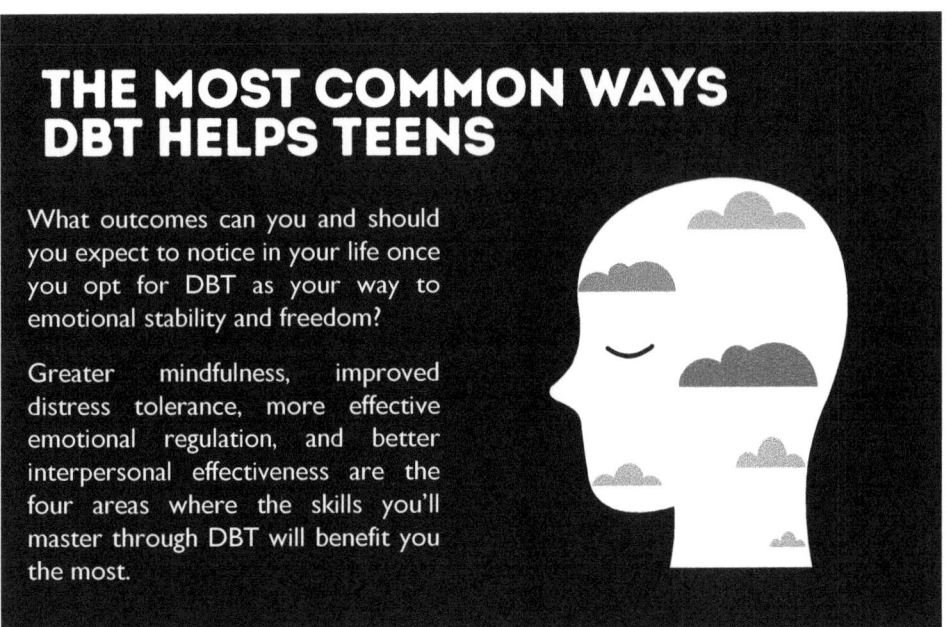

THE MOST COMMON WAYS DBT HELPS TEENS

What outcomes can you and should you expect to notice in your life once you opt for DBT as your way to emotional stability and freedom?

Greater mindfulness, improved distress tolerance, more effective emotional regulation, and better interpersonal effectiveness are the four areas where the skills you'll master through DBT will benefit you the most.

MINDFULNESS

When you are more mindful, you'll notice that your emotions are things you experience, not who you are. You may feel sadness, but it doesn't mean you are a sad person. You may feel anger, but it doesn't mean you are an angry person. Emotions are fleeting and something we experience, but they don't define who we are.

When you are more mindful, you'll enjoy a greater awareness of the feelings that pass through you and become better at letting whatever you feel flow through without holding onto these feelings and assuming them to be part of your identity.

I remember it was an exhilarating, freeing moment when I realized that although I may feel anger in that specific moment, rejection, disappointment, or any other emotion, I don't need to hang onto these emotions. They are just something I feel, and the feeling will pass soon.

Other added benefits to being more mindful include improved focus; you'll get better at memorizing information and notice a reduction in your stress and anxiety levels. Mindfulness also does wonders to relieve the symptoms of depression (Cherry, 2022).

DISTRESS TOLERANCE

We all go through tough moments from time to time. While being in the middle of such a challenging time in your life—it may be a tricky subject at school, being socially rejected, the divorce of your parents, the death of a beloved grandparent, or maybe even a romantic breakup —you are often bombarded with two sets of negative emotions.

The first set is a healthy reflection of what you are feeling; hurt, rejection, disappointment, sadness, or any other feelings the situation may stir. The second set of negative emotions is less promising. These are the negative emotions you feel because you must endure challenging times.

Ready for an example? Sandra's parents are getting a divorce. They waited for her 16th birthday party to happen, and 2 days later, they told her that they were splitting up and that she, her younger brother, and their mom would be staying behind in the family home while her father moves into an apartment in the city at the end of the month. Sandra is sad, shocked, concerned, and already missing her dad, even though there are 10 more days before he leaves. These are all natural emotions to feel, and gradually, Sandra will work through them. While experiencing these negative emotions, Sandra also feels sorry for her parents. She knows that they must have pondered on this decision for quite some time before making their final choice and that, even then, they held back on breaking their sad news until after her birthday, careful not to spoil the magical moment for her.

Now, we have a different version of Sandra's life. She is still in the same position but deals with more negative emotions. She feels that it is unfair that this is happening to her. Sandra accuses her parents of being selfish and not considering her feelings. She mostly walks around angry at home, as she feels that her parents are wrong and messed up by allowing their marriage to fail and that now she has to pay the price for their mistakes. Sandra considers herself to be the victim of her parents' divorce.

Can you see that Sandra's entire outlook on her parents' divorce doesn't consider their feelings in the second scenario? That she doesn't even recognize that they, too, are going through a difficult time and that she is selfishly making it all about her? Therefore, she'll want to punish everyone with her anger.

In the second scenario, Sandra lacks distress tolerance; in the first scenario, her behavior reflects that of someone who can empathize and manage her distress well. In the first version, Sandra can effectively work through her emotions and find healing for the hurt her parents' divorce is causing in her life without making it harder for them and her little brother. In the second, Sandra is not addressing her actual emotions, as every emotion she experiences is overcast by her anger, anger that also makes the situation much worse for her parents and sibling. Can you see how greater distress tolerance can make a vast difference in your life and your relationships? There is a saying that the problem is not the problem—the way we see the problem is the problem.

EMOTIONAL REGULATION

Do you tend to lash out at others when you are tired or stressed? Do you avoid social interaction when you suffer humiliation? It can happen that you've developed a go-to response for every situation in your life, and this response may not necessarily be the most effective approach nor the one that will even resolve the emotions you are experiencing. DBT teaches the needed skills to acknowledge feelings for what they are and the skills to address each emotion most appropriately and effectively.

Through DBT, you'll also learn how to shift your focus from every situation's negative aspects to see the positive in every event. Even from what you perceive as the worst scenario, good can come—you only need to know how to see these positives. I'll be the first to admit that seeing the positive can be challenging when disaster strikes, but there is always some good in every situation.

Can you recall any past events that you've felt were the worst that could happen to you, but now that time has passed, you can see that there were also positive things that resulted from the situation?

INTERPERSONAL EFFECTIVENESS

How well do you rate your ability to maintain your relationships? Interpersonal effectiveness is linked to the ability to manage your emotions and expectations within a relationship with those of another (Cherry, 2022). It is the foundation of strong bonds. You are bound to have stronger, happier, and healthier relationships by improving this skill.

Keith and Megan had been dating for a couple of months when it was time for his prom. As Megan was a year younger than Keith, she knew that while she had specific ideas about what she wanted to look like when going to the dance, this was Keith's moment to shine. Therefore, she didn't expect the focus to be on her. While dressing in vintage clothes was not her preferred choice, she decided to hold on to the dress she dreamed about for her prom the following year and opted for a dress that complimented Keith's vintage outfit. As long as he has fun at his prom, she'll be happy too—she just wants to enjoy the time with him and make some beautiful memories. It is how she showed interpersonal effectiveness by balancing her needs with those of Keith.

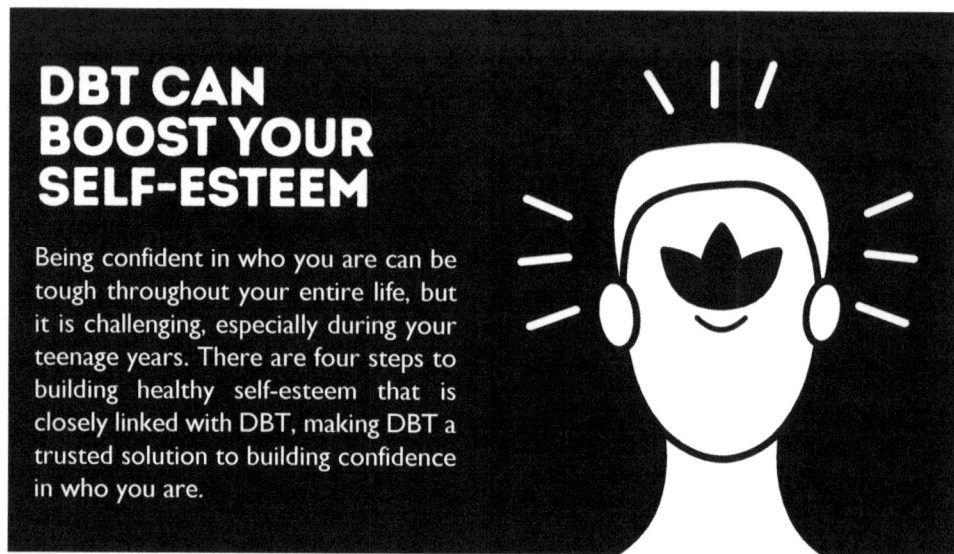

DBT CAN BOOST YOUR SELF-ESTEEM

Being confident in who you are can be tough throughout your entire life, but it is challenging, especially during your teenage years. There are four steps to building healthy self-esteem that is closely linked with DBT, making DBT a trusted solution to building confidence in who you are.

BE FAIR

DBT encourages a fair approach to all in life. Being fair can contribute hugely towards your relationships as it will keep you from shifting blame or judging others. Being fair also demands that you are kind to yourself by not putting your needs and desires on the back burner all the time.

Yes, there will be times when being fair asks you to give someone else's needs preference above yours, but this shouldn't be the case the entire time. Fairness means that you can always be sure that you are doing the right thing, even when it is not pleasant.

DON'T OVER-APOLOGIZE

The therapy teaches that there is a time and a place to apologize in life but never over-apologize. Never feel the need to apologize for saying no. It may be that you want to soften the blow when you do say no, but this may only lead to a buildup of resentment that transforms into excessive anger again. This is a lesson that Buddy had to learn the hard way.

He couldn't wait for the new year to start as he was so keen to join the drama club at his new school. Buddy saw himself on the stages of the world and wanted to start his career right away. When school started, his friend Jimmy asked him to join the swimming team as Jimmy didn't have the confidence to go to the swimming club alone. First, Buddy said, "Sorry, Jimmy, I just can't. Drama and swimming are meeting at the same time, and if I go with you, I won't be able to be part of the drama club."

However, while Jimmy didn't have the confidence to go swimming on his own, he did know how to be persistent until Buddy changed his mind. Initially, Buddy tried to pretend he liked it, but gradually it became more evident that he regretted his mistake. One day, while walking home, Jimmy made a silly joke, and it caused Buddy to respond in anger. All the resentment he felt towards Jimmy for choosing Jimmy over his dreams erupted in a rage that Buddy had no control over. Buddy didn't go back to swimming. He also didn't join the drama club. The two were no longer friends.

Buddy shouldn't have felt bad over his choice to pick his dreams. He wouldn't have robbed Jimmy of anything if he did, but his failure to say no cost him a lot.

DETERMINE & CELEBRATE YOUR VALUES

Self-esteem and values are also two concepts that are closely linked. DBT helps in this regard, as it encourages you to identify your values. These values will determine every choice you make in the future. The stronger you are set in your values, the more likely you are to stick to them. Each time you choose to act in line with your values, your self-esteem expands, turning you into the confident person you want to be.

When you are confident in who you are, it becomes much easier to accept that anger is something you feel, not who you are. When you've grasped that, dealing with your anger—and all other emotions—becomes much easier.

DIGGING DEEPER

It is time again to grab your DBT journal.

At the core of DBT, we'll find mindfulness. It is the essential first step you need to take to identify your emotions; to create distance between what you feel and who you are; and to define your values. The concept of mindfulness can often sound more daunting than it is. You can practice mindfulness throughout the day, wherever you go, but before you can do so on your way to school, while taking your shower, or during any meal, you need to experience what it entails. Now is that moment.

I want you to find a place to sit without being disturbed. If you can find such a spot somewhere in nature, it would be even better.

Find a comfortable position and take a few deep breaths. Then, without thinking, write in your DBT journal what you are feeling, smelling, seeing, and hearing—are you sitting on a lawn, perhaps? Then, write how the grass touching your legs feels—is the air hot, humid, cold, chilly, or soothing? Are there any strong-smelling flowers around you? Do you hear laughter, the conversations of others perhaps? Now, if you listen more attentively, do you hear birds, insects, or the buzzing city in the background? How do all these things make you feel? Are you feeling content, happy, nervous, excited, or relaxed?

It doesn't matter how long it takes you; be sure to capture every detail of the moment. Pin down your external experiences and your internal realizations. During this time you've spent being aware of your surroundings, you've been mindful, you employed greater awareness, and were living in the present moment. The more you practice mindfulness, the more it will become your way of living. Are you ready to observe the world with different eyes? Start doing so today.

CHAPTER 3:
THE BEGINNING OF CHANGE

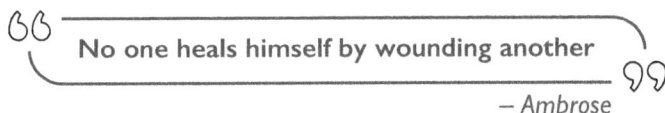

66
No one heals himself by wounding another
99

— Ambrose

You know it, and I know it. After going through the motions of experiencing extreme rage, after the hurtful outburst of anger, there is no healing. You don't feel any better than before. Sure, you feel less tense since you've let off some steam, but in most cases, steam is just hot air that burns those who come too close to it. Steam doesn't heal your hurt; it only hurts another. The moment it is all over, the regret and shame for your behavior kick in almost instantly. The self-castigation starts, and so does the buildup leading to your next explosive expression of anger. You are the only one capable of putting an end to this vicious cycle. Only you can choose to take control of your anger and emotions. Only you can stop hurting those around you.

Are you ready to learn the required skills for expressing your anger healthily and constructively rather than leaving a trail of destruction as far as you go?

HEALTHY WAYS TO EXPRESS ANGER EFFECTIVELY AND MEANINGFULLY

For the longest time, I thought the way we express anger was the same for everyone and that there is only one way to show that you are angry. I just assumed those around me who didn't express anger in the manner I did were just not ever as angry as I was. Maybe they just didn't ever have any reason to show anger.

DBT helped me to realize that I was completely wrong for most of my life. Through therapy, I realized that there are ways to show your anger that can be less hurtful, even productive and good, if you use healthy techniques.

After all that I've learned about anger and how to effectively manage my rage, the solution I came up with was to create and establish my "anger response plan." You are most likely familiar with an evacuation plan. Every school should have one, and if school management is diligent in keeping safety protocols, you've likely been part of several evacuation plan simulations or drills. Some kids in my school considered these drills a nuisance as they meant that they had to get up and leave the school building. However, others, including myself, liked these drills as they ate into the time we had to spend in class. I also felt that fire drills gave an exciting twist to the day. It is probably also why the idea of having a similar plan in place to address anger was so attractive to me. The core purpose of a fire drill is to minimize injury and to ensure that in the case of an actual emergency, everyone is clear on what to do to reduce the risk of injury, fatalities, and damage to property. Once the alarm triggers a response—and the alarm can go off at any time—the immediate response simply kicks into gear without thinking about what to do next.

CREATING AN ANGER RESPONSE PLAN

I am sharing the steps of my anger response plan as it includes several helpful techniques and steps to express your anger more effectively and to help you to maintain control over your emotions and behavior.

BE ALERT TO THE SIGNS

The sound of an alarm is the trigger to respond during a fire drill. When it comes to anger, the signals you'll receive may be more subtle than the shrill sound of your school's fire alarm. Yet, as you become more mindful of your emotions and the sensations you experience throughout the day, you'll get better at recognizing them long before you crash and burn.

The common signs of a rise in anger are your heart racing, feeling shaky, or your tone of voice may change when you talk, becoming higher and shriller. Others may grind their teeth, start pacing around, feel hot, as well as be more critical, judgmental, and snappy. In most cases, if you usually have a great sense of humor, your sense of finding things funny will dissipate

DETERMINE THE ROOT OF YOUR ANGER

Now, you are alerted to the state you are in, and it is time to determine from where the cause of concern is originating. The sooner the fire can be located, the sooner you can extinguish the flames before it turns into a fierce rage. So, ask yourself, what is making you angry? Maybe you are hungry, tired, overwhelmed by conditions beyond your control, hurt, disappointed, going through hormonal changes, feeling rejected or left out, or any other reason you can think of that is not sitting well in your mind.

I've found that writing down my thoughts helps a lot to get to the root of my concerns if I struggle to determine the exact cause of what is fueling this anger inside me. Mostly, I write in my journal—similar to your DBT journal—but there have been times when I captured my emotions in a letter. Then I can directly express my feelings towards the person I've identified as the one causing me to feel this inner strife. DO NOT SEND THE LETTER, though—at least, not the first draft. During the first draft of such a letter, you are likely still ranting and blowing off steam in an out-of-control manner. Once you finish the letter, get up and go for a walk. Come back and reread it with a perspective of how you can say what you want to say more nicely. Maybe you feel that you don't have to send any letters at all anymore. That is good. If you still feel the need to get your word out, then start from scratch and capture your emotions again without the anger you've already let go of in the first draft.

COUNTING, COUNTING, & MORE COUNTING

Are you familiar with the advice of counting to 10 when you are angry? I've concluded that counting to 10 is useless for me. What helps me is to count to 100. Yet, it is not only about thinking about the counting but to think about something that doesn't upset me for 100 seconds.

So, set your timer for 100 seconds—that would be 1 minute and 40 seconds—and while the timer is ticking, think only about something you enjoy. It can be a book, a movie, a person who makes you laugh a lot, a funny joke you've heard, or anything else. Avoid cheating, as by doing so, you are only cheating yourself. Repeat the 100 seconds until you've managed to think for 100 seconds only about something pleasant. I promise your anger will be much more manageable once you are done.

TAKE A TIMEOUT

There is nothing wrong with taking a timeout when you need it. Whenever you feel more signals alerting you of the rise of anger internally while being in a conversation or even within a particular situation, take a timeout. Excuse yourself and put the distance you need between yourself and the cause of your anger.

Use this timeout to take a couple of deep breaths in a neutral environment. Get active and go for a quick walk around the school, jog in your neighborhood, or maybe take the family dog for a walk. Physical activity and time in nature have a soothing effect on emotions. Once you are ready, you can approach the conversation or situation again; as you'll be much calmer now, you'll remain in better control of the emotions stirred inside.

SOOTHE YOURSELF

We never know when the emergency alarm is going to rip through the present moment with a shrill sound. However, I've learned that by being more mindful and aware of what I am feeling, I can take certain steps to increase my overall calmness:

I listen to music. When I was younger—much younger—the sounds blasting from my stereo were quite angry. Now I know better; this type of music isn't an expression of my anger; it only increases the anger that I am already feeling. Since I've switched to listening to calmer tones, I can feel my anger melting away. I am not saying you need to listen to Simon and Garfunkel or perhaps a few sonatas—not that there's anything wrong with these, and I love them too—but go for the milder side of your music collection to calm your mood.

Practicing gratitude has also helped me a great deal, and therefore, I still hold onto this routine. I've established a habit of writing one thing that I am grateful for on a piece of paper, and then I fold the note and chuck it into a large jar that I keep on my nightstand. Whenever I feel that my anger is rising, I go to my jar and read some of the notes I wrote. When I remind myself again of all the good that I have in my life, anger usually comes in second.

Finding a creative outlet for my anger has also panned out well. The added benefit is that I have several interesting sculptures in my home that serve both as reminders to myself that my anger doesn't have to control me and as a dramatic touch to my décor. Whether it is songwriting, painting, sketching, or like in my case, sculpting that speaks to you, rely on your creativity to positively channel your energy.

DRILL IN YOUR ACTION PLAN

This brings me to a second benefit of having my sculptures to mind. They serve as reminders that I am capable of managing my anger. I compare them to the evacuation plans that you'll see in large apartment blocks, hotels, resorts, and your school, to name only a few locations, where these plans are visible to all to see. Even if you've never been part of an emergency drill in these buildings, walking past these plans serves as a reminder that there is a way out of every bad situation—you just need to stick to your plans. Find a format that you are comfortable with to remind you that you too have a plan in place to get you out of the sticky situation of being angry while preventing any injury.

THE PROS & CONS OF ANGER

I've touched now several times already on using anger constructively or effectively, but let's put the positive use of anger under the microscope to see what the pros and cons are that the emotion brings about.

THE CONS OF ANGER

It almost feels like I want to ask you what you want first: the bad news or the not-so-bad news? Quite simply, I've experienced that for every so-called "pro" to the expression of anger, you can establish the same results, or even better, by following a different approach than one fueled by an underlying rage. Yet, let's start with the bad news before moving on to the not-so-bad, right?

As you are more than likely already very familiar with the cons of anger, I think merely listing them will suffice. You are, of course, also welcome to add more of the cons you've experienced in your life:

✔️ Anger is bad for your health. It increases your blood pressure and heart rate and the excess pressure on your cardiac system increases the risk of heart attacks and strokes (Promises Behavioral Health, 2022).

✔️ It crushes your relationships.

✔️ Our anger outbursts impact the way others see you; they lose respect for you and become weary of being around you.

✔️ These outbursts and their severity tend to cause you humiliation and feelings of regret over what you've done or said. These feelings have a negative ripple effect on your self-esteem and confidence.

✔️ Anger leaves you feeling on the edge all the time.

✔️ It robs you of experiencing joy; laughter and fun; opportunities; and meaningful bonds.

✔️ When anger is extremely out of control, it can get you a criminal record, resulting in costly settlements.

✔️ While being blinded by your anger, you can cause irreversible harm that you have to live with for the rest of your life.

✔️ Anger increases feelings of isolation, anxiety, stress, and the possibility of depression ("What Is Anger?" n.d.).

What other cons can you add to the list?

THE NOT-SO-BAD NEWS

To be fair, there can come some good from anger too. Anger is such a potent emotion, loaded with energy, that it can give you the boost to act on what you've been procrastinating on for far too long. Therefore, anger is also helpful for instigating change. For example, certain social atrocities may go unnoticed by those in power and are able to bring about change until the anger of the masses evolves into protests which then shed the essential light on the concerns to bring change:

> Anger may get you to take up an exercise routine; clean your house or room; and start ticking things off your to-do list that becomes very lengthy as time passes.

> It also gives you the courage to speak up when you might have shied away from a topic or person for too long.

> You discharge emotionally.

> Your anger can lead to the punishment of those who did you wrong.

> Anger tends to get you attention, but is it the kind of attention you desire?

You may have a few points you want to add to the list too. Yet, you could've achieved all of the above without putting your mind and body through the impact anger has on it and without taking the risk of facing potentially dire consequences. There are far more productive and wholesome ways to achieve all of the above positive outcomes of anger. It is why I am not so much in support of using a high-risk emotion as a tool to establish any desired result.

RESPONDING VS. REACTING

Have you received this advice in the past and thought what does it even mean? Aren't the two terms synonyms? I remember my confusion about what I was being told the first time I was instructed to respond instead of reacting. I remember the situation so well even though it happened more than 10 years ago already.

I think the reason why this memory stuck so much with me is that I can't believe that I treated my family, the people who love me deeply, so badly.

I was about 16 and couldn't wait for the upcoming summer break. I was tired of being on the edge the entire time, hated school, and just had a massive fallout with a friend. While it sounded super uncool to go with your family on holiday, I knew that when we are on holiday, my parents are way less on my case, meaning there was far more freedom in my life. My mom's family had a cabin at a lake and we would join them. As it was such a small community living in that area, it was quite safe to move around freely, and nobody minded if I would be out the entire day swimming or simply reading while sitting under a tree. I remember how we would sometimes stroll in the streets even after dark, as it was so safe there. So, I was holding on to the idea of breaking free from the norm to get me through the last couple of days of school.

 Then the news broke. My dad's mom had a stroke, and suddenly we were heading toward the opposite side of the state for the entire holiday. He was an only child and his dad passed away a few years before, so he wanted to be there with his mom to care for her when she went home from the hospital.

I hated the town she stayed in. She was very old and her house was stuffy, and I always felt that she didn't like me much. My immediate reaction to this disappointment was to be angry. I felt like the entire world was out to get me and that nobody cared, and I wasn't going to tolerate this treatment anymore. I was horrible. Instead of being there for my dad—and my mom—I made everyone's lives miserable. Nobody could talk to me without me biting off their heads. One day, my anger erupted so badly, I slammed a door after losing my voice while screaming at my parents, and I knocked over a crystal vase that belonged to my gran, the gran who was dying. I'll never forget the expression on my dad's face when I looked up from the shattered pieces on the floor. I wanted to clean it up and he just told me to go. I remember feeling sorry, guilty, lonely, isolated, and hurt at the same time—it was horrible. My parents decided to take me to my family at the lake house and they went to my other gran. She passed away a few days later without me seeing her or ever saying goodbye. The irony is that after all the hurt and heartache, my parents still spend most of the holidays at the lake house, but there was this awkward thing between me & my dad, a thing that took years before it finally got resolved.

It could've been different if I only responded rather than reacted.

The difference between reacting and responding to a situation is that reacting happens rapidly. We are exposed to a trigger and, without delay, we react. We don't allow time for the mud to settle, for emotions to calm down, or for clear thinking to return to the surface.

Responding is different. When we respond, we wait before saying or doing anything. We hold onto what we want to say to see if our words or the way we express ourselves will improve. It requires delayed action.

The process of reacting can be dissected into three steps: stimulus, anger, and action.

Responding consists of more processes. Here, we have a stimulus, anger, a pause to process, and we plan a response—only then does the action take place.

Knowing what I know now, I can see how the situation with my grandma could've been entirely different. Yes, I was tired and deserved a break. However, there was no way that my parents would've known what would happen to my dad's mother. For him to want to go to be by her side was only normal, and of course, my mom would also want to be there to support him and her mother-in-law—I mean, it was only the right thing to do. If I would've given the time needed to respond, I could've supported my parents too, and still considered the time away from the norm as a break. I could've understood that they were tired, stressed, and concerned too; that my dad was sad and probably also felt some regrets for not being there immediately when his mother needed him. I would've realized all of this if I allowed time for the mud to settle and not only think about myself.

DIGGING DEEPER

Are you ready to up the efforts needed to establish change? I have two exercises that will benefit you.

In the first exercise, I want you to create your anger response plan. It would mean that you have to write down the steps you need to follow when the anger alarm is bringing your life to a stop. Have fun while doing so and give this plan any format that speaks to you.

You can make a poster; have a complete outline; write down an action plan; lay out your actions in the form of speech bubbles; add color and images; and claim this plan as yours. The following questions will guide you along the way:

✔ What signs register as warnings that an emergency is heading your way?

✔ What processes or routines can you put in place to buy yourself the time to determine what is causing you to feel this anger? When this warning signal goes off in a building, the desired response is to leave the building in an orderly manner. So, determine your go-to reaction when you notice these signs.

✔ Identify the possible obstacles you may experience along the way and determine how you can overcome these with ease.

✔ List several actions you can take to soothe yourself, to give the mud time to settle, and to get logic to overcome emotion so that you can respond rather than react.

✓ Once you are done, place this plan where you'll see if it often—at best, daily. This way, whenever you are getting triggered, you don't have to think about how you want or need to respond; you can simply follow the instructions set out on your anger response plan.

The second task I want you to complete is to remember a time when you reacted. List the cons that resulted from your reaction and ponder if there were any possible cons. Now that you know better, you can do better. So, if you can replay the specific situation, what would you do differently, as you would be responding rather than reacting? Now, list the possible pros and cons of the situation.

When your changed approach to the conflict situation leaves you feeling proud of yourself, then pat yourself on the back. It is time to reward yourself—you may not have noticed it yet, but you've already taken huge steps to improve your behavior and become the master of your emotions.

Maybe you are familiar with Robin Sharma and his bestselling book—the first of a couple more—The Monk Who Sold His Ferrari, or perhaps you've never heard of him. Regardless, he says that things happen twice: first in our minds and then in reality. If you've reached a stage where you can plan and maybe even dream about your changed behavior when angered, you are already halfway there.

The more you think about the person you want to be when you are angry or how you want to respond when you are triggered, the more natural your desired way of managing your anger will become to fulfill the next time when all the pawpaw hits the fan.

CHAPTER 4: MASTERING YOUR BODY

> 66 Holding on to anger is like grasping a hot coal with the intent of throwing it on someone else; you are the one who gets burned. 99
>
> — *Buddha*

The human body is a complex and intricate network in which the mind, body, and soul all impact each other. Anxiety and stress are often accompanied by a sense of having butterflies in the stomach; similarly, fear can make us shiver, feel nauseous, or have difficulty breathing. These are all examples of how our emotional state can impact us physically. Comparably, anger also manifests physically, and the same happens when we are exposed to anger triggers. I've learned that the physical responses of my body to these triggers often alert me of the fact that I am being triggered. By becoming acquainted with these physical responses, I've found a tool to become alert to what is going to happen if I don't act to change the course in advance. By familiarizing yourself with the most common physical responses of anger triggers, and by identifying the triggers unique to you, you give yourself a little more time to steer the explosive situation in a different—and safer—direction.

UNDERSTANDING THE PHYSICAL MANIFESTATION OF ANGER

Are you up for a quick biology lesson? Anger, like any other emotion, is caused by chemicals released in the brain. These chemicals instruct the body to prepare itself physically for a specific type of situation. The part of the brain responsible for the release of the hormones linked to anger, is the amygdala, a small part of the brain shaped like two almonds.

Once the body senses a situation that might be a threat, the amygdala responds by releasing hormones that prepare the body to fight. Part of the preparation includes releasing hormones giving the body an energy burst that will last for up to a few minutes. While the entire process I've described here can happen within the wink of an eye, after the energy has been released, it can take much longer until your body returns to a calm state ("Physiology of Anger," n.d.).

It is due to this process—the release of chemicals—that anger and every other feeling surpass the emotional aspects of our being and also affect us physically.

RECOGNIZING THESE PHYSICAL RESPONSES EARLY ON

Sometimes, it can be hard to determine exactly what you are feeling, judging purely on your emotions alone. However, through mindfulness and by employing greater awareness of the sensations in your body, actions, and any changes in your behavior, you can gather much quicker when anger is rising inside.

I've touched on these physical changes in the previous chapter, but as there is more to say, let's linger on this for a moment.

Anger often manifests in the following manners, but it doesn't mean that it will happen exactly the same for you. Therefore, you need to rely on awareness of physical sensations to become familiar with how your anger triggers manifest physically:

A clenching jaw can be caused by muscles that are pulling tighter and are ready for action.	As digestion is not a physical process necessary to protect yourself in a state of fear, the stress hormones will slow down the circulation to your digestive system to allow greater blood flow to your muscles, bringing them the oxygen they need to fight. As a result, you may experience stomach cramps and aches.	The increased need for oxygen in your muscles demands that your heart rate speeds up to increase circulation. So, it is normal to experience an increased heart rate. By having your heart rate speed up, the blood in your veins is under more pressure, causing an increase in blood pressure that may lead to a headache.	Higher blood pressure is also causing you to feel flushed and sweaty, trembling and shaky. As there is suddenly such a spike in heart rate and blood pressure, it is normal to feel dizzy or light-headed.

While these are the most common ways which anger manifests physically, you are likely to experience several other emotions too. If you are not familiar with identifying the emotions you are experiencing, it is easy to get confused in the heat of the moment and—instead of recognizing the irritation, resentment, anxiety, sadness, guilt, or any other emotion for what it is—to just consider it as anger, leaving you to feel like the anger you are dealing with is much greater than in reality.

These changes also impact your behavior and the following are common behavior changes related to exposure to anger triggers:

You may be cupping your fist with your other hand, indicating you are ready to fight.

You may reach for alcohol or nicotine to "calm your nerves" or to "relax."

Excessive rubbing of the head, especially the forehead, is another sign.

Changes in your tone of voice include a shrill tone or speaking louder, even screaming & shouting.

HOW TO USE STOP EFFECTIVELY

STOP is one of the many skills and techniques I've learned in DBT. As it showed to be a very effective approach to overcoming anger, I've practiced it so often that it has become second nature for me.

Essentially, STOP sums up action steps—or inaction steps—that will help you to respond and not react. STOP is designed in such a manner that it gives time to let the mud settle and for reasoning to surface. Let's break it down:

Stop: Yes, the first action you need to take according to STOP is to stop yourself from reacting toward any of the physical, emotional, or behavioral changes you've noticed. Example time: Let's say your friend blows you off at the last minute when you had plans to go to a party together.

For the entire week, you've been looking forward to it, and you and your best buddy decided to go together as you both had bad breakups this year and decided to go solo for a while. Then the night before the event, you get a text simply stating, "Sorry dude. You're on your own. I'm taking Shelley."

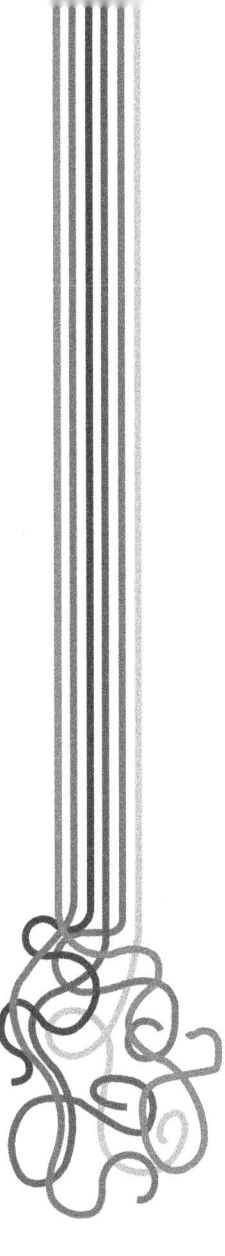

✓ Of course, you are upset. There is no way how you'll find a date before then and you are not going on your own. You are furious and have a selection of words to tell him how much his behavior sucks. Stop!

✓ The best way I can describe it is instead of jumping right onto the matter by sending a text, visualize yourself freezing for a moment.

Take a step back: In your vision, when you unfreeze, take a step back. Your momentum is broken and nothing is propelling you forward anymore. You can take a step back from the trigger to reconsider your position in the situation. Take a few deep breaths and maybe ask yourself if you would've done the same to him if it was you. After all, Shelly is both extremely pretty and super nice. Would you have said no to that? Don't you want your friend—best friend—to be happy after going through such a bad breakup, a pain you've experienced yourself firsthand?

Observe: Now, it is time to shift your focus internally by taking stock of the emotions you are experiencing. So, we know you are disappointed because you don't see how you can go to the party alone. You are angry because your friend chose a girl above you. You think you might have made the same choice and would like him to understand your situation. You are happy for him to get this nice girl to go to the party with him. You are curious as you wonder how it all happened since you saw him at school.

✓ This can indeed be a confusing stage in the process. But, ask yourself what you would recommend someone in your position to do if you were an onlooker on it all. Say, what happened to you, happened to a friend, what would you say to that person and how do you think they should deal with the situation?

Proceed Mindfully: Now you have your answer and know what to do. The initial emotions you've experienced are no longer so intense and you can think clearly and logically about the situation. So, you text him back, "What??? How did that happen? Happy for you dude. Check you anyway at the party. Say hi to Shelley."

Practice this technique as much as possible and see how most of the most intense emotions you experience—that usually cause outrage—dissipate naturally when you decide to STOP rather than act.

HOW TO USE DBT DISTRESS TOLERANCE SKILLS

The STOP skill is one of a larger collection of distress tolerance skills aiming to provide immediate relief to the symptoms you are experiencing at the moment when your anger is highly explosive. These skills are all designed in a manner to help you to accept the reality of your situation with greater ease and to reduce the chances of you taking any impulsive actions you'll most likely regret later on.

By familiarizing myself with these distress-tolerance skills, I could see how it was often my inability to accept the situation that was at the root of my anger explosions—it is with shame that I remind you of my story about how I didn't support my dad at all when his mom had a stroke). These skills can help you to escape any suffering you may expe-rience, caused by your lack of acceptance.

TIPP Like STOP, TIPP is also an acronym for temperature, intense exercise, paced breathing, and paired muscle relaxation.

Visualize yourself being right on the edge of an anger explosion. You are standing on an edge of a volcano, and the moment you lean slightly forward, you'll fall, activating an eruption of hot melted rock that will fly up high into the sky and cause destruction wherever it lands. What are you going to do? Fall forward, or use TIPP to take you in a different direction to defuse the situation , sparing people and places you surround yourself with?

Temperature: The term "hot-headed" came into existence for a reason. While in a state of extreme anger, you are most likely having increased blood circulation to your head, leaving your face feeling warm and red. By cooling yourself down physically, you can calm your mood too. One such way is by going to the bathroom and splashing your face with cold water to ease your emotions.

Intense exercise: As anger is such a potent emotion, you need to discharge the level of energy gathered inside. The most effective way to do this is through exercise that requires as much energy as what you have to give. Sprinting, boxing, jumping jacks, or getting into the pool to swim a couple of laps will all help you to release this energy & decrease your internal pressure without the need to blow your top.

Paced breathing: I've said that the mind and the body are complexly connected and that one has an impact on the other. As stress hormones in your brain can cause your breathing to become shallow and rapid, you use your breathing to reverse this state. Stand upright and place your hands on your belly and then close your eyes and focus on nothing except breathing deeply. Notice how the air passes through your airways and how it fills your lungs, causing your belly to lift your hands. As you exhale, the opposite effect occurs. By slowing your breathing, you reverse the release of stress hormones, leading you to greater emotional calm.

Paired muscle relaxation: You know the feeling. Everything inside of you feels highly strung. You feel like a violin string, ready to snap. The discomfort, almost pain, is the worst in your neck and shoulder areas. By deliberately tightening your muscles and then letting them relax, you'll gradually feel the stress seep out of your body. The best is to start at one end of your body—let's say your toes, and then stretch your toes and work your way towards your feet, ankles, calves, thighs, buttocks, and back until you get to your head and face. Stretch and let go and feel your muscles ease into greater relaxation, your heart pace returning to normal, and your mood alleviating to where it is safe again at the volcano.

ACCEPTS

Another helpful DBT skill to add to your toolbox for anger management is ACCEPTS, which is an acronym that stands for activities, contributing, comparisons, emotions, pushing away, thoughts, and sensations.

The core purpose of ACCEPTS is to use it in a manner that will distract your mind and free it from obsessing over the cause of your anger.

Let's see how it works:

Activities: Identify several activities as your go-to activities when you feel you need to escape from your thoughts or your mind will explode. For the longest time, my go-to was watching Friends replays. I would immerse myself for hours in the lives of Joey, Rachel, Monica, Phoebe, Chandler, and Ross. For you, it may be your favorite series currently airing on Netflix, or hanging with a friend. A friend recently shared how she would escape from her own thoughts by going horse riding. I can just imagine that it can be quite a thrilling experience effectively taking your mind away from your anger.

Contributing: Volunteering is a fantastic way to overcome your stress and concerns. You don't even have to become a volunteer if you don't feel like it, as your help will be as much appreciated when you help a sibling with their homework, a friend with their assignment, your dad in the garden, or by volunteering your help with the laundry, making the literal and figurative load on your mom's shoulders lighter.

Comparison: If you want to compare yourself, then do so by using a former version of yourself as the benchmark. Compare how well you are handling your anger now in relation to a previous event, or compare how much your life improved over the past couple of months.

Emotions: There are several things you can do to change the most predominant emotion you may be experiencing. Music is a powerful tool to change our emotional state. Watching a thriller, scary movie, or comedy will also help to change your mood. I've always been a sucker for romcoms and these are still my go-to movies when I need an emotional reset.

Push away: Just for a moment, or maybe a little longer, decide to actively push away everything that is upsetting or angering you. Allow yourself some space between the origin of your anger and yourself. By allowing this space, you'll likely notice how your perspective on matters changes.

Thoughts: Change your thought patterns by thinking about the dialogue in one of your favorite movies, singing the words of a song you like, grabbing the crossword puzzle, or even sudoku printed on the local paper lying on the kitchen table. It doesn't matter what you do, just change your train of thought.

Thoughts: Change your thought patterns by thinking about the dialogue in one of your favorite movies, singing the words of a song you like, grabbing the crossword puzzle, or even sudoku printed on the local paper lying on the kitchen table. It doesn't matter what you do, just change your train of thought.

GROUNDING YOURSELF

Grounding is another helpful approach to discharging yourself. I know there are many people who are sensitive towards textures and they hate walking barefoot on grass. Others just hate walking barefoot at all. I am one of those people who love the sensation of walking barefoot on a soft lawn after a hard and challenging day. The sensation of the cool soft strands of grass immediately discharges my emotions and I feel almost instant relief.

Through greater awareness of the texture of the grass, the sensation it leaves between my toes, and the softness underneath my heels, I become focused on the present moment. This remains my favorite form of grounding.

How does grounding work? The technique helps you to shift your focus to the present moment and to live in the now. The present moment is a space where there is no reason for concern or a place for regret—it just is. Through grounding, you can ease anxiety, depression, stress, and even PTSD symptoms. These techniques effectively lift your mood and contribute to your overall well-being. The best of it all is that they are really fun exercises.

One way to ground yourself is to look around where you are sitting and to notice the objects within arm's reach. Pick these objects up, one after the other, but take your time with every item and feel the texture. How heavy or light, rough or delicate is the item you are holding? What color is it? Is it hard, squeezy, cold, smooth, fluffy, or bendy?

Sniff your favorite scent. Like music, scents are also potent mood changers. Here, you can choose to sniff your favorite perfume or explore a range of aromas. There are usually a bunch of things to sniff in the kitchen, especially when you tackle the spice rack. Vanilla, coffee, cinnamon, mint, basil, thyme, teas… there are so many to name. Focusing on nothing but the scent you are smelling is another outstanding grounding technique.

DIGGING DEEPER

You are smart, intelligent, capable, and highly resourceful, right? You don't need to just do everything I am telling you to do, even though it will help you a great deal in finding the route to inner calmness & excellent anger management.

You can establish grounding techniques that are unique to your personality. As I've explained how walking barefoot on grass does wonders for my soul, but isn't something everyone will do, I want you to determine three go-to grounding techniques that bring you the best results.

It will mean that you may have to do some of your own research to discover more known DBT grounding techniques, or you can recall what are the simple actions that make you feel grounded. You may not have had a name for the technique before nor have known how to refer to the impact it has on your mood, but now you know. So, list three different grounding techniques that work for you. Name them, describe them, and be sure to include them in your DBT journal.

Then, practice them so that you never have to think about what to do when you are feeling your emotions rise. You simply do what comes naturally to you as you've done this so many times; it becomes your second nature.

Next, I'll tell you how to become a master of your mind.

CHAPTER 5:
IN TUNE WITH YOUR MIND

> When you know yourself you are empowered.
> When you accept yourself you are invincible.
>
> — Tina Lifford

It came to me as quite a surprise the first time I learned that DBT identifies three minds in us all. Nonetheless, once I understood the concept, it made so much sense to me and it supported me greatly to become a master of my emotions.

There are three parts to the mind: the rational mind, the emotional mind, and the wise mind. Ideally, you want the wise mind to be the controlling force in your life, but the wise mind can only exist in the presence of the other two. To live a life where you are in control of all three, you need to be more mindful of what is happening in each of these minds individually as well as grasp and understand how these minds impact each other and the outcome you'll get.

The rational mind guides and contains logical thinking and rationale. On the other end of the spectrum, you'll find the emotional mind that is mostly overreacting as it is allowing emotions to take control. The wise mind presents itself where the rational mind and the emotional mind overlap.

> Now, let's dig into this to see what each of these minds looks like and explore the role they play.

THE EMOTIONAL MIND

It is in the emotional mind where the heat leading to an emotional eruption simmers and stews. By all means, there is a place and a purpose for the emotional mind as it is what enables you to empathize with others; it also enables you to show and feel sympathy and to have compassion.

It is in the emotional mind where the heat leading to an emotional eruption simmers and stews. By all means, there is a place and a purpose for the emotional mind as it is what enables you to empathize with others; it also enables you to show and feel sympathy and to have compassion.

I am not saying that emotion is bad. What I am saying is that when there is limited or no control over the emotional mind, it becomes dangerous.

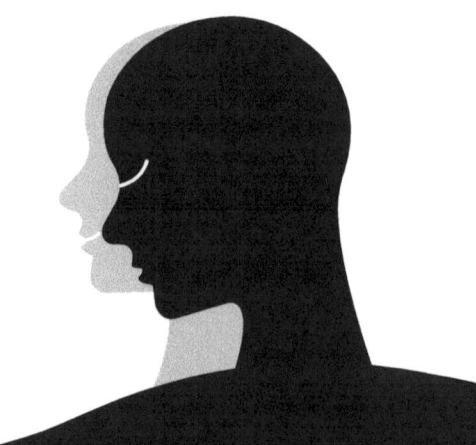

If your emotional mind is the force in charge of your actions, you are likely to be a passionate person, fighting tooth and nail for what you stand for or believe in. But are you effective in getting what you desire?

Felicity is 16 and identifies as an activist. Activism is good. It highlights social atrocities, stands up for the underdog, and restores injustice in the world, often by creating awareness around the issue. Typically, activists would be made up of people who are passionate about a specific cause. Their behavior is fueled by their intense desire to right a wrong. The way they behave is a product of their deep-rooted commitment to the cause.

Felicity was a bit different. Her activism wasn't rooted in her beliefs or passions. No, she found causes to have an excusable explanation for her actions. I remember her mom saying to me that it sometimes feels as if Felicity is looking for a cause just so that she can let go of her emotions while she shielded her behavior with the excuse that she was an activist. I got the feeling that even though she did care to a certain degree about the causes she was adding her voice to, it was more about her emotions that were out of control than the cause itself.

The cause was merely an excuse for her behavior when she stormed into a top-end restaurant immersed in fake blood and having what appeared to be animal intestines draped around her neck as part of her protest against people eating meat. Another incident occurred when she broke into a private lab to free the animals where she believed a huge cosmetic house was running tests on them and that she was going to expose them. Felicity wound up getting arrested for breaking in and trespassing on private property, and it wasn't her first and wouldn't be her last arrest.

The problem was that Felicity wasn't vegan or vegetarian, and she wore makeup from the best-known cosmetic brands too. She merely adapted her activism to find a cause giving her an outlet for her intense emotions. Her emotional brain was dictating her every move and her mother rightfully feared that soon she would take it too far, landing her in hot water.

THE REASONABLE MIND

If the emotional mind is warm and passionate, the reasonable mind is cold and calculated. When the reasonable mind is in charge, your moves will be precise and controlled—overtly so. To act according to reason is good when present in healthy quantities. For example, say your mom asked you to pick up a few things from the grocery store after school. You have two choices: You can either walk home on the same route you normally do and then go to the grocery store, or you can walk a slightly different route and stop at the grocery store on your way home. The latter is a reasonable choice for it will help you save time and effort.

When the level of reason you showcase becomes so overpowering that it casts a shadow on all you say and do, it is problematic though. Then, others will likely refer to you as cold, heartless, lacking compassion, and hard to connect with. You'll struggle to have any meaningful relationships. It will make it hard for your future coworkers to work with you as you come across as someone who lacks an understanding of what is at the heart of humanity. Yes, sure, you may likely never experience an emotional explosion, but that doesn't mean that these feelings aren't brewing toxically underneath the surface.

His reasonable mind ruled Denver. As it was hard for others to form any connection with him, he would always end up alone during teamwork exercises. If someone was instructed to work with him, his entire class openly pitied that person. Denver was the person who told the principal every time when the janitor slept on the job. He went as far as to take pictures of the sleeping man and threatened to take the matter to the school board if the principal doesn't remove the janitor for his inadequate performance. Yes, the janitor was wrong, but he only slept because his wife was dying of cancer; when she had a bad night, he would be up the entire time to help her be more comfortable with her pain. Denver's complaints eventually resulted in the janitor losing his job. He couldn't afford medicine for his wife anymore, and two weeks later, she passed away.

The entire school was heartbroken for they mostly cared deeply about the man, but Denver persisted that the janitor was wrong and deserved the action taken against him.

Can you see that even if you are ruled by the rational mind and never have an emotional outburst, your action can still be extremely hurtful?

THE WISE MIND

At the sweet spot where rationale and emotion overlap, you find the wise mind. It is a place where balance exists and where intuition has an important role to play. The internal equilibrium creates a welcoming place where the inner voice can be heard. The wise mind can make smart moves resulting from rational thinking and inspired empathy and compassion for others.

It attaches value to gut feelings and seeks deeper meaning in life, events, and relationships. It is the optimal mental space to settle in.

The wise mind is available to all to access and is what elevates your words, behavior, and actions to make a meaningful impact on the world and the lives of others.

> How will learning the skills to employ the wise mind benefit Felicity & Denver?

The biggest revelation Felicity couldprobably have is that one attracts more flies with honey than vinegar. If she changed her approach to activism to only stand up for the causes she truly believes in, her efforts to establish change will be fueled by her passion for the cause and not by the desire to cause "meaningful" disruption. As these efforts will also be less diluted, they will be more effective. Say she decided to stick to promoting a meat-free environment as her cause of choice, then her strategy could've changed in the following manner:

> She'll stop eating meat and meat products herself.

> Felicity would commit her time to sharing accurate information about the impact commercial farming has on the environment and the cruelty that is often inherent to commercial farming.

> She would select her target audience to be people who are on the verge of making the transition, rather than disrupting a crowd so badly that they choke on their last bite of a chop or steak.

> She would refrain from actions causing damage to the properties of private people and entities and from disrupting their operations in such a manner that it damages their brand identity.

Denver had to move more toward having an emotional side to his approach:

Felicity would commit her time to sharing accurate information about the impact commercial farming has on the environment and the cruelty that is often inherent to commercial farming.

She would select her target audience to be people who are on the verge of making the transition, rather than disrupting a crowd so badly that they choke on their last bite of a chop or steak.

She would refrain from actions causing damage to the properties of private people and entities and from disrupting their operations in such a manner that it damages their brand identity.

Can you see that in both cases the outcome is far more positive for all involved when the concern is approached with a wise mind?

Having a wise mind is not a genetic privilege nor based on class, gender, religion, or cultural distinction. It is an approach towards life, events, and others that we can all adapt to, learn and acquire.

DBT presented me with the steps I had to take to adapt my thinking and approach toward life from being ruled by my emotional mind to operating from a wise-mind perspective.

ESTABLISH CHANGE THROUGH RAIN

In DBT there are indeed many acronyms, each as meaningful as the next, and all of them are potent drivers of change to establish a meaningful life. RAIN is no different.

RAIN stands for recognize, accept, investigate, and not-identify. By following the steps captured in RAIN, you'll be able to successfully maintain an entirely different approach toward how you manage your emotions. RAIN is a way to practice mindfulness when your circumstances make it challenging slip into a state of awareness.

The two most common unbalanced ways people approach emotions are either to allow them to run wild without applying any control over what is taking place, or to suppress the feeling so deeply that they lose circulation and become numb. Neither way resolves these feelings and the lack of addressing these feelings in an appropriate manner can resolve even greater concerns that will demand your attention.

Walk with me through the four steps of the process:

Recognize: It requires that you take a moment to recognize and identify the emotion that is welling up inside when you are becoming more emotionally charged. Instead of denying the presence of the emotion, acknowledge it without any judgment or self-criticism. Embrace the emotion by taking time to become aware of the physical sensation it leaves in your body. Instead of running away or suppressing, or even losing yourself in the emotion, just observe it and the impact it has.

✓ I love visualization and mostly find myself thinking in pictures. Yes, when I hear the word "cat," the image of a black cat immediately comes to mind. I've always found that images make it easier to explain and grasp certain concepts. So, I want to use an image here, too, to explain RAIN in a simpler manner.

✓ Now, back to the first step of RAIN: Visualize yourself standing on the edge of a lake. You can see the water, the trees seaming the edge of the lake, and maybe there are snowcapped mountains in the background. It can also be an ominous lake with a thick fog hanging low above the dark and murky water. You have the freedom to decide what your lake looks like, just remember that the lake in this image represents a specific emotion.

✓ As we know that you are observing the lake by looking at the details around it, it is certain that you aren't running away from the feeling nor suppressing it; but, you are also not going into the lake and immersing yourself in the water. No, you are standing on the edge, observing. You can name the lake—let's call this "lake rejection." So, appearance wise, this is probably leaning more toward the ominous and desolate side of options.

✓ By taking this step, you are creating distance between yourself and the emotion, making it easier to observe it and accept its existence.

Allow: As you accept the existence of the lake—or feeling—you let it be. You might not like the lake and it will surely not end on your list of preferred go-to holiday destinations, but you allow it to be present in your visualization. As you do this, your inherent resistance toward the lake's existence disappears gradually.

✓ So, you acknowledged and accepted the feeling you have—rejection in this example—without getting caught in it, allowing it to drag you down to a place of deep internal emotional torment.

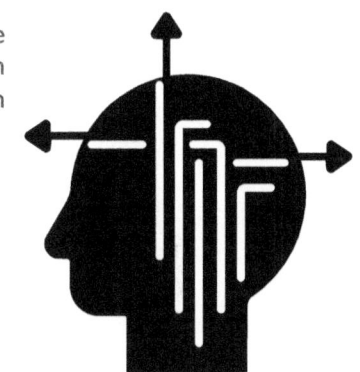

Investigate: Fear is often rooted in the unknown. Therefore, it is something you can overcome by becoming more familiar with the things that scare you.

✓ At times, the scary things in life are dark & ominous, and at other times, it can be the hurt caused by rejection. However, we can explore the lake and notice that the water is in fact not dark and scary; it was merely a cloud in front of the sun casting a dark shadow on the surface. Similarly, you can notice that you were not rejected and that the friend who declined an invite is actually dealing with a very personal matter over which they are highly embarrassed and didn't want to share.

✓ You can also ask questions like why do you perceive the lake in this manner? Would it look different if you take 10 steps to the left or the right from where you are standing now? It mostly likely does. What do you need right now to take care of yourself in your situation?

✓ By asking these questions, you alert your conscious thinking to find solutions on how to best approach the manner to resolve the emotion you've identified.

Nonidentifcation: At the heart of this step is the realization that you are merely an observer of the lake, a visitor to that space in your mind. You aren't the lake itself. See, when I state that, you are probably thinking, Of course, I am not the lake. However, when we replace the term lake with a certain emotion, like rejection, it is so easy to consider ourselves to be rejected rather than merely experiencing the emotion—rejection.

✓ Remember, as much as you are not the lake, you are also not any other negative emotion threatening to take control of your mind, words, and actions. This may be the last step in the process, but it is crucial to maintain the distance, to acknowledge what you are experiencing but also understand that it is only a feeling or an experience. It is not who you are.

USING MEDITATION TO PROCESS EMOTIONS

I admit that when you are experiencing intense emotions, it may not be the best time or place for meditation. Yet, when you commit to regular meditation with the intent to improve your emotional management and have made the practice part of your daily routine, you are gradually equipping yourself with the tools needed, so that when that intense moment presents itself, you are prepared.

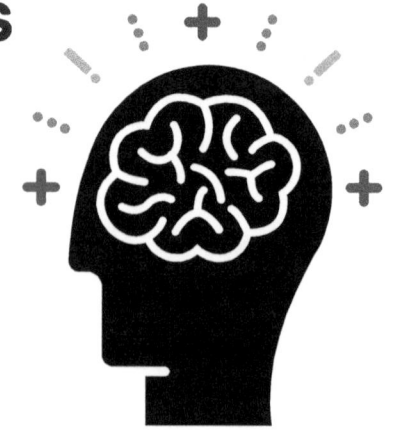

Through meditation, you can adjust your natural response to strong emotions, calm yourself, and process emotions that may still be suppressed and need to be aired before you can address them effectively.

There are several different forms of meditation and you can choose any way you like to meditate, or try a couple of methods and pick one that suits your personality and unique style best. Yet, at the foundation of many different meditative practices are the following steps:

1. Find a place where you can sit undisturbed.

2. Settle in a comfortable position, either lying down on your back or sitting in a position in which you are comfortable.

3. Decide how long you want to meditate and set a timer so that you don't have to watch the clock.

4. You can even wear comfortable clothes that won't distract you.

5. Many struggle initially to meditate effectively, but the more you do it, the better you become. As it can be hard to sit still for so long, start by setting your time for only five minutes—you can increase this later on.

6. Decide how long you want to meditate and set a timer so that you don't have to watch the clock.

Remember that the purpose of meditation isn't to clear your mind and think about nothing at all but to maintain your focus on one thing only. Every time that something else pops into your mind, you just gently nudge it away and return to what you've decided to focus on in the first place.

This "thing" you focus on can be a dot on the wall in front of you, an image you visualize, the tones of music—if you prefer to have music playing like the sounds of chimes or Buddhist bowls—your breathing, or even visualizing how anger leaves your body with every exhale and how clear and pure peace enters every time you inhale.

Gradually, you'll feel how relaxed your body is, but an even more significant event occurs on a mental level. You'll find that the more you meditate, the more you peel through the different layers of your anger, your emotions, and your being. You gain a deeper inherent clarity, calmness, and insight in matters that you've always struggled with. Through this connection, taking time out to commit yourself to self-development and growth, it is as if all forces come together to assist you on this noble quest.
I want to share with you what happened to me when I started meditating for the first time.

I had a quiet spot and found an app that would play lovely, soothing sounds. I would set my timer for 15 minutes and just lie down and breathe in and out until I could feel my muscles relaxing. Then, I would listen to the sounds, and whenever everyday life entered my thoughts, I would push them away.

Initially, when the image popped into my mind it made little sense to me. However, the same image kept on returning day after day. It was the image of a rusty old metal pole that towered high above my head, but it was more than that, as every day I would see how bits of rust would flake off the pole and gradually become less rusty. After a couple of days, I realized that these rusty bits were memories linked to my heavy burden of emotional baggage. Each time, the pole looked better than the previous time. After about two weeks, I could see the pole had a shiny surface.

I remember that by the time the pole turned into a bright and brilliant surface, I felt much lighter too. I was calmer and could approach explosive situations with reason and thought that allowed me to respond instead of react.

Nature gives preference to balance. It is continuously working towards sustaining an equilibrium, and the moment you open yourself to still the turbulent emotions inside, it gradually happens all by itself to you too. To me, that is how meditation became really beneficial on my journey to overcome my anger with the guidance of DBT.

What your meditation journey would look like is not going to be the same as mine. Your imagery will be completely unique to you, and how you benefit from the ancient practice will be answering your custom needs. But, you need to start to reap the benefits that can free you from the weight lying on your shoulders without proper emotional management. Claim your image, your healing, and the sense of progress as you work your way through the many layers of complexities making up your being.

DIGGING DEEPER

I am so tempted to make this assignment centered around meditation, as I know it will benefit you so much, but I don't, because I want these exercises to lead you to practical solutions you can apply in the heat of the moment. So, please start meditating today as you'll be doing yourself an immense favor.

Meanwhile, I also want you to grab your DBT journal and remember an incident where you reacted with an emotional response:

Instead of reliving the entire event in your mind, visualize the event from the top, but use RAIN to process what happened.

Accept that these emotions exist and that it is normal to feel them from time to time.

Recognize the emotions you've been feeling.

Nonidentify with these feelings by acknowledging that they are in you but not who you are.

Investigate these emotions.

Great!
Next, we are going to explore more fun ways to keep your cool and to allow your wise mind to flourish.

CHAPTER 6: KEEPING YOUR COOL

66 ———————————————————

Emotions flow in and out, they don't define us.

99

– Julie Reed

One of the hardest realities of life to learn—whether you are 13, 30, or 83—life will always have hard times and good times, throw challenges at you, and place obstacles in your way. The worst of it all is that these things interrupt your rhythm usually when you least expect it.

Tracy's life was fine. She got good grades at school, just got chosen for the cheerleaders, and was looking forward to starting the final year of high school with a bang. One day as she walked in from school, she found her mother in tears on the couch with her dad sitting on the other side of the room looking

very concerned and his hands folded in his lap. He was leaving them for another woman. Yes, Tracy knew that he didn't leave her, he was leaving his marriage with her mother, but it still felt like he was walking out on both of them, choosing someone else above her. What made it even worse for her was when she learned that her dad's mistress is the mother of one of the kids in her school—that sucked. Tracy told me that it felt like she was falling without stopping into a deep dark pit.

Darren's football career was going great. He knew he would be on the field to play the coming weekend when several college scouts would be in the crowd. His sister begged him to go horse riding with her that Wednesday, and while he has been very comfortable on a horse his entire life, his horse got spooked by a bee and the mare threw him off. Darren broke his leg in two places and was out for the season. Darren never returned to football at all again.

It can even be something as simple as oversleeping; getting dressed when you are already late and a zipper breaks; or not being able to find your favorite scarf, shoes, or clean underwear. These things happen. We can't stop them. They happen to you and to me, and all we can do about it is to learn the skills to maintain our balance and not allow them to throw us off track.

There is a saying that if you have $86,400 in your bank account—that is how many seconds you have in a day—and someone steals $10 of it, you are not going to throw the remaining $83,390 away. Why do we do it with our time then? Money can be replaced; time can't.

HOW TO KEEP YOUR EMOTIONS IN CHECK

Emotional balance refers to your ability to balance the positive and negative feelings you have and to sustain this balance regardless of what is happening around you. The image I get when I think about emotional balance is that of a surfer riding the waves with ease regardless of what the water is doing underneath the board.

I guess the same is true for a skier, skateboarder, or when you are on a hoverboard; these people are all highly skilled to sustain their balance with mostly nothing but a few core movements. They make it look so easy, but they are only so successful because they practiced it a lot.

You can do the same and achieve the same effortless appearance when you are sustaining your emotional balance, but it will require practicing the correct skills.

SET THE STAGE

What I mean when I say you need to "set the stage" is that you have to take preventative measures to avoid being caught in the perfect storm. This would mean that you get enough sleep—a tired mind is much easier to get overwhelmed by negative emotions. By practicing mindfulness, you'll be more aware of the feelings you have and be able to identify them as well as address the root of these concerns. When you notice that your emotional state is manifesting physically—you may have a constant headache, regular stomach cramps, or just feel physically drained or highly strung—act on these symptoms and address them immediately. Take a time out, go for a walk in nature, or have a coffee with a friend. Whatever it is you do, give your mind and body a timeout to relax and recover. Taking regular breaks prevents major emotional explosions or even implosions, causing you to collapse internally.

Another way that can help you to set a stage that is far more resilient is to stay connected with those you love and who care about you too. These people are your support network and can hold you up when you are feeling weak. Take care of yourself and be kind to yourself. Take that long bath when you feel you need it, or have that night out with friends to get a break from all the stress you experience at school.

Never underestimate the importance of gratitude. Make being grateful a part of your daily routine and see how much easier the challenge along your journey becomes to handle confidently. Emotional balance is also easier to sustain when you have physical balance too; yes, work hard, but also take breaks to be active. The fitter your body is, the more capable you'll be to address emotional and mental challenges with ease.

When you are active, trying to do so outside for nature is still the most effective environment to calm down turbulent emotions.

By setting the stage with these actions, you know you have a strong foundation to overcome obstacles with confidence and without allowing their emotional charge to overpower you.

Setting the stage is the most important step you can take to ensure effective emotional regulation, but it isn't all you can do.

TAKE STOCK OF THE IMPACT OF THESE EMOTIONS

While setting the stage will help you overcome these challenges, it won't indemnify you from being hit by these storms. So, when you are hit by a storm, assess the impact of the emotions you are feeling:

Are you so upset by your friend being constantly late for appointments that you'll allow your anger to ruin a life-long friendship?

Are you so hurt by the actions of a loved one that you want to amputate them from your life forever?

Are you feeling so despondent about not making the team that you aren't even willing to support them next to the field, or try out ever again?

Whatever emotion you are feeling fueling your anger, determine the amount of damage caused in your life or relationships and compare this to the value you attach to whatever is at risk to decide whether you can let go of these emotions or are willing to rather risk losing it all. In a sense, it is not only a damage assessment but also a risk forecast.

MANAGE INSTEAD OF REPRESS

The speed and grace of the surfer won't be possible if they tried to repress the impact of the waves on the board. Quite frankly, I think any other approach than merely managing the state of the water and the waves will crush the surfer, as the force they are up against is simply so overpowering. The same is true for emotions: For a while, it may appear as if you are doing great by repressing your feelings, but in the end, their force will overwhelm you. The solution would be to apply all the techniques you've learned so far, like breathing deeply or writing in your journal, to manage what you are feeling.

USING OPPOSITE-TO-EMOTION ACTION

This is another very helpful exercise DBT taught me, and I am sure you'll gain a lot of value from it too. The best thing is that you may already be doing this in your life, so the exercise will only help you to get better at it and guide you towards how many other situations you can use it.

It is something I do almost on a daily basis, and I can specifically recall a moment when I applied it earlier today.

I was working late last night, got to bed way past my usual bedtime, and overslept this morning. I admit that I wasn't setting the right stage for emotional balance and I nearly paid the price for my negligence in this regard. I was heading out, and my neighbor knocked on my door. She is a very old lady with a high demand to make small talk. She wanted to borrow some sugar and immediately plunged into giving me the latest updates on all 23 of her grandkids. I didn't have time to listen to her and desperately wanted to snub the conversation with a rude comment, but I applied the opposite emotion, and said, "Debra, what about I pop in later this afternoon and then you tell me all about it over a cup of coffee?"

It worked. I managed to arrive on time at my appointment and didn't hurt anyone's feelings or get any haters in the process.

The exercise requires that you identify what you are feeling at that very moment. Then, consider how you want to react. Next... you do the opposite.

I was frustrated and annoyed by my neighbor. I wanted to tell her that I don't have time for all her stories and that she talks way too much, but I politely scheduled another time to give her all my attention.

The mean girl at school asks you if you bought your dress at Goodwill. You are hurt and angered by her comment as you think you have a great personal style. You want to grab her by her hair and pull her through the mud. But you stop, look at her, and politely say, "No, but thanks for noticing anyway," as you walk away from the explosive situation.

Or, maybe you were not chosen for your team at school. You are angry at the coach and feel that nobody on the team deserves it as much as you do. You never want to play again, but you continue to go to the practices and improve your game while supporting them next to the field when they play.

ESTABLISH CHANGE THROUGH RAIN

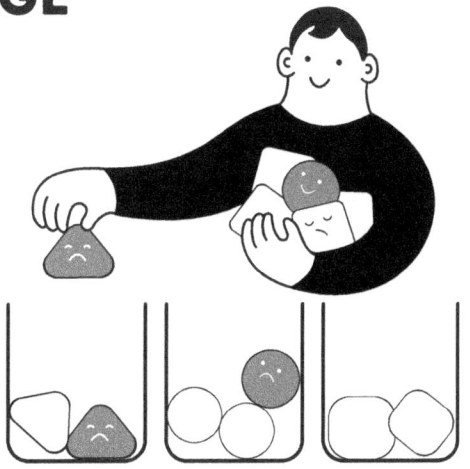

The more you are mindful, the better your awareness of your emotions becomes and the better you'll get at managing them. It is just like driving a car. Maybe you've got your driver's permit already, or maybe you are still working towards achieving that milestone. Either way, when you first got in behind a steering wheel, it was most likely a daunting experience. You are in charge of a powerful machine that can hurt or even kill others—or yourself.

There are pedals, levers, and a stick you have to control. Then, you have to find the balance between pressing the fuel pedal hard enough to move forward but not too hard so that you speed. It is daunting, and I haven't even gotten yet to discussing the road rules and signs, lanes, pedestrians, and other vehicles sharing the same road. Yet, after spending a bit of time driving, you get familiar with the vehicle and how to negotiate it through heavy traffic.

The first time I got safely to my destination, I felt a sense of accomplishment for doing it and relief that I didn't hit anyone nor damaged the car. Now, it is easy.

The same is true when it comes to your emotions. The more you are aware of them, dissect and explore them, the easier it becomes to manage them effectively even while moving through a minefield of possible emotional outbursts. Yet, it is not the only benefit you'll reap when you start to explore your emotions. No, you'll also prevent yourself from feeling the burden of meta-emotions.

What are meta-emotions? Meta-emotions are the feelings you feel caused by other feelings you are feeling. I know, that is a tongue-twister, but it sounds more complex than it is.

Sarah and Claud have been dating for three months. Sarah is smitten. Claude is her first love and she is just so happy to be in a relationship. After school, she gets home and falls onto her bed to check her phone. She immediately notices a notification that Claude sent her a text.

CLAUDE

" Hi, S. I've been thinking and I think we need to give each other space and see other people. Cool. CU. PS. I'm taking Amy to the dance. "

What? Sarah is immediately in tears while the following questions run through her mind:

What did I do wrong?

Why did he leave me?

We were still good only a few hours ago, what happened?

Nobody will like me ever again.

I am such a loser.

Am I not pretty enough?

Is it because I didn't sleep with him yet?

I should've said yes when we spoke about sex, but I wasn't ready.

Did he just break off with me over a text?

Who does he think he is?

Who is Amy?

Argh, why did I cry?

No wonder he left you, Sarah. You cry over nothing.

Why do I always cry? I hate it when I cry. I am so ticked off at myself right now!

Initially, Sarah felt hurt, heartache, and rejection. These are all reasonable emotions and it is normal for her to feel that way. But as time passed, she developed a meta-emotion: anger. Now, she is angry at herself for being sad over her loser ex-boyfriend who didn't even have the guts to break it off with her in person.

Sarah's initial emotions were validated. The meta-emotion, anger, is only an added burden, something to leave her feeling ashamed.

When you are mindful of what you are feeling, and understand why you are feeling a certain way and that it is okay to feel that way, you stop meta-emotions from developing.

What Sarah could've done was explore what she was feeling. Then, she could have determined that she felt shocked as it came out of the blue. She would've noticed that she was feeling heartache, for she truly liked Claude a lot. She might even have felt that he betrayed her every time he told her how much he likes her, for clearly, he was lying. If anger did show up, then it would've been anger towards Claude for fooling her to think that his feelings were sincere, for breaking it off with her in a text message, and for not keeping his word by going to the dance with her. While there are several reasons to be angry at him, getting angry with herself for displaying perfectly normal feelings would do her no good.

ACCEPTING THE PAIN AND MOVING ON

I can hear you say, "So, what must Sarah do, for not being angry at herself is not helping much now, is it?"

Well, the reality of life—heads up, this can be a hard one to swallow—is that we can't control everything that happens to us and we are bound to get hurt at times. We can try our best to prevent this from happening, but there are no certainties that it won't happen from time to time. So, yes, Claude hurt Sarah. But, we often increase the intensity of the hurt when we decide to hold onto it.

Sometimes, we need to acknowledge the things or people that are already gone from our lives rather than desperately try to hold onto the idea of changing the situation. Similarly, the only usual remedy in life is to accept that you've been caused to experience pain and that you have to move on, for staying will only make the hurt worse and last far longer.

DBT offers you three skills to help you through this challenging time and ease the suffering you experience. These three skills are all part of the process of accepting reality, supporting you to manage your emotions more effectively even when in tough times.

While it may feel like you would be better off rejecting or ignoring your feelings, both options are toxic coping mechanisms. The following three methods are far more emotionally healthy alternatives.

RADICAL ACCEPTANCE

When you take a moment to put your feelings aside, what does reality look like? It is important to understand the details of the reality of your situation because that is what you need to accept. The longer you are going to fight, resist, or reject reality, the more you are only wearing yourself down emotionally, mentally, and physically. The moment you stop to interact with the pain, shame, rejection, disappointment, or any other negative emotion, it becomes better and the healing can begin.

It can be a hard thing to do, but it is very much the same as scratching off the scab from a wound. Every time you scratch the injury, it starts to bleed again. However, by doing so, you are also increasing the risk of infection and causing the wound to leave an even more pronounced scar than if you only left it to heal.

When you apply radical acceptance, you can distinguish between the things you can control—like your choices, outcomes, words, and behavior—and you stop wasting your energy on the things you can't control—the choices, outcomes, words, and behavior of others.

I want you to always remember that you are supposed to feel your emotions, acknowledge them, embrace them, accept them, learn from them, and heal from them. Never are you ever asked to become a slave to your emotions. The choice remains yours.

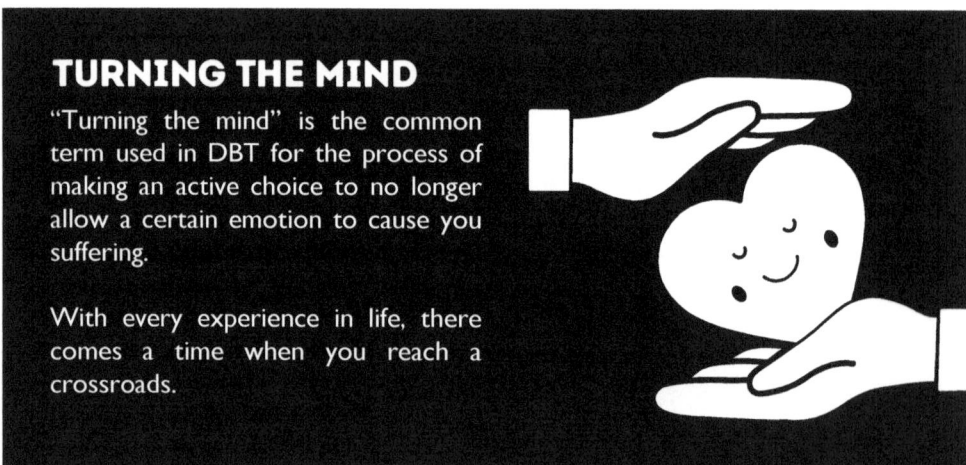

TURNING THE MIND

"Turning the mind" is the common term used in DBT for the process of making an active choice to no longer allow a certain emotion to cause you suffering.

With every experience in life, there comes a time when you reach a crossroads.

On the one hand, you have the choice to remain controlled by the emotion and to allow the pain to continue. Gradually, the pain has developed meta-emotions, and you now have an even heavier burden to carry with you. When you look down the other pathway, you see acceptance leading gradually into growth and healing. Down this pathway, your pain decreases over time, and you become wiser, stronger, and better equipped to deal with the challenges life will continue to throw at you—not because of your nature, but because of the nature of life.

TURNING THE MIND

Willingness is often underestimated as a part of the healing process, or any growth for that matter. I can share the most significant and powerful steps to help you to achieve the results you desire. Yet, they are all utterly meaningless if they aren't met with willingness. To overcome the pain you are feeling, accept the feelings you have, learn from your emotions, and become skilled at managing your emotions in a manner that you can enjoy a balanced life demands your willingness to let go, learn, accept, apply, and enrich your life. It demands no less of a willingness than what it demanded of the surfer gliding smoothly and effortlessly at top speeds, mastering the powerful waves of the ocean.

Like how salt adds flavor to food, willingness brings success to your efforts to establish change.

Are you willing to do what it takes to master the waves of emotions caused by the unexpected twists and rocks on the journey of life?

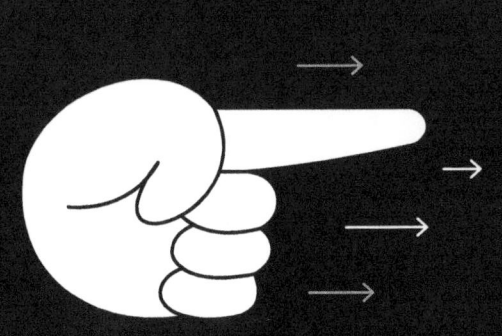

DIGGING DEEPER

Time to grab your DBT journal again. This time, I want you to pick a situation in your life that you are struggling to accept and let go of the emotions it causes you to feel. I find the following exercise very helpful (Skyland Trail, 2019):

1. What are you fighting against, or what is the reality of the situation? For Sarah, the reality is that maybe Claude just didn't feel the same way. It is also that someone who breaks off a relationship via a text is really not the kind of person you want to be with.

2. Remind yourself that the reality of the situation can't be changed. For Sarah, the reality is also that she really liked him and he was her first love, yet he hurt her badly and there is nothing she can do about it now.

3. As it is usually the case that something led to the situation you find yourself in, determine what that "thing" was that caused it all. Maybe Claude always liked Amy, but because she wasn't interested, he went for Sarah instead, and only then did Amy become interested. I know it is horrible, but this is just an example.

4. Take a few deep breaths to calm your thoughts and relax your body.

5. Compile a list of the things you feel like doing if you choose not to accept reality.

6. Determine why these are all bad moves to make. You might have to think about what may happen in the future if you take these steps too.

7. Become aware of the feelings you have and the sensations they cause in your body.

8. Consider how much you have to live for if you remove the pain from the equation for a moment. Sarah still had a lot of friends, a loving family, good marks, a great social circle, and did well in sports.

9. Become aware of how focusing on the positives in your life make you feel.

10. Decide to instead focus on these good things in your life and enjoy the feelings they create.

Every time you fall back into a state of misery, remind yourself that you did put a lot of thought into the process and that you've made a choice about what you are doing. Then, gently nudge your thoughts back to what is good in your life.

CHAPTER 7:
USING YOUR WORDS

It was playwright Edward Bulwer-Lytton who advised the world about the power of words when he said that the pen is mightier than the sword. Strangely enough, we tend to fear war, nuclear attacks, or any other form of physical harm, while often the power of our words is widely underestimated. Your words can hurt or heal, but they also have the power to bring about change, repair, restore, build, encourage, transform, or be effective in any other way you choose. How good you'll be at achieving the outcome you've set out for will depend on how skilled you are at using your words.

The degree to which you are effective in communication will largely determine the quality of your relationships, how successful you are in achieving your dreams and even impact your overall happiness. DBT taught me the communication skills needed to have healthy relationships, and I am passing this wisdom on to you. The four skills I consider to be vital to my overall happiness are called THINK, FAST, GIVE, and DEAR MAN.

THINK

THINK is one of the more recently added skills to DBT and is an acronym for think, have empathy, interpretations, notice, and kindness. The main aim of THINK is to minimize the bad emotions you feel toward others. It is hard enough to be in control of your words when you are not in a good space, and when you are feeling negativity toward another person—may they be a family member, friend, romantic partner, or even a stranger—it can be almost impossible to manage what you say effectively. Therefore, this strategy is so helpful. It simply eases all the negativity in your mind around someone and makes effective communication so much easier:

THINK:

This part of the process asks that you put yourself in the other person's shoes. Consider how they feel or think. What are they thinking about you?

Do they see you as a threat? Maybe they are hurt by something you aren't even aware of.

A while ago, I was waiting in line at the DMV when I overheard a conversation taking place behind me. It was two ladies, both moms of teenage boys who were sharing their sorrows with each other. They were mentioning how angry their kids are and how concerned they are about the future, as neither knew why their children were so angry nor what to do about it. I remembered how my path randomly crossed with DBT, and I decided to turn around and share a bit about my story and how DBT can help. They were very interested but asked that I spoke to their kids, and I agreed. The topic of communication came up while I chatted with one kid, who got visibly upset when I shared this strategy, about how he needs to think about the other person's perspective. He felt it is unfair that I could suggest that he has to go to all the effort of changing his perspective. He was a football player and loved the game, so I explained THINK in the following manner: Imagine you are playing the game of a lifetime. Whether your team will go to compete on the state level depends on winning this game and the stakes are high. But, your team remains a bit behind the entire time as you can't read the opposition's next move. Time after time, they catch you off guard. You know you'll lose. Then, during a break, you get the opportunity to see how the other team sees you. You get to think like they think and where they see your weak spots. This knowledge gives you the edge to pick up your game, win, and go to the state championship. Will you consider this as an effort or as a golden opportunity to achieve the outcome you desire? Obviously the latter, right? The same happens when you put yourself in the shoes of someone else. You get to understand what they are feeling and can address the matter more effectively from your side. By changing your perspective, you give yourself the edge in a conversation.

HAVE EMPATHY:

When you understand the other person's side, it becomes easier to feel what they feel. When you have a greater understanding of their side of the story, it is easier to feel empathy for them and to tone down the intensity of your emotions.

INTERPRETATION:

Stepping into the other person's shoes will also help you to grasp a greater understanding of why they are doing what they do. It gives you a much deeper insight into the situation, which is often all we need to gain a better understanding and resolve the matter without causing any more hurt to another or ourselves.

NOTICE:

When you look at the other person, what do you see? It is hard to see someone else for who they truly are if your vision is tainted with a negative perspective and when you can't see beyond your own emotions. Therefore, shake your assumptions and look at the person for who they really are.

KINDNESS:

Keep all of the above in mind when you respond, and then do so with kindness. Kindness doesn't mean that you are breaking yourself to accommodate the other or that you disregard your emotions to spare theirs. No, it means that you are setting your boundaries but are doing so with kindness. Rather than saying, "I can't stand to be near you and I don't want to see you ever again," respond with, "I am hurt and angry and I can't resolve this matter now. Give me some time to cool down and, when I am ready, I'll reach & and we can talk then." It is really as simple as that.

FAST

Fair, (no) apologies, stick to your values, and truthful is the framework of FAST. FAST is all about setting your boundaries and protecting them to secure your self-respect when conflict arises:

FAIR:

Fairness towards yourself and others is woven into the fibers of having self-respect. Someone who portrays self-respect is fair in their behavior, words, and even thoughts. They will treat others in the same manner as they want to be treated and, by doing so, they steer clear from being dramatical or judgy in their approach towards others. They don't distinguish people based on any presumptions and always ask themselves what is the right thing to do, for them and you.

(NO) APOLOGIES:

Yes, there will be times—and probably many times too—when you have to apologize. You just don't ever have to apologize for something you didn't do.

STICK TO YOUR VALUES:

If you aren't going to stand for anything, you'll likely fall for everything. So, define your values and stick to them.

Don't associate yourself with people who contest your values the entire time—nobody needs that added stress in their lives. Rather, spend your time with people who are like-minded and supportive. It is also important that you are true to your values. If you state that education is important to you, then make the most of your education and don't be a slacker at school. If you value change and state that you want to see an improvement in the world, then be the change you want to see. There is no better way to celebrate what you stand for and what your values are than actually living according to them.

TRUTHFUL:

Be honest to yourself and others but also about yourself and others. Being truthful will sometimes be hard. It means that you can't exaggerate, be dramatic, or oversimplify your situation. At times, being truthful can leave you feeling embarrassed or ashamed. Yet, if you want to live your life with dignity, confidence, joy, and have healthy relationships, it will demand some investment from your side. Neglecting the four steps of FAST is the fastest way to ruin your relationships and your reputation.

GIVE

GIVE—the key to healthy and happy relationships, regardless of who the other person is—stands for gentle, interested, validate, and easy manner.

While GIVE will help you to sustain your relationships, it is also beneficial when you meet new people:

GENTLE:

Take a moment to consider your general approach towards people. Would you describe it as forceful, making a statement, being on defense—even attacking—or are you gentle? The way we approach and address others often determines the way they'll respond. If you are going in with force, then they may offer instant resistance. Similarly, if you open with an attack, the immediate response is to become defensive and close up toward the person launching this attack. However, choose to approach them gently and people are generally more open to sharing, collaborating, or discussing the matter you want to address. Similarly, the way you approach someone whom you meet for the very first time, determines the first impression you leave with them. You'll get much further in life and enjoy far greater success with a gentle approach toward people.

INTEREST:

Have you ever experienced that deeply satisfying feeling when you've spoken to someone and they just made you feel heard? The entire time you were talking, you could see they were listening to every word you said. Their body language and expressions communicated that they absorbed your message, and they followed through on the conversation by asking you questions to learn more and gain a deeper understanding. You, too, can be that person when you show genuine interest in the other person.

VALIDATE:

Validation means that you verbally express that you understand what the other person is saying. You'll use statements that echo the feelings they are expressing. Do not undervalue validation in a conversation. Just imagine a situation where you are telling your best friend, "I am so angry right now. It is the third time now that my lab assistant left me to clean up our station on my own. It is not fair. We both worked on the project but when the period is over, she leaves me with all the dirty equipment."

✓ Which of the following replies would mean the most to you?

"Aha. Is that cute guy still in your class? He looks so hot in his lab coat."

Or, "No way! That's not right. How unfair. I mean, can't the teacher see what she is doing? I would be so angry as well if I were you. Maybe you should tell her next time straight out that it is her turn to clean up."

✓ See the big difference validation can bring to any conversation? Use it to your benefit

EASY MANNER:

I have to share this story with you. I was about 15 when my school sent a couple of us to go camping with several students from the surrounding school to explore nature. It was a type of adventure camp and we lived in tents and had to study nature. It was fun, but then I had a tent mate, Eileen. She was worried about everything and so intense about every little detail. Whenever we had to do something together, she would get so stressed out and, eventually, turned me into a nervous wreck too. While we promised to keep in contact after, I blocked her number on my phone the moment our bus departed.

A much better approach towards others would be to present yourself as easygoing. When you are easygoing, you still take life seriously and know what is important, but you are also confident enough in your skills and abilities that the challenges ahead don't freak you out. Your approach will also likely calm others down, making life a lot easier for everyone.

DEAR MAN

Sometimes, you need effective communication skills to say something or to make a statement, and at times, you need these skills to ask for something in a manner that will support your effort to get what you are looking for. It is in these situations when DEAR MAN can be especially helpful.

DEAR MAN is another DBT acronym for describe, express, assert, reinforce, mindful, appear confident, and negotiate:

DESCRIBE:

Okay, I think this is relatively straightforward. When you want something from someone, you need to describe to them what you want, or how else would they know what it is that you are asking? When you want to go to the movies with friends but would need your parents' permission to go—and some pocket money too—the best approach is to describe what you want from them. Do so politely but be clear about it. Look at the following three examples and see if you can see which would be the most effective to get the results you desire in this case.

✓ "Emma, Jason, everyone is going to watch a movie tonight. It sounds like so much fun. I wish I could go too."

✓ "I think it is time that you spoil me, as I've been slaving away the past couple of months. My friends are all going to the movies tonight and I deserve to go too."

✓ "My friends are all going to the movies tonight and I would really want to go too. Would it be okay if I go? I would need about $30 though, but don't worry, Emma and Jason will fetch me and drop me off, so I'll be home by 11."

» The first two attempts were not really describing the details of the event or even asked for anything for that matter. The first is more a hint and the second a demand. The third option clearly and politely states what is desired.

EXPRESS:

Part of the success of the third option is that it expresses exactly what you desire. You stated what you want to do, how much money you would need, and what the logistics around the situation would be like.

ASSERT:

You can say why something is important to you and be assertive without being arrogant, demanding, or aggressive. Most people respond better when you clarify why you think you deserve that they grant your request without coming across as if you think they'll be utterly wrong if they don't. Assertiveness is often coming across more in your body language and the tone you use than in your words. So, keep eye contact and stand up straight.

REINFORCE:

You should use reinforcement as the sequel to your request. First, you asked for something, and when your request is granted or it seems like matters are going in a positive direction for you, you can reinforce why granting your request is good. Examples will be, "I'll be back by 11," or "I promise I'll mow the lawn," "do the laundry," or "the dishes." Then, of course, stick to the promises you make.

MINDFUL:

Whether you are identifying your emotions, enjoying a meal, or asking for what you want, remain in the moment and be mindful. In this example, it will be beneficial to remain mindful, as you'll be able to better observe your parent's response, facial expression, or any nonverbal sounds. You'll also be able to think on your feet and know when you need to start negotiating so that you don't miss out on the opportunity.

APPEAR CONFIDENT:

Would you be more inclined to give someone what they ask of you when they come across confident and are presenting their request with clarity and the conviction that you'll see the matter in the same way as they do, or when they barely get their words out?

If you've given your request thought and followed every step of the DEAR MAN approach, then there is no reason why you can't be confident. For example, is there any reason why your request to the movies may be declined? Did you pick a good time to ask for this? Have you taken all possible factors into consideration of why it may not happen? If so, then you've covered all that you had to do.

NEGOTIATE:

Negotiation is only necessary when it appears like you are not going to get what you want. Don't start negotiating before that moment appears, but it will help to prepare yourself beforehand for if the moment occurs. Make sure you have a valid argument and good reasons for why you think your request should be granted. What would such a negotiation look like? Maybe offer to do something in return, to earn the money you are asking for, or commit to not asking anything for the rest of the month.

Always make sure that you know the person you are asking this favor from and understand what is important to them; you'll know how to speak to their hearts and minds more effectively.

If you approach communication like an art, realizing the power of your words, the tone you use, your body language, and your facial expressions, you'll be much more effective in sustaining healthy and lasting relationships. The added benefit is of course also that you'll be able to avoid a lot of anger or negative energy from your life, making it much easier to manage your emotions.

DIGGING DEEPER

Each of these communication skill sets is aimed to address a specific kind of communication and will be of value to address a specific need you may have:

THINK is ideally used in conflict situations and to resolve the matter before it spins out of control.

FAST will help you to express yourself with confidence & help to establish boundaries to protect your values.

GIVE will support your efforts to grow your existing bonds stronger and to make new friends.

The steps of DEAR MAN will help you to get what you ask for in life.

Each of these will help you get through your teenage years with much greater success and living with—but also causing far fewer—emotional scars. Yet, once you've mastered each of these techniques, they'll become the various foundations of communication you'll need to be successful in your career and adult relationships too.

Therefore, I want you to practice each of these skills from now onwards and not favor one above another. To help you to get comfortable with at least one straight away, I want you to think about what is that one challenging conversation that is coming up soon. It can be a difficult conversation you need to have with a friend with whom you had an argument and still need to make things right. Then, you'll need to use THINK. Perhaps a friend is disregarding your values and you have to assert yourself with FAST. You can also feel uneasy about going to a new school soon, and the fact that you have to make new friends. GIVE will be helpful, and if you want to ask a favor from a parent, friend, or teacher, then use DEAR MAN.

You pick the situation relevant to your life right now and plan in your DBT journal how you'll approach the conversation based on the different steps of the relevant DBT communication skill.

Capture the options you have under every step and visualize how this conversation is going to work out. Once you've had the conversation, return to your journal and record what you think went really well as well as what you can do to improve your approach.

CHAPTER 8: PUTTING IT ALL TOGETHER

You have no control over all that has happened in your past. You can't undo the things you did, nor can you unsay the things you've said during those moments of erupted anger when you've lost all control. There is no point in pondering on these moments covered in shame, humiliation, embarrassment, or guilt. What you can do, though, is to take control over your words and actions, manage your emotions, and improve the image you have of your future.

Even the slightest change you make today has the possibility to ripple out and have a gigantic impact on your life lying ahead. One day, an excited woman met a complete stranger in a miserable state at a coffee vendor, and by taking the time to share all she knew about DBT, she changed the life of that woman and all who love her. I know that woman is me. If it wasn't for the stranger getting a coffee, I wouldn't have gotten to the point of writing this book for you to read. Can you see how far our actions ripple out, affecting people we don't even know?

HOW TO USE THE SHARED KNOWLEDGE AND SKILLS EFFECTIVELY

You have been introduced to some of the most effective and impactful DBT skills, but it may be confusing to determine where to go next. Sometimes, it helps to get a bird's eye view of the path you are not taking to assist you in clearly defining the road you are taking. I think giving you this bird's eye view on DBT will be the final skill I'll be adding to your toolbox.

Essentially, DBT consists of four modules each addressing an area of concern. The four stages are mindfulness, improving distress tolerance, getting better at managing your emotions, and improving your relationships through interpersonal effectiveness.

All four of these modules or stages flow from one to the other. For example, when you become more mindful, you'll get better at identifying your emotions, determining the actual cause of this stress, and managing your distress, consequently improving your relationships. It is why making changes by focusing on one area will improve the others too. But, if you want to enjoy more significant results, it is best to include daily changes in your life that will impact each of these areas individually. It is also why I've given you practical examples of each of these four stages.

As you know, my initial introduction to DBT was rather random, and a lot of what I've learned during the first couple of weeks was through self-study. As I wasn't exactly sure what I was doing, my approach to DBT was rather fast and loose. I lacked discipline, and most of it was rather unstructured or properly planned. I knew I didn't want to be so angry anymore and that my anger and the outbursts that went along with it were hurting the people I love as well as myself. However, when I found the structure I was looking for and could determine what I wanted to achieve by practicing the skill sets I've shared with you, I had direction and focus and my efforts became more effective.

Therefore, I want to recap on what it is you would want to achieve in each of the four DBT modules, to give you the direction which will assist you in making the progress you desire.

MINDFULNESS

Mindfulness improves your skills to observe your environment, both externally and internally. It helps to familiarize yourself with what you feel, ask what causes you to feel this way, and determine whether you are able to make any changes to better your situation or whether healing lies in acceptance. Then, it will also help you to remain mentally present in the moment, which will reduce your worries and anxiety over the future as well as your regrets over past events.

We can divide mindfulness skills into three stages. The one category includes ways to help you cope with your current situation. This is possible by improving the way you observe things, circumstances, and people without judgment. It is all about unbiased awareness. The second focuses on getting better at describing the things you observe. Effectively and accurately put into words what you experience can be challenging at times, but practice makes it far easier to achieve. The third leg is participating and would include yourself as an object to observe. Yes, you are not only getting more efficient in observing and describing external, but also internal, awareness.

The second category of mindfulness skills is coping skills. Firstly, they teach you to become less judgmental in your approach and the words you use. Secondly, it also includes being one-minded in the sense that you learn to focus on one thing at a time and avoid multitasking. Thirdly, it can enhance your effectiveness, your ability to learn how you can become more effective, and clarifies what practices help you the most to achieve a greater sense of mindfulness.

DISTRESS TOLERANCE

Life happens to all of us, regardless of our age or situation. In other words, during the times we get hurt, face stressful times, and are rejected and disappointed, we still need to keep our chin up high—crashing and burning is not an option. Through distress-tolerance skills, you'll get better at dealing with life when it becomes so hard. Grounding yourself is one of the very helpful techniques to master in this module.

EMOTIONAL REGULATION

The skills captured in this module aim to help you to master your emotions instead of succumbing your power to what you are feeling. It requires that you learn to assess every emotion to determine whether it is real or not, as well as whether it is a meta-emotion or a primary one. You also need to discern between which emotions you can change and which demand acceptance as they are relative to circumstances beyond your control. Once you've gotten a firm grasp on your emotions, it is vital that you learn to react to them in the most appropriate manner. Here, the opposite emotion skills are often the hardest to follow, but they also bring exceptional results.

IMPROVING YOUR RELATIONSHIPS

Nobody can make you happy—not your parents, siblings, romantic partners, or even your best friend. They can all contribute to your happiness, but you need to be happy within yourself to have lasting and happy relationships with them all. The more you improve your internal environment and become more content and in control of your life you are, the better these relationships will become too.

Furthermore, remember that when a volcano bursts open and spews molten rock into the air, it is not the volcano that gets hurt in the process. No, the volcano feels a welcome release of built-up pressure. It is, however, the vegetation and any houses in the area that get scorched, & it is the communities that get displaced by the hot lava covering everything they treasure.

The same happens when you are exploding. Immediately, you feel an immense release of anger and other suppressed emotions, but the pain and damage are caused to those who are close to you, your family, friends, and all those who love a volcano enough to put themselves in harm's way. So, by becoming a master of your emotions, being more mindful, and getting better at managing yourself during times of distress, you are also taking care of the relationships you have in your life. You are effectively deciding to become a dormant volcano, no longer threatening those around you.

Even though I am no expert in soil science, I am an avid gardener and have learned that volcano ash is an extremely rich fertilizer, and many plants flourish in nutrient-rich soil once the volcano has stopped erupting and turns dormant. None of the relationships you've destroyed or harmed through the many, many explosions during the years are unsalvageable. Once you become dormant in your anger, you can transform these relationships and help them to flourish just like the rich vegetation we'll find in volcano ash.

UNLEARNING OLD HABITS

The process of learning new skills and habits is a dual process, as you are effectively also unlearning old habits. For every skill that you are working on and getting better at, you are letting go of an existing habit that you've relied upon probably for quite some time.

Just like a caterpillar needs to shed old habits to move onto the next stage and become a butterfly, you, too, have to go through a transformation process to be able to fly. Nature is of course a huge aid in the caterpillar's quest for transformation and it is not so lenient to us mortals, but the following steps will be helpful to you:

ACKNOWLEDGE THAT YOU HAVE A PROBLEM.

Change is hard—very hard at times—and you need to have absolute clarity on why you want to make these changes in your life. Consider what your life would be like in a couple of years from now if you continue in the same manner, and compare that to what your life can be like if you make the necessary changes.

IDENTIFY THE HABITS THAT YOU KNOW YOU NEED TO SHED.

Determine why they are so toxic and what the consequences would be if they remain in your life any longer.

KNOW THAT THE JOURNEY TO SUCCESS COMES WITH MANY UPS AND DOWNS.

It is hardly ever the case that anyone sets out to bring significant change to their lives without regressing at some stage. Therefore, understand that change comes in a cycle.

First, you won't know that your behavior is a problem. Then, you become aware of how bad your anger outbursts are for you and those around you. Next, you are trying to devise a plan to change this situation, which is likely where you are now. The fourth stage comprises action. Now, you are knee-deep in learning new skills. However, as you gradually feel the conditions that initially drove you to change ease, it is easy to become slack. It is when you may skip your mindfulness exercises or meditation, or feel too tired to write in your DBT journal. So, the next stage is often regression, and then you start all over again; or, as you know about the blind spots in the cycle of change now, you can choose to continue your efforts and enjoy change.

START BY TAKING SMALL STEPS.

Small but consistent steps will get you much further than taking huge leaps which you can't sustain.

KNOW WHEN TO ASK FOR HELP.

We all need help at times, and now that you've learned the DEAR MAN skills, reach out & ask for help when you need it.

DIGGING DEEPER

Are you ready for your last guided exercise from me?

I want you to spend a bit of time on this exercise, so maybe find a spot where you can sit undisturbed and truly have the time to dig deep.

Now, list the habits you think you need to change. Then, for every habit, answer the following questions:

- ✓ What am I doing that is a problem?
- ✓ Why is it a problem?
- ✓ To whom is this a problem?
- ✓ What is going to happen if I don't change my behavior?
- ✓ What is going to happen if I don't change my behavior?
- ✓ What can my life look like if I do make the necessary changes?

- ✓ Does the value I attach to my current problematic behavior even measure up against what I can gain from making these changes?

- ✓ What obstacles can I expect along the way? In this question, consider the fact that you may lose some people whom you've considered to be friends.

A few years ago, I met Carl. Carl's anger was fueled by the people he surrounded himself with every day at school. They were a group of youngsters who would gather and energize themselves by watching the impact of their destructive behavior. They were responsible for several graffiti incidents at their school and the other students almost feared them as they were such an explosive bunch of kids hanging out together. Yet, Carl wanted to change and he had to prepare himself to lose these people. For a certain time, he became the person they zoomed their focus on, but in Carl's words, "Knowing what I know now, it was all worth it."

Linked to the previous question is my last and final question: Who would you like to be friends with in the future you are preparing for yourself?

When you have absolute clarity on all these points, there is no more reason to hang onto your old life, simply because it is familiar. Then, you are heading in the right direction, you only need to take that very important first step.

CONCLUSION

66
The past cannot be changed. The future is yet in your power.
99
-Mary Pickford

One of the most frustrating things is to acknowledge you have a problem, to start working on it—like reading this book—by practicing the steps as you go along, and then... you don't see any immediate change.

This has been such a major challenge for me, and I can only imagine that it is even worse for you. When I was a teenager, life was just a little slower than it is now. The reality is that technology has transformed us into a generation of people used to instant gratification.

When I say instant gratification, I mean that if you want to know if a centipede really has 1,000 legs, you ask Google and yield multiple answers within seconds. When you see a pair of sneakers you like online, you press add to cart, complete the transaction, and within a couple of days, it arrives at your door. We don't have to wait long for anything really, except the processes that remain dependent on the human mind.

The mind hasn't evolved with technology. Sure, we are capable of working with all the advanced tools we have access to, but our minds didn't change much over the past couple of centuries.

This means the expectation of when you can see results and the reality of how soon your efforts will bring you the desired outcome are even more out of line than a couple of years ago when it was me standing in your shoes.

So, as you've reached this point in the book, I think it is safe to assume, you are desperate in your situation and are committed to taking the steps necessary to bring about the change you desire. You've also attached a certain credibility to everything I've shared from my experience with DBT and are optimistic that it will instigate change in your life. Therefore, I am asking you to be patient, kind to yourself, persistent in your efforts, and know that change is a choice you have to make every day of your life. Still, I would wake up every morning knowing and telling myself that living the life I deserve is a choice I have to make several times during my day.

DBT takes time and so does change. How much time it will take depends entirely on you. Every person is unique in personality, circumstances, the severity of their anger, and their expectations of the future. For some, DBT brings the results they are seeking within six months. Others sometimes work relentlessly for a year before they can notice significant differences. What makes it even harder is that at times these differences can be so subtle that it is easy to miss them. Therefore, keep track of your emotions and incidents in your journal as much as possible. Here, you'll be able to measure the change in your behavior far more effectively. Keep in mind that there are certain types of behavior and problematic symptoms that may stay with you even long after you've already invested a year into resolving them. The difference is thought that even if these symptoms remain around for longer than you want, you've disempowered them from having any control over your life as you are now fully equipped with all the skills you need to manage your emotions, especially anger, effectively.

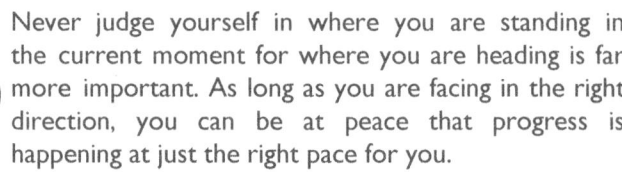

Never judge yourself in where you are standing in the current moment for where you are heading is far more important. As long as you are facing in the right direction, you can be at peace that progress is happening at just the right pace for you.

You have the tools to empower yourself, and when you've reached this point of the book, I know that you've created a strong and sturdy foundation for weathering the storms life will send across your way with ease and success. Now, go forth, and gently introduce the world to the newer & greater version of you.

GLOSSARY

These definitions can also be found in my other book: DBT Skills and Mindfulness for Teen Anxiety: A Neurodivergent Friendly Guide for Emotional Regulation to Understand, Manage, and Prevent Toxic Emotions; Overcome Fear, Panic, and Worry

ACCEPTS:

ACCEPTS is a DBT skill that stands for activities, contributing, comparisons, emotions, pushing away, thoughts, and sensations. It is a skill used to distract your mind from obsessing over the cause of your anger.

AMYGDALA:

The amygdala is the area in the brain where we process memories, and it plays especially an important role in how we remember memories. It has the size and shape of two walnuts and is situated deeply in the brain's center.

BORDERLINE PERSONALITY DISORDER (BPD):

BDP is a mental disorder characterized by difficulty with emotion regulation, interpersonal functioning, and the stability of behavior. People with BPD may experience intense emotions, fear of abandonment, impulsive behaviors, and unstable relationships. DBT is an evidence-based form of treatment for BPD.

DEAR MAN:

DEAR MAN is a dialectical behavior therapy skill that stands for describe, express, assert, reinforce, mindful, appear, express, assert, reinforce, mindful, appear confident, and negotiate. It is used to help people learn how to be assertive in their communication with others.

DIALECTICAL BEHAVIOR THERAPY (DBT):

DBT is a type of talk therapy for people who experience emotions like anger intensely. The type of therapy relies on learning various skills to treat a range of mental health concerns like BPD, but it can also improve mental health in a range of other ways.

DISTRESS TOLERANCE:

The term refers to the ability to tolerate distressful emotions and experiences without making them worse. This includes learning how to control your reactions when faced with a difficult situation and developing the ability to ride out the storm until it passes.

FAST:

FAST is an interpersonal effectiveness skill acronym for fair; apology; sticking to values and facts; and truth. It can be used to help you stay focused on the important issues in a conversation and speak your truth respectfully.

GIVE:

GIVE is an interpersonal effectiveness skill acronym for gentle, interested, validating, and easy manner. It can help you communicate effectively in difficult situations.

GROUNDING:

Grounding refers to a set of skills to help you stay in the moment while feeling overwhelmed by feelings. By remaining in the present at the moment, it becomes easier to deal with distress.

INTERPERSONAL EFFECTIVENESS:

Interpersonal effectiveness refers to the ability to get what you want while maintaining, or even improving, relationships. It is a set of skills designed to help you communicate effectively and navigate social situations with ease.

MINDFULNESS:

Mindfulness is the practice of focusing on the present moment without judgment or analysis. It involves cultivating an awareness of your thoughts, feelings, and environment in order to gain insight into your feelings and sensations.

OPPOSITE ACTION:

This is an emotion regulation skill used to help you shift your emotional state in a way that is helpful and adaptive. It involves taking action that is the opposite of what your current emotion might suggest, such as forcing yourself to act cheerful when sad.

RADICAL ACCEPTANCE:

Radical acceptance is a practice of embracing and accepting the present moment without judgment or resistance. It allows you to acknowledge your feelings and experiences without getting caught up in the need to change them. In DBT, radical acceptance is one of the four core skills and can increase self-compassion.

RAIN:

RAIN is a DBT skill that stands for recognize, allow, investigate, and nonidentification. It is used to help people to face strong emotions by turning toward what they experience in a nonjudgmental way.

STOP:

STOP is an emotion regulation skill acronym that stands for stop, take a step back, observe the situation objectively, and proceed mindfully. It can help you stay mindful in difficult moments and make decisions based on what is best for you.

THINK:

THINK is an interpersonal effectiveness skill acronym that stands for think, have empathy, interpretations, notice, and kindness. It can help you communicate effectively in difficult situations.

TIPP:

TIPP is a distress tolerance skill acronym that stands for temperature, intense, exercise, paced breathing, and progressive muscle relaxation. It can help you cope with difficult emotions in a healthy way.

VALIDATION:

Validation is the process of recognizing and understanding another person's feelings and experiences without judgment or criticism. It can build relationships and foster greater empathy, understanding, and compassion between people. In DBT, validation is a core skill that can help you better understand yourself and others.

WISE MIND:

This is a concept that combines the logical and emotional aspects of the self. It encourages you to use both your rational and intuitive sides to make decisions, rather than relying on one or the other. In DBT, the wise mind serves as a guiding principle for making mindful, balanced decisions.

THE DBT SKILLS WORKBOOK FOR TEENS

ANXIETY RECOVERY

Develop essential coping skills for anxiety
relief and effective self-regulation using
Dialectical Behavioral Therapy and
Mindfulness techniques

M.A. MARTINE

INTRODUCTION

D o you struggle with your emotions or mental health issues that make you feel like life is too hard? Perhaps, as a teen, you have thought about what it would be like to have control over those overwhelming and confusing feelings? Or maybe you have tried different methods to manage your mood, but you are still looking for a better solution. *DBT Skills and Mindfulness for Teen Anxiety* is here to help!

This book offers an excellent introduction to dialectical behavioral therapy (DBT) and gives you the tools you need to live a healthier and happier life. It contains skill-building exercises, helpful tips and strategies, and much more. With the help of this book, you can gain insight into how to manage your emotions and become an expert in self-care.

DBT was originally developed as a treatment for people suffering from borderline personality disorder (BPD), but has since been adapted to many other conditions. It is a type of cognitive behavioral therapy (CBT) that focuses on helping people to recognize and manage intense emotions, thoughts, and behaviors. DBT uses a multi-faceted approach, combining mindfulness techniques, skills training, and behavior modification to create lasting change in a person's life.

DBT teaches practical tools that can be used to manage intense emotions and difficult situations. It helps you learn how to stay present in the moment without letting your thoughts take control of your behavior. Although the skills in DBT require time, patience, and practice, they have helped many people transform their lives and live above the limitations of their emotional and mental health problems.

When I was a teen, I struggled to solidify relationships with others or think positively about myself. I didn't get along well with my classmates and I often felt overwhelmed by my anxieties. Instead, I was constantly overthinking, second-guessing myself, and avoiding tough conversations. I would spend hours questioning how to respond to a text message from a friend, and I couldn't bear the thought of talking to someone who might reject me.

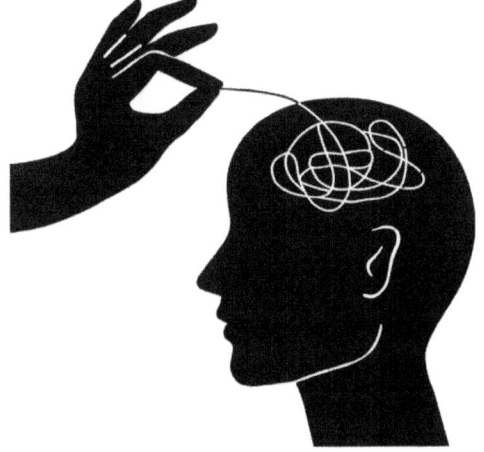

This constant turmoil led to a lot of self-destructive behavior. In high school, I became depressed. To numb the negative thoughts, I started drinking and partying. This pain and agony continued into my college years, where I ultimately dropped out.

Unfortunately, my relationships with others weren't the only challenges I faced. I also dealt with depression, anxiety, and addiction during my teenage years. It wasn't until I started practicing mindful activities that I was able to find relief from these issues. For me, personally, yoga and meditation were incredibly helpful in calming down my nervous system, helping me become more aware of my thoughts and feelings, and guiding me in learning how to better regulate my emotions.

Mindful activities are beneficial for all teens, regardless of their current mental health state. Taking the time to be present and connect with your emotions can help improve overall well-being and bring about positive changes in life. So, whether it's taking a mindful walk, doing yoga, or writing down your thoughts and feelings, there are many mindful activities that can help teens cope with stress and anxiety.

I wasn't a teen when I started DBT. I was well into my 20s when I realized something was amiss. While it's never too late to try therapy or psychological tools like DBT, had I used these tools as a teenager, I would have been better equipped to manage my feelings and relationships. That's why this book is such an important resource for teens who are struggling with the same issues I experienced. *DBT Skills and Mindfulness for Teen Anxiety* helps young people identify, understand, and manage their intense emotions like anger, sadness, and anxiety so that they can reach their full potential.

The book explains DBT skills in an easy-to-understand way, using language and examples that apply to teens. It takes a positive approach by focusing on developing healthy coping strategies rather than problem-solving. Readers will discover the importance of self-care, learn how to pay attention to their own emotions, and be better able to communicate their needs in healthy ways. With the help of this book, teens can learn to manage their emotions and develop healthier relationships with others, which will give them the confidence they need to succeed in life.

It was only after I started to use the skills that I share with you in this book that my life slowly began to change. After learning DBT skills, I could recognize my emotions more clearly, feel more in control of my thoughts and behaviors, and become much more confident in expressing myself in relationships with others. With the help of mindfulness, distress tolerance, and other DBT skills, I could step back and recognize my thoughts for what they were—just thoughts—and take control of my emotions and reactions. Through practice, the concepts became second nature, and I started living life according to my own values without feeling dragged down by negative emotions.

This book is here to provide you with the same skills and understanding that helped me thrive. Learning DBT skills can help you gain valuable insight into how your emotions and thoughts influence your behavior, and help you make positive changes in your life. It is important to remember that DBT requires practice and consistency in order to be successful. It can take time before the skills become second nature, but with dedication and motivation, you can gain control over intense emotions or mental health issues.

IN THIS BOOK, YOU WILL LEARN:

- ✅ the four modules of DBT and how to use them in your life

- ✅ mindfulness techniques to help you stay present in the moment

- ✅ coping skills to manage difficult emotions and behaviors

- ✅ how to effectively communicate with others

- ✅ tips and advice for overcoming self-destructive behavior

- ✅ practical tools for managing anxiety, depression, and other mental health issues

- ✅ how to identify your triggers

- ✅ how to build healthy relationships

- ✅ how to regulate your emotions and become a master of self-care

Unfortunately, these skills don't always come easy to us. Perhaps we endured trauma that has resulted in intense emotions and difficult behaviors. Or, maybe we just didn't have the right resources or support when we needed it the most. No matter what the situation is, this book will help you relearn healthy skills that can prompt you to take control of your emotions and improve your mental health.

DBT Skills and Mindfulness for Teen Anxiety is a great resource for discovering and mastering the skills you need to live a life free from intense emotions and mental health struggles. If you are committed to making changes and living a life free of self-destructive behavioral patterns, this book will help you achieve your goals. Good luck on this journey!

PART ONE

UNDERSTANDING AND BENEFITS

CHAPTER 1: WHAT IS DBT?

Before we dive deep into the ins and outs of dialectical behavior therapy (DBT), I would like you to take a moment and do an internal assessment.

Take this time to consider a problem that you're having. It can be anything from depression, anxiety, or stress, to difficult relationships. Maybe you struggle to communicate with your family or friends or to make decisions. Now ask yourself—what is your goal? How would you like to overcome this issue and move forward in life? What tools would you need to overcome the hurdles you're facing?

Now, there's one more thing I want you to consider: What lesson can you learn from your struggles? In other words, what can you take away from the experience that will help you in the future? For instance, if you're struggling to communicate with others, what lessons do you think you can learn to help you with communication in the future? In what ways would you be able to look at your challenges from a loving and accepting perspective?

These questions can be hard to answer, and that's why DBT is here to help. DBT is a type of therapy that uses mindfulness, interpersonal effectiveness, distress tolerance, and emotional regulation strategies to help people address their challenges. Basically, it helps you become more aware of your thoughts and feelings so you can better manage them and find positive solutions to your problems.

Dialectical behavior therapy is all about providing you with the skills and tools to overcome any problem or difficulty that life throws your way. It's a form of cognitive behavioral therapy, or CBT, which works by helping you understand how your thoughts and behaviors are connected. DBT helps teach you different strategies for managing difficult emotions, developing healthier relationships, and improving communication skills.

It also helps you learn how to recognize and accept your own emotions and the emotions of others. With DBT, you can begin to understand why it's important to take a thoughtful approach for solving problems and making decisions. DBT isn't just about problem-solving—it's also about taking care of yourself and learning how to accept your struggles as part of life. DBT works by teaching you new skills

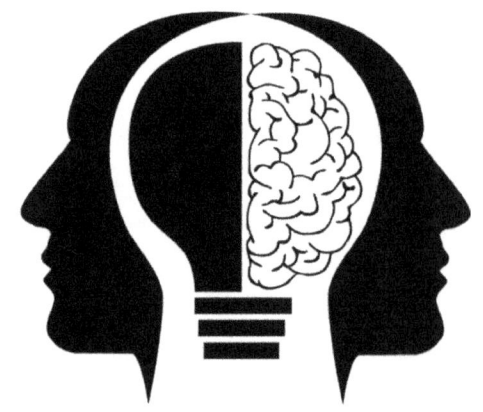

and strategies that can be used in both the short-term and long-term. In the short-term, DBT helps teach you how to better manage immediate stressors or challenges. In the long-term, DBT helps you learn to accept yourself and build healthier relationships with others.

THE HISTORY OF DBT

Dialectical behavior therapy is an evidence-based psychological therapy that was devel-oped by psychologist Marsha Linehan in the 1980s (Schimelpfening, 2022). It combines cognitive behavioral therapy with elements of Eastern spiritual practices and philoso-phies, such as mindfulness, acceptance, nonjudgmental attitudes, and other principles from Buddhism. DBT works to help people identify and manage their own emotions, become more aware of the reactions of others, build better relationships, and make more mindful decisions.

DBT teaches people skills like emotion regulation, distress tolerance, and interpersonal effectiveness (Schimelpfening, 2022). The idea behind this type of therapy is that by teaching an individual these skills, they will better manage their emotions and reactions in difficult or stressful situations. By taking the time to learn and practice these skills, people can work toward becoming more accepting of themselves, as well as others. At its core, DBT helps people recognize self-destructive behaviors. From there, they can change or develop new skills to cope with life's challenges in healthier ways.

By understanding how their thoughts affect their behavior and by developing healthy coping skills, individuals can gain greater control over their own lives and ultimately create a more positive self-image.

WHAT IS DBT
USED FOR?

Dialectical behavior therapy can treat a variety of mental health issues, such as depression, substance abuse, anxiety, and post-traumatic stress disorder (Schimelpfening, 2022). It is also often used to help people
with borderline personality disorder (BPD) or those who have difficulty controlling their emotions. DBT can help these people gain insight into how their thoughts and reactions affect their behavior and relationships. It also provides them with the tools to create positive change in their life.

WHY DOES DBT WORK?

The success of DBT lies in its ability to help individuals manage difficult emotions and behaviors. By teaching people skills like emotion regulation, distress tolerance, and interpersonal effectiveness, they can learn how to control their emotions and reactions in difficult or stressful situations. This can help them become more accepting of themselves and others, which ultimately helps improve their self-image and overall mental health.

HOW DOES DBT WORK?

Dialectical behavior therapy works by teaching people skills such as emotion regulation, distress tolerance, and interpersonal effectiveness. It also incorporates mindfulness-based practices such as meditation and breathing exercises that help to increase awareness of one's thoughts and emotions. In addition, individuals in DBT will also receive individual counseling sessions with their therapist in order to discuss their goals and progress.

Overall, by teaching individuals skills such as emotion regulation, distress tolerance, and interpersonal effectiveness, people can understand how their thoughts affect their behavior and create positive change in their life.

WHAT ARE THE PROS AND CONS OF DBT?

The pros of DBT include:

✔ It can help individuals gain insight into how their thoughts, reactions, and behavior.

✔ It teaches valuable skills, such as emotion regulation, distress tolerance, and interpersonal effectiveness.

✔ It can be done in both individual and group settings, making it easy for people to get the help they need in a safe and supportive environment.

The cons of DBT include:

✔ It can require a lot of time and effort from the individual in order to get the most out of it.

✔ It may not be suitable for everyone depending on their needs, goals, and lifestyle.

✔ It is not always covered by insurance and can be expensive.

DBT EFFECTIVENESS

The evidence for the effectiveness of dialectical behavior therapy is extensive. Studies have shown that DBT can be a powerful tool in helping people reduce symptoms of depression, anxiety, and borderline personality disorder. It has also been found to help those struggling with substance abuse, eating disorders, and post-traumatic stress disorder.

DBT has been effective in reducing self-harm behaviors, suicidal thoughts, and improving interpersonal relationships. It also helps people develop a better understanding of their emotions and how to manage them. Furthermore, DBT works by helping people recognize the interconnectedness between their thoughts, feelings, and behaviors.

Another effective aspect of DBT is that dialectical means to find a middle ground between two opposites, and this is exactly what DBT teaches (Pieper, 2022). It encourages you to accept the difficult emotions and thoughts that you're feeling while also trying to find a way to move forward. Dialectics teaches you that your emotions and thoughts might not be accurate, but you can still accept them, anyway. Additionally, this therapy teaches you that others may have a different point of view, yet still be valid.

In short, dialectical behavior therapy is a powerful tool that can help you navigate through challenging times in life and work towards long-term goals. With DBT, you'll learn how to better manage emotions and thoughts, develop healthier relationships with others, and gain self-acceptance. The tools and strategies learned through this therapy can be used for a lifetime.

HOW DOES TEEN AND ADULT DBT DIFFER?

While the core principles of DBT are the same, certain aspects make Teen DBT different from Adult DBT. The crucial difference is that it focuses on helping teens to identify and manage their emotions in age-appropriate ways. This includes teaching teens how to recognize, cope, and develop healthy ways of expressing their feelings. Teen DBT also places greater emphasis on the importance of parental involvement in order to ensure that teens are getting the help they need.

In summary, dialectical behavior therapy has been found to be an effective treatment for a variety of mental health issues and Teen DBT is tailored to the needs of young kids, with greater emphasis on parental involvement and teaching teens age-appropriate ways of managing their emotions.

 # WHAT ARE THE BENEFITS OF TEEN DBT?

The benefits of Teen DBT include improved ability to manage emotions, reduced symptoms of mental health issues such as depression, anxiety, and PTSD, enhanced interpersonal relationships, and greater satisfaction with life. Additionally, this type of therapy can provide teens with insight into their thoughts and behaviors in order to create positive change. Furthermore, teen DBT places great emphasis on parental involvement, which can help ensure that teens are receiving the help they need. Some additional benefits they may receive are:

- ✔ increased self-awareness

- ✔ improved communication skills

- ✔ improved problem-solving strategies

- ✔ reduced impulsivity and aggression

Overall, Teen DBT can be a valuable tool in helping teens to navigate the often tumultuous journey of adolescence. With the right guidance and commitment, it can help them develop healthy coping mechanisms and gain insight into their thoughts and behaviors.

THE PREMISES OF DBT

Dialectical behavior therapy is based on the problems you are facing. In the DBT, those problems boil down to two culprits:

- ✓ Faulty, negative, or unhealthy thought patterns: DBT teaches individuals to identify and challenge faulty thoughts. It helps them develop healthier thought patterns that lead to positive behavior outcomes.

- ✓ Unhelpful learned behavior: DBT focuses on developing new skills and strategies that allow individuals to handle difficult situations positively.

For example, our thought patterns can lead us to believe that we need to be perfect in order to be accepted. We may then develop behaviors designed to prove our worth, such as overeating, skipping class, or working too hard. DBT helps teens recognize and challenge these thoughts in order to come up with healthier strategies for dealing with difficult emotions like stress and anxiety.

On the other hand, unhelpful learned behaviors can lead to further issues. For example, if a teen is skipping school, it's likely that they are engaging in other negative behaviors like drug and alcohol use. DBT helps teens recognize the connection between their behavior and its consequences, so they can develop new skills and strategies to handle difficult situations positively.

Overall, these two premises form the foundation of DBT and help individuals learn healthy behaviors and thought patterns that can lead to lasting change in their lives. People struggling with psychological problems can learn better ways of coping with them, relieving their symptoms, and becoming more effective in their lives.

Dialectical behavior therapy can accomplish this, and it's an effective tool for teens to learn how to manage their emotions in order to change their lives. Completing these four stages will cause an individual to have better control over their emotions and behaviors, increased sense of purpose, improved relationships with others, and increased satisfaction in life.

GROUP VERSUS INDIVIDUAL SESSIONS FOR TEENS

When learning DBT skills, teens have the option of joining a group or having individual sessions. Individual sessions provide a safe and intimate environment for teens to work through their issues. During individual sessions, teens can speak openly about their feelings without worrying about being judged or ridiculed. This allows them to explore their emotions in a safe space so that they can come up with healthier solutions on how to handle them.

Group sessions usually involve about 8–10 participants and a therapist who guides the session. This is an effective way for teens to practice their DBT skills in a safe and supportive environment and connect with other teens who are struggling with similar issues. However, it can be difficult for some teens to share their experiences in a group setting. Through both individual and group sessions, teens can explore their emotions safely and find lasting solutions for difficult situations.

Some pros are:

Teens can benefit from the support of group members.

Group sessions provide teens with a safe environment in which to practice DBT skills.

Teens learn how to manage emotions in social situations.

Some cons are:

Some teens may not feel comfortable expressing their feelings in a group setting.

It's difficult to get quality feedback from everyone in a group setting.

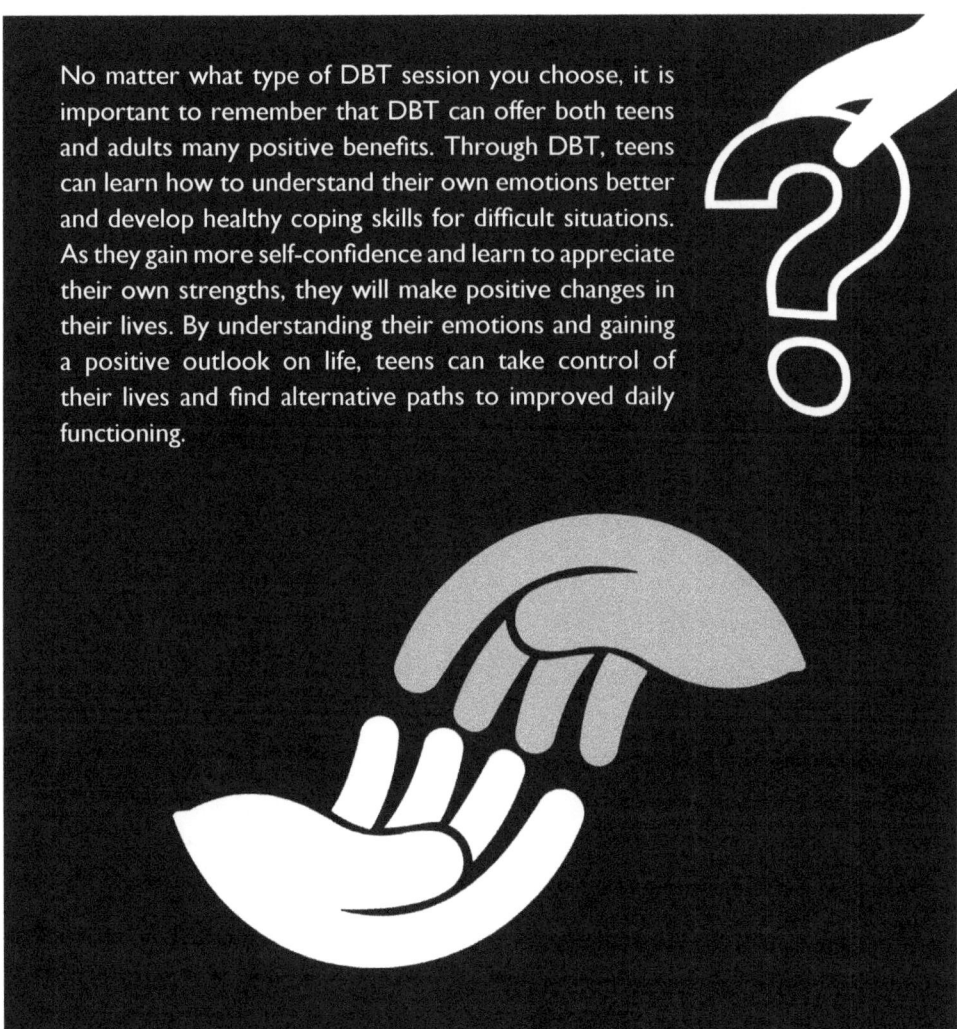

No matter what type of DBT session you choose, it is important to remember that DBT can offer both teens and adults many positive benefits. Through DBT, teens can learn how to understand their own emotions better and develop healthy coping skills for difficult situations. As they gain more self-confidence and learn to appreciate their own strengths, they will make positive changes in their lives. By understanding their emotions and gaining a positive outlook on life, teens can take control of their lives and find alternative paths to improved daily functioning.

CHAPTER 2: HOW DOES DBT WORK?

Now that we've reviewed what DBT is and how it can be beneficial for teens, let's look at how DBT actually works.

In the last chapter, we reviewed the four domains of DBT: mindfulness, emotional regulation, distress tolerance, and interpersonal effectiveness. Each of these domains is composed of unique skills that can help teens manage their emotions in healthy ways. These skills are necessary to help us solve problems. In this chapter, we'll review how these skills work with one another to build upon each other and form effective solutions.

However, before we jump in, I want you to reconsider the problem you thought about at the beginning of Chapter 1. Recall that I asked you to think of a problem or challenge that you're having currently and what your goals are. Now, think back to that same problem and how you want to solve it. What are your go-to problem-solving methods?

Do you usually try to talk it out with someone or do you prefer to just let it all sink in? It's helpful to reflect on how we usually approach solving problems because these are our natural instincts. It's important to recognize that, while these methods may work sometimes, they don't always lead to the best solution. That's where DBT comes in.

DBT is a method of problem-solving that helps you think logically and make decisions based on facts, not emotions. It teaches you how to recognize your own emotions and how to regulate them so they don't get out of control. This way, you can be proactive about problem-solving instead of simply reacting emotionally.

FOUR SOLUTIONS TO ANY PROBLEM

When it comes to problem-solving, you theoretically have four options: stay miserable, tolerate the problem, feel better about the problem, or solve the problem *(4 DBT Problem-Solving Options You Can Use to Solve Any Problem,* 2017). Each of these options corresponds to a different domain within DBT.

With each of these solutions comes pros and cons. For instance, if you choose to stay miserable, you'll remain stuck in the same spot. You won't use skills to improve your life and the problem won't get any better. So, let's say the challenge you're facing is a disagreement with your parents. If you choose to stay miserable, you'll remain at an impasse and nothing will change.

The second option is to tolerate the problem. This involves accepting the situation for what it is and learning to cope with it. This can be beneficial if there aren't solutions to your problem and it isn't a situation where you have control. For instance, with a disagreement with your parents, you may need to accept that it's out of your hands and practice distress tolerance skills. While this isn't the most welcomed response, it eases some of the frustration and can be a healthy way to cope.

The third option is to feel better about the problem. This could involve using coping skills, such as mindfulness or emotional regulation, to process your feelings and gain some perspective on the situation. In this case, you might not solve the problem directly, but you can alter the way you feel about it, which will ease some of the emotional distress. For example, you could practice mindfulness to stay present in the moment and learn to better recognize your own emotions.

The fourth option is to solve the problem. This requires a combination of skills from all four domains. You'll need to use distress tolerance strategies to remain calm and open-minded, interpersonal effectiveness skills to communicate effectively, emotional regulation strategies to manage your emotions, and mindfulness skills to stay grounded in the present. In the case of a disagreement with your parents, you may need to use these skills together to come up with a solution that works for everyone.

In this way, DBT provides us with a roadmap to effectively solve problems by addressing them from all angles. Once you have practiced these skills and gained more understanding of how they fit together, you'll be able to build upon them and create your own successful problem-solving strategies.

By utilizing the four solutions of DBT, you can be more proactive in solving your problems. It will take practice and dedication, but with persistence and support, you can learn how to effectively use these skills and make positive changes in your life. Don't forget that finding a solution isn't always easy and sometimes it may feel like you're stuck in a rut. But with DBT, you can learn how to take steps toward making meaningful changes and finding the best solution for any problem.

THE FOUR MODULES OF DBT AND PROBLEM-SOLVING

In order to understand how DBT works, it's important to first look at the four modules within this type of therapy. The four domains—mindfulness, emotional regulation, distress tolerance and interpersonal effectiveness—are each composed of unique skills that can help us better manage our emotions. Together, these four modules work together to form an effective system for problem-solving.

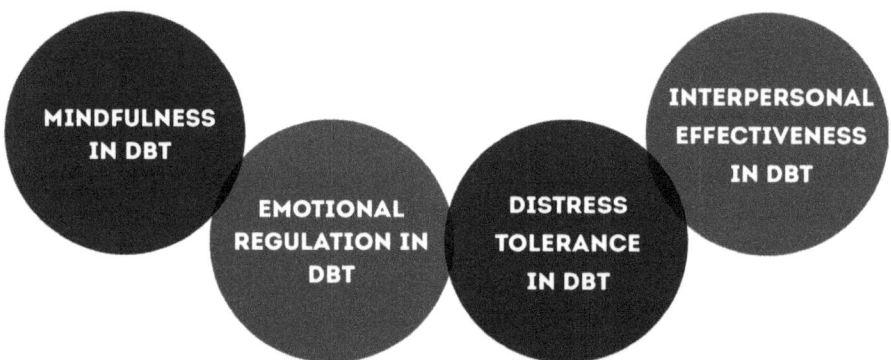

MINDFULNESS IN DBT

This technique can teach you to concentrate on the present moment and be aware of their emotions without judgment (Schimelpfening, 2022). You may notice your mind wanders, but mindfulness teaches you how to refocus when this happens. This can be useful for finding solutions to any problem because it helps us to stay in the present moment and objectively observe the situation.

Mindfulness also applies to activities like meditation, which can help us communicate with our intuition and practice self-care. This is important for problem-solving because it allows us to step back and gain perspective on the issue at hand. Also, by participating in the moment, we can observe our reactions and use this knowledge to better understand the issue.

Overall, mindfulness teaches you how to do one thing at a time and focus on what works for you. You allow yourself to observe your behavior, thoughts, or emotions without acting on them.

EMOTIONAL REGULATION IN DBT

This module focuses on helping you identify, understand, and control your emotions (Schimelpfening, 2022). You may learn to recognize what triggers your emotions, how to express them without damaging relationships or engaging in self-harmful behavior, and how to create positive change in yourself.

This domain teaches you how to become aware of your emotions and learn how to manage them (Schimelpfening, 2022). It involves identifying our feelings and understanding where they come from, as well as learning how to process the emotions in a healthy way. This can be beneficial for problem-solving because it allows us to identify and process our reactions before we take action.

The function of emotions is to protect us, but also to make sure that we're in harmony with our environment. We can use this knowledge to better manage our emotions and create a more positive outlook on the problem at hand.

However, these emotions can also come with an action urge. For example, when we feel angry, we are likely to want to act on that feeling right away. By practicing emotional regulation, we can learn how to identify and manage these action urges in order to find better solutions to the problem.

> Emotion regulation teaches you to understand and label emotions, reduce emotional vulnerability, and decrease emotional suffering.

DISTRESS TOLERANCE IN DBT

This technique teaches you how to tolerate uncomfortable or painful situations without trying to escape from them or make them worse (Schimelpfening, 2022). It is especially helpful for people who struggle with impulsivity and self-destructive behavior.

It involves learning how to accept the situation for what it is, as well as understanding our triggers and dealing with any self-destructive behavior that may be present. This can help us find solutions because it gives us an alternative to dealing with our emotions in an unhealthy way.

Distress tolerance also includes skills such as radical acceptance and self-soothing, which focus on accepting the current situation without judgment and taking care of yourself while you are going through it. This can help us move forward with a more positive outlook on the problem at hand and find better solutions. Teens with anxiety, depression, or other emotional issues will benefit from distress tolerance.

INTERPERSONAL EFFECTIVENESS IN DBT

This technique focuses on teaching people how to relate to and interact with others, including staying assertive while respecting the needs of other people (Schimelpfening, 2022). If you don't know how to say no without feeling guilty or how to express your opinion without being aggressive, this module can help.

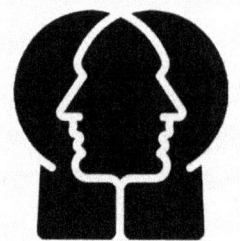

It involves learning how to effectively express our needs, set boundaries, and advocate for ourselves. This can help us with problem-solving because it gives us the tools to communicate our concerns without losing sight of what we need.

Interpersonal effectiveness includes skills such as assertiveness, which teaches us how to express our needs without sacrificing our values and respect for others. This is important for problem-solving because it gives us the confidence to stand up for ourselves while also taking into consideration the feelings of those around us. Ultimately, interpersonal effectiveness helps teens learn how to maintain the relationships that are important to them while also taking care of their own needs.

Overall, DBT is a comprehensive form of therapy that teaches you how to manage your emotions and reactions in difficult situations. By using all four modules, you can learn how to effectively regulate your emotions, establish healthy relationships with others, and develop greater distress tolerance. In this way, DBT can be a powerful tool for creating positive change in your life.

STAGES AND GOALS IN DBT

The four stages of dialectical behavior therapy provide a framework for goal-setting and progress. These are:

Stabilization: The focus here is on developing skills to help individuals with immediate crises and reducing behaviors that are self-destructive or harmful. They might be depressed and at their lowest of lows.

Emotional pain: This stage focuses on teaching individuals how to manage painful and overwhelming emotions when they arise. Their actions may have improved, but they still struggle with their emotions.

Goal setting and maintaining progress: This stage focuses on helping individuals to set realistic goals and develop strategies for achieving them. This promotes stability, which is important for long-term success.

Spiritual fulfillment: This stage is about helping individuals to find peace and satisfaction in their lives. It focuses on developing a sense of purpose, meaning, and connection with the world around them.

 **DBT HELPS YOU IDENTIFY YOUR STRENGTHS AND WEAKNESSES**

DBT can help teens identify their own strengths, which are often hidden beneath the surface. When exploring new ways of managing emotions and dealing with difficult situations, it helps to know what positive characteristics you already possess. This can give teens more confidence in themselves and can provide a foundation for growth through DBT.

It focuses on teaching teens how to recognize when they need help and how to ask for it. This helps them become better at problem-solving and developing solutions to challenges in their lives. It also helps them develop healthier relationships with others by understanding how their behavior and emotions affect those around them. In addition, DBT also helps teens identify areas of difficulty and potential triggers that may lead to self-destructive or impulsive behaviors. With this knowledge, they can develop skills to better manage difficult situations and protect themselves from harm.

For instance, if a teen is a natural problem solver, they can use that skill to create solutions for difficult situations. Or, if they're an empathetic listener, they can put that skill to good use when communicating with others. Additionally, understanding their weaknesses can be just as important. It's essential to recognize triggers that lead to impulsive behavior and know how to manage them before they become overwhelming.

Overall, by gaining a better understanding of yourself, you can learn how to better manage your emotions, create healthier relationships with others, and become more in tune with your life goals. DBT helps you develop greater insight into your thoughts and feelings, which translates into improved daily functioning.

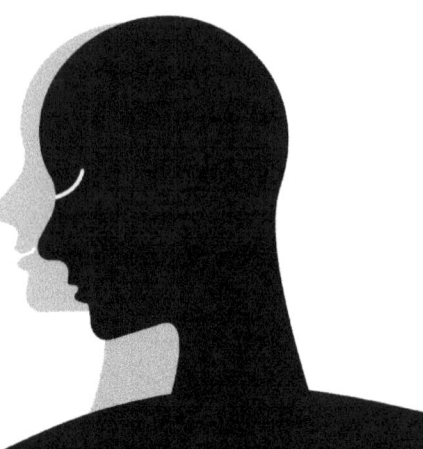

DBT BUILDS A POSITIVE SELF-IMAGE AND SELF-ESTEEM

DBT is a therapy that helps teens build a positive self-image and self-esteem. By understanding their strengths and weaknesses, they can develop greater confidence in themselves and be better equipped to handle difficult situations. Through DBT, teens learn how to identify their needs, set goals for themselves, and create strategies for achieving them. By engaging in the four stages of DBT, individuals can learn to accept their own positive qualities.

Part of DBT is acceptance. Acceptance is key because it helps you to appreciate and see yourself in a more favorable light. Once you've come to terms with your strengths, you will be better equipped to handle difficult situations without resorting to unhealthy behaviors.

DBT helps individuals to recognize and embrace the unique qualities that make them who they are. This allows teens to be more comfortable with themselves and promotes a positive self-image. As you learn to appreciate yourself, your self-esteem will also improve.

For example, if you are naturally creative, DBT can help you learn how to use your creativity to make positive changes in your life. Instead of pushing away the parts of yourself that make you unique, DBT encourages you to embrace them and turn them into strengths. DBT is a powerful form of therapy that can help teens build self-confidence, manage emotions, and create healthier relationships with others.

DBT is an effective tool for problem-solving because it provides us with skills and tools to manage our emotions, tolerate distress, and interact with others in a productive way. With practice, teens can learn how to use these skills to better deal with their emotional problems and create better solutions for the issues they face.

In DBT, teens learn to take control of their emotions and reactions, which can lead to healthier decision-making and problem-solving skills that will stay with them throughout their lives. By using the skills learned through DBT, teens can gain the confidence to handle difficult emotions, take action in a more effective manner, and break out of patterns of unhealthy coping.

With this newfound knowledge, they can feel empowered to tackle their problems head-on and create solutions that will help them in the long run. They'll also be better equipped to navigate relationships and build a strong support system that will help them when they feel overwhelmed. Ultimately, DBT can help teens find a more positive outlet for their emotions and learn how to create better solutions for the issues they face.

CHAPTER 3: IDENTIFYING THE PROBLEM

Now that we've identified the skills and tools available to us through DBT, let's look at how we can use them to identify the problem we're facing.

The first step is to take a few moments to think about what problem you want to solve. This could be anything from dealing with anxiety or depression, managing anger or stress, or working on improving relationships. Take your time and think about what it is you want to address. The first step is to identify the issue that is causing distress or discomfort in your life.

Once you have identified the problem, it is important to figure out what caused it. This could include anything from past experiences or trauma, environmental factors, unhealthy coping mechanisms or relationships, and much more. Thinking about these causes can help you better understand why you are feeling this way and give you a better sense of what needs to be addressed.

Once you have identified the issue and its potential causes, it is time to think about potential solutions. This could involve using DBT skills such as mindfulness and distress tolerance to better manage your emotions, or interpersonal effectiveness skills in order to communicate more effectively with others.

 **COMMON EMOTIONAL AND MENTAL CONCERNS FOR TEENS**

One in seven teens will experience a mental health disorder in their lifetime (World Health Organization, 2021). This can range from anxiety, depression, and trauma to bipolar disorder and schizophrenia. No matter what your issues are, it is important to know that you are not alone and there are people who care about you and want to help.

It is important to remember that every teen's experience will be different, so the following list of common emotional problems is not exhaustive. Some teens may struggle with:

- ✓ **Anxiety:** Anxiety is probably the most common emotional problem teenagers face. It can manifest as excessive worry and fear, physical symptoms such as an increased heart rate or stomach problems, feelings of dread or avoidance of certain situations, and more. Some ways to identify whether you are struggling with anxiety are to pay attention to how your thoughts and feelings influence your behavior.

- ✓ **Depression:** Depression is a serious mental health disorder that can affect how teens think, feel, and act. It often includes prolonged periods of sadness and/or loss of interest in activities, as well as changes in sleeping or eating patterns. It is important to recognize the symptoms of depression and reach out for help if you are struggling.

- ✓ **Anger:** Excessive anger is a common problem that many teens have trouble managing. It can lead to difficulty in relationships, as well as problems with academic performance or legal issues. In order to better manage your anger, it's important to identify the triggers and beliefs that are causing it, as well as finding healthier ways to express it.

- ✓ **Stress:** Stress is a normal part of life and everyone experiences it from time to time. It can manifest in physical, mental, and emotional symptoms. It is important to identify the source of your stress, manage it in healthy ways, and create a plan to reduce it.

- ✓ **Low self-esteem:** Low self-esteem can lead to difficulty in relationships, difficulty making decisions, and feelings of worthlessness. It is important to identify the sources of your low self-esteem and learn how to challenge them. This can include things like recognizing your strengths and accomplishments, setting goals for yourself, and focusing on positive aspects of yourself.

- ✓ **Loneliness and isolation:** Many teens feel isolated or alone, even when surrounded by friends. This can lead to feelings of sadness and worthlessness. It is important to identify the source of these emotions, reach out for support from friends or family, and develop healthy relationships with others.

✓ **Worry and panic:** Worry and panic can lead to a sense of fear or dread, as well as physical symptoms such as an elevated heart rate. It is important to recognize the source of these worries and find healthy ways to manage them. This could involve activities such as mindfulness or deep breathing exercises, writing out your thoughts, talking to someone you trust, or engaging in physical activities.

✓ **ADHD:** Attention deficit hyperactivity disorder (ADHD) is a common condition among teens and can lead to difficulty in focusing or staying on task. It can also cause impulsive behavior and hyperactivity, which can interfere with relationships or academic performance. Working with a doctor to develop an appropriate treatment plan is important for managing the symptoms of ADHD.

✓ **Autism:** Autism is a complex neurodevelopmental disorder that can affect social interaction, communication, behavior, and more. It is important to understand the signs of autism in order to appropriately support those who are living with it. Working with professionals and getting resources, such as therapy or medication, can help manage the symptoms of autism.

✓ **Bipolar disorder:** Bipolar disorder is a mental health condition that can cause significant mood swings between periods of mania and depression. It is important to recognize the signs and symptoms of bipolar disorder in order to get the right treatment. This could include medication, therapy, lifestyle changes, or other treatments.

✓ **Borderline personality disorder:** Borderline personality disorder is a mental health condition that can cause intense emotional instability, difficulty managing relationships, and impulsive behavior. It is important to recognize the signs of BPD and reach out for help in order to get treatment. Treatment could include cognitive behavioral therapy or dialectical behavior therapy.

✓ **Schizophrenia:** Schizophrenia is a mental health condition that can cause hallucinations, delusions, and disorganized thinking. It is important to recognize the signs of schizophrenia in order to get necessary treatment. This could involve medication, therapy, and learning coping skills for managing symptoms.

✓ **Trauma:** Trauma can manifest in physical and emotional symptoms, such as flashbacks, nightmares, difficulty concentrating, and more. It is important to seek help when dealing with trauma in order to get the right treatment. This could involve talk therapy or other forms of counseling.

The goal of all these approaches is to improve your understanding of yourself and provide you with the tools to better manage your emotions and mental health. Although these are just some of the common emotional issues teenagers face, it is important to remember that everyone's experience is unique. Therefore, it is important to identify the issue you want to address and find solutions that work for you. DBT can be a powerful tool in helping teens manage their emotions and create positive change in their lives.

DBT VERSUS DEPRESSION AND SUICIDE PREVENTION FOR TEENS

Mental health issues like depression and suicidal ideation are serious concerns for teens. In order to address these issues, it is important to understand how to identify your concerns and then apply the proper techniques to combat the symptoms.

Our mental health has always been important. However, after the COVID-19 pandemic, it is even more evident that we must take our mental well-being seriously. It may not be a surprise to learn that as the covid cases rose, so did cases of depression and suicidal ideation in teens and adults. Therefore, it is so important to understand how to deal with these issues and get the help you need.

SUICIDE AND SELF HARM AMONG TEENS

Suicide is the second leading cause of death among teens. It is extremely important for parents and caregivers to be aware of the warning signs of suicidal thoughts or behavior. Some of these signs include changes in sleeping or eating habits, withdrawal from friends and activities, talking about suicide, or feeling hopeless. If you notice any of these signs in yourself or someone you care about, it is important to talk to a trusted adult or mental health professional.

Self-harm is another serious problem for teens. Self-harm can include cutting, burning, or any other behavior that is done to intentionally injure oneself. This behavior is often linked to feeling very overwhelmed and releasing the pain of emotions. It is important to understand why this behavior happens in order to find healthier ways of coping with difficult situations.

While self-harm and suicide can be common among teens, it is important to remember that there is help available and you can get better. DBT can be a great tool for understanding your emotions and developing new strategies for managing them. For instance, distress tolerance and emotion regulation tools can help you overcome extreme emotions and suicidal thoughts. Additionally, interpersonal effectiveness tools can help you express yourself better in relationships so you can feel comfortable asking for help. These skills can help you cope with difficult emotions and make positive changes in your life.

DBT VERSUS ANXIETY, WORRY, OR PANIC ATTACKS

Anxiety is a common emotion among teens. It can manifest in physical symptoms such as difficulty breathing, sweating, nausea, and more. It is important to understand how to recognize when you are feeling anxious so that you can manage it before it becomes too overwhelming.

One type of anxiety disorder is generalized anxiety disorder (GAD). GAD is characterized by persistent and excessive worrying that interferes with daily life. People with GAD may also have physical symptoms such as restlessness, fatigue, muscle tension, or irritability. Additionally, there are many other anxiety disorders, like social, panic, and obsessive-compulsive disorder.

DBT can help you understand your anxiety, identify the source, and learn new strategies for managing it. Mindfulness skills can help you become more aware of your thoughts and feelings so that you can respond in healthier ways. Additionally, DBT teaches emotion regulation, which is a set of tools for managing powerful emotions such as worry or fear. These skills can help you recognize when anxiety is escalating and give you the tools to manage it before it becomes overwhelming.

Depending on the problems you're facing and the skills you're using to address them, DBT can help you find healthier ways of coping with difficult emotions. For example, distress tolerance has tools for accepting painful emotions so that you can be more aware of them and cope with them better. Meanwhile, emotion regulation has several acronyms that can help you identify the source of your feelings and respond in a healthier way. These skills can help you better manage anxiety, worry, or panic attacks.

No matter what challenges you're facing, DBT can provide valuable tools for understanding and managing your emotions. With practice, you'll be able to develop new strategies for coping with difficult situations and feel more in control of your emotional health. With the help of DBT, you can make changes in your life and begin to heal from whatever difficulties you may be facing.

DBT VERSUS EMOTIONAL INTELLIGENCE AND MATURITY

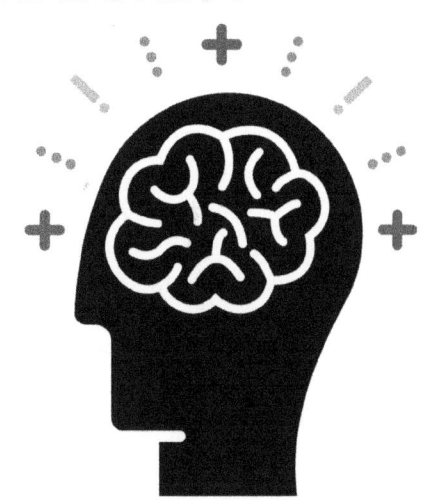

While DBT can be a valuable tool for managing emotions, it is important to also remember that your emotional well-being is connected to other aspects of life. Emotional intelligence and maturity both play an important role in how you relate to yourself and others.

Emotional intelligence involves understanding how your thoughts, feelings, and behaviors affect others and developing the skills to manage them effectively. This can include understanding when to express your feelings, learning how to communicate needs healthily, and managing conflict with empathy.

Maturity is also important for self-care. Maturity involves taking responsibility for yourself and your actions, setting realistic goals for yourself, and making decisions that show you can take care of yourself.

The major components of emotional intelligence are self-regulation, self-awareness, empathy, motivation, and socialization. DBT can help you develop skills such as mindfulness, distress tolerance, and emotion regulation, which are all important for emotional intelligence. Additionally, DBT gives you space to practice and strengthen these skills so that they become more natural over time.

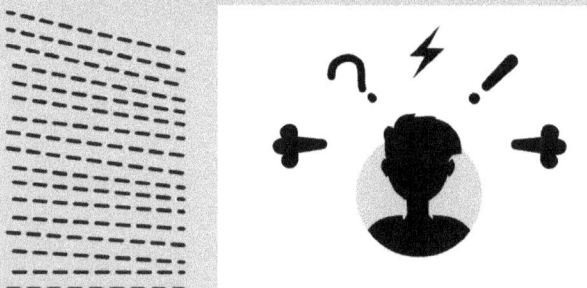

Self-regulation is the art of mastering your emotions in order to stay focused and productive. It involves understanding the intensity of your emotions and working to curb them when needed. DBT teaches several strategies for self-regulation, including mindfulness, distress tolerance, and, of course, emotion regulation.

While DBT can help you build skills such as distress tolerance and emotion regulation, self-regulation also involves setting boundaries for yourself, which is a key part of maturity. Self-regulation helps you to stay in control of your emotions, make decisions that are best for you, and take responsibility for your actions.

COMMON CHARACTERISTICS OF AN EMOTIONAL EPISODE

The common characteristics of an emotional episode include feeling overwhelmed, angry, irritable, or anxious. You may experience physical symptoms such as tightness in the chest, increased heart rate, difficulty concentrating, or trouble sleeping. There may also be a sense of helplessness or hopelessness. You may find yourself feeling disassociated from reality—as if your emotions are out of control.

OBSTACLES YOU MAY FACE

There are several obstacles that may stand in your way of regulating your emotions. These can include unhelpful thoughts or beliefs, poor self-esteem, learned behaviors from childhood, and difficulty recognizing or accepting your feelings. You may also find it difficult to put effective strategies into action or maintain them over time.

 The good news is that DBT can help you overcome these obstacles and build the skills needed to better manage your thoughts, feelings, and behaviors. The key to managing an emotional episode is to identify its source and take steps to manage it. DBT can help you with this process, providing tools for understanding what triggers the emotion and focusing on calming techniques, such as deep breathing or mindfulness exercises. DBT also teaches skills for responding rather than reacting when emotions become overwhelming.

SELF-AWARENESS

Self-awareness is an important part of emotional intelligence and is essential for managing difficult emotions. It involves understanding your feelings, thoughts, motivation, behavior, and reactions. DBT helps you develop this skill by teaching mindfulness techniques such as focusing on the present moment and paying attention to your physical, mental, and emotional responses in any situation. Ultimately, self-awareness allows you to acknowledge your emotions, recognize your triggers, and practice radical acceptance.

EMPATHY

Empathy is the ability to understand and relate to another person's feelings. This quality comes in two forms: recognizing others' emotional episodes and understanding how their situation or challenges can lead to feelings of helplessness or hopelessness. DBT helps you cultivate empathy by teaching skills, such as active listening, understanding perspective-taking, and validation. Empathy is a valuable skill for creating healthy relationships with others and developing an understanding of the world around you.

EMPATHY AND FORGIVENESS

Empathy can also lead to forgiveness, an act of releasing resentments so you can move on from a situation. DBT teaches skills for developing empathy and understanding the importance of self-forgiveness. Accepting and forgiving yourself for your mistakes is essential for growth, healing, and healthy relationships with others. Additionally, forgiving others allows you to create healthier relationships and move away from feelings of resentment or anger.

EMPATHY AND MORALITY

Empathy is also closely associated with morality. DBT teaches you how to make ethical decisions, consider the consequences of your actions, and weigh up the potential benefits and harms. Ethical decision-making requires an understanding of how our choices impact others and ourselves, as well as recognizing that we all have a moral responsibility to treat others with respect and compassion.

Motivation drives us to take action. It can come from a variety of sources, such as the desire for success, positive reinforcement, or recognition from others. However, the goal is to do what's best for you in a way that is supportive, even if it's not a popular choice. DBT can help you find motivating factors, such as identifying your passions and interests, setting achievable goals, and building self-esteem. DBT teaches skills to help you build motivation and find your inner strength. These include focusing on goals, recognizing progress, and celebrating successes. Ultimately, having motivation makes it easier to persist in times of difficulty and reach your desired outcome.

SOCIALIZATION

It's important to develop social skills in order to interact with and relate to others. Socialization is learning how to communicate, cooperate, and understand other people's points of view. DBT helps you build these skills by teaching strategies for active listening, understanding nonverbal communication such as body language or facial expressions, and conflict resolution. Additionally, DBT helps you develop empathy for others and respect for their perspectives, allowing you to build better relationships with those around you. Here are the popular ways to socialize:

Contribute to the conversation:	Humbly:	Intelligently:	Generously:
Participating in group conversations can help build relationships, expand your knowledge, and allow you to share ideas. There are three ways we can contribute to a conversation: humbly, intelligently, or generously.	We can make sure our contributions are meaningful and respectful. This time can be spent brainstorming or asking thoughtful questions, as we search for viable solutions.	When we contribute intelligently, we learn to break down the situation. We distinguish the facts from the fiction or focus on the crucial information while putting aside the details.	Knowledge is power and if we have it, we should share it. Contributing generously means that we speak life into our community and teach others what we know.

WORKING THROUGH CONFLICTS

Conflict is a part of life and it's important to handle it in a way that is constructive, respectful, and understanding. DBT teaches techniques for working through conflicts such as problem-solving, compromise, negotiation, and active listening. Additionally, it teaches you to recognize and respect the feelings of others in order to reach a resolution. These tools can help you navigate any situation and come to a satisfactory conclusion for all parties involved.

As you can see, many aspects of life can contribute to the challenges, emotions, or relationships you experience. However, DBT skills can help you gain insight into yourself and others, so you can better identify your problem. Once you understand the problem, you can learn how to handle con licts constructively and ind motivation to keep going in life.

By learning and implementing DBT skills, you can gain insight into yourself, your relationships with others, and how to interact more effectively in society. Although

the journey won't be easy, it is worth the effort, as these techniques can help you reach better outcomes for yourself and those around you. With practice, the tools will become easier to use, and you can be on your way to a healthier and happier life.

THE THREE AS

In DBT, the Three As are a set of principles to help guide your behavior:

Acceptance: Accepting yourself and others for who they are, without trying to change or judge them.

Awareness: Paying attention to the present moment and recognizing thoughts, feelings, and actions.

Action: Taking wise action that considers both short-term and long-term consequences.

The goal of the three As is to help you create a life that works for you by making thoughtful decisions based on these principles. With practice, the Three As can become second nature and help you live your best life!

WHAT DO THE THREE AS LOOK LIKE IN ACTION?

When you practice acceptance, you don't have to agree with someone's opinion or behavior. You can be compassionate and understanding while still being honest and respectful. Acceptance is important because it allows us to validate one another's feelings without judgment.

For awareness, you can start by simply noticing the present moment and being aware of your thoughts and emotions. Take time each day to be still and observe what's happening in your body, mind, and heart. This helps you make decisions based on a balanced perspective instead of letting your feelings take over.

Finally, when it comes to action, you can make decisions that are both mindful and wise. This means looking at the long-term consequences of your actions and avoiding impulsivity or hasty decisions. Taking the time to step back and think before you act can help keep you on track and lead to healthier outcomes.

By practicing the Three As, you can become more aware of your thoughts and feelings while remaining compassionate and mindful. Over time, this will help you make better decisions that benefit both the short-term and long-term goals in your life.

PART TWO

PREPARING
AND STARTING

A LOVE LETTER TO THE READER

Dear reader,

Before you start the second session, I wanted to share with you a letter that would've helped me as a teen if I had the courage to write it.

Take a moment and think about the last time you looked at yourself in the mirror. Like, a time when you truly looked at yourself and appreciated what you saw. What did you see? What were the things you liked about yourself? What do you think other people love about you? Is the person staring back at you the person you want to be?

When I was a teen, my biggest fear was that nobody liked me; that I wasn't worth loving or even being seen. Does that sound familiar? Do you know what it's like to feel alone in a room full of people?

Now, do you know how to combat those feelings? When you dive deep within, can you pinpoint your positive qualities? Your courage, your talents, and your determination? Can you identify the pleasant moments in your life—the moments that make you smile when you remember them?

Or do you instead focus on the negative attributes? Your f aws and imperfections? The parts of yourself that you think are inadequate or don't meet the standards of others? The part of you that you wish was simply *better*.

If it's the latter, then I want to tell you something: You are more than capable of rising above your self-doubt and insecurities. Even if the only person standing in your way is yourself, you can still push through and be the best version of yourself. You are worth it and you deserve a chance to shine brighter than ever before!

The negative thoughts you have of yourself likely come from a place of fear—from a place of rejection and worry. However, you don't have to be scared anymore. You can draw strength from your courage and use it to become the person you want to be. As you begin the following sections, you will learn and implement tools to help you on your journey toward self-love, self-appreciation, and building healthy relationships with others. These tools will help you gain a better understanding of yourself and your worth, so know that even if it gets tough, there will be something amazing waiting for you on the other side.

I've been in a similar position. I struggled with self-doubt and insecurities. I begged friends and family for the answers I thought would ix me, only to realize that the answers weren't in them but within myself. It took a lot of time, energy, and resilience to get where I am today, and I know you can get there, too, if you just trust yourself and have faith in the process.

You don't have to let your fear keep you from becoming the person you want to be. I believe in you and your potential. And I know that with a bit of courage and determination, you can learn to fall in love with yourself and the world around you. I'm rooting for you.

Take this time to love yourself and take pride in who you are. You're worth it!

Sincerely,
Your biggest
fan.

CHAPTER 4: MINDFULNESS OVER MIND-FULLNESS

Before we jump into mindfulness, I would like you to take a moment to practice being mindful. Don't worry, it might sound a bit strange and maybe even a little confusing, but it's actually really simple.

First, settle into your seat comfortably. You can sit, stand, lie down—it doesn't matter. However, you should be able to be still and relaxed. Take a few deep breaths to get centered and focus on your breath.

Pay attention to the sensations of your body, like how your feet feel pressed against the floor or how you can feel your own heartbeat if you pay attention closely enough. Or feel your lungs and chest expand and then contract as you breathe. Now, shift your attention to the world around you. Notice the temperature of the room and any sounds that might be in the background, like a refrigerator humming or the birds outside chirping.

Don't judge these sensations—don't think they're good or bad, just observe them with curiosity. This is mindfulness. It's a practice of being present in the moment and being aware of both yourself and your environment without judgment. Mindfulness helps you accept your thoughts, feelings, and experiences without reacting to them right away. This can be incredibly helpful when it comes to managing difficult emotions like anxiety or sadness. When practiced regularly, mindfulness can help us better regulate our emotions and stay grounded during times of distress.

WHAT IS MINDFULNESS?

When our mind is full of worries, stressors, and anxieties, it's hard to think clearly or feel relaxed. This is where mindfulness comes in. Mindfulness is the practice of focusing your attention on the present moment and purposefully letting go of judgments or worries about the past or future. It helps us to become aware of our thoughts and feelings without attaching any value to them and to view the world objectively.

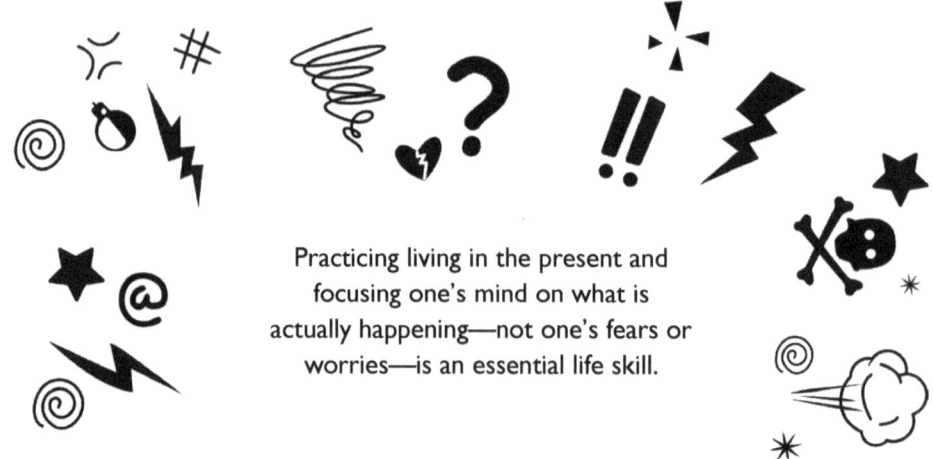

Practicing living in the present and focusing one's mind on what is actually happening—not one's fears or worries—is an essential life skill.

When your mind is rattling with worries, it can be hard to make moral decisions or communicate effectively because it is hard to stay in the present when your mind is full of concerned thoughts.

Making time for mindfulness can allow you to focus on what matters and help you put perspective into situations that are out of your control. It also helps you become more aware of yourself. When done regularly, mindfulness can help you reduce your stress levels, improve your relationships, and become more productive.

At the end of the day, mindfulness is all about taking a step back from the negative thoughts that interfere with our day-to-day lives and replacing them with positive ones. It means learning to recognize when we are getting overwhelmed or our thoughts are taking us too far down a negative path, and then actively choosing to focus our attention and energy on more positive things.

It has been proven in research to reduce stress and anxiety, increase emotional intelligence, and give us a greater sense of inner peace. Additionally, it can help us become more mindful and aware of our own emotions and the emotions of others, allowing us to better navigate any situation with an open mind. When you focus on your worries and anxieties, it takes you away from the present and prevents you from living in the moment. Practicing mindfulness can help break that cycle and allow us to live a fuller life.

MINDFULNESS HELPS YOU RECOGNIZE THE PROBLEM WITHOUT FURTHER WORSENING IT

When you practice being mindful, you're going to notice your emotions and thoughts, which can help you identify the source of any discomfort or stress. Once you know what's causing these feelings, it will be easier for you to address them and make changes that lead toward a more balanced life.

Mindfulness is an important skill that everyone should learn, as it allows us to take control of our lives and focus on what truly matters. There are many ways to practice mindfulness, such as meditation, yoga, or mindful breathing techniques—whatever works best for you.

Our emotions are powerful. In fact, a one-second emotion can ruin our whole day, maybe even more. For instance, if a classmate pushes you at school, your angry reaction can cause an entire argument to ensue, which could escalate the situation and then affect your mood throughout the day.

Mindfulness helps us combat this by teaching us to be mindful of our thoughts and emotions. It may not seem like it, but we do have control over our emotions and the way we react to situations. In fact, the first few moments after a situation occurs are the most important, as they determine how we will handle it. However, with mindfulness techniques at our sides, we can learn to be wise and make better decisions in these moments. We also learn to respond rather than react, which can be very useful when it comes to preventing situations from escalating.

So, next time something happens which causes you to feel an emotion like anger or sadness, take a few moments and practice mindfulness. Be aware of your emotions and thoughts, and instead of reacting in the heat of the moment—take a deep breath and think before responding.

Mindfulness helps us break free from negative thought patterns and instead focus on what's happening in the present moment. With practice, you can become more mindful of your emotions and reactions, improving both your mental and physical well-being. So, why not give it a try? You just might be surprised by the results!

Learning how to observe our thoughts and feelings without getting attached to them can help us manage negative emotions while also finding more positive ways of responding in challenging situations.

Taking the time to practice mindfulness allows us to be more aware of our thoughts and feelings, make better decisions collectively, and focus on what matters most in our lives. It's a powerful tool that can help us reduce stress, increase our emotional intelligence, and feel more inner peace. Plus, it helps us become better at noticing how we're feeling before negative situations worsen.

MINDFULNESS AND ACKNOWLEDGING ANXIETY, WORRY, DEPRESSION, AND SUICIDAL TENDENCIES

Mindfulness isn't only the art of being aware or "in the moment," it's also about not judging yourself. Of course, our thoughts play a huge role in how we feel. Unfortunately, there's really no way around this. If you constantly think to yourself that you're stupid, incapable, unwanted, unloved, or anything else negative, then it's only natural that you'd feel frustrated and down. Then, eventually, your actions will begin to follow suit. It's not always intentional, but it's a ripple effect. A ripple effect we need to be aware of—which is what mindfulness aids us in doing.

Alas, we cannot always control our exact thoughts. We can reframe them, push them away, or even use some of the DBT tools like the "opposite action" where you do something that is the opposite of what your thoughts are suggesting. However, these techniques only work if we're open-minded, refuse to be judgmental, and we don't get attached to them. Otherwise, we'll be stuck in a never-ending loop.

You see, our thoughts come, and if they're negative, then they make us feel bad. However, depending on how bad they are or how truthful we think they are, then we might judge the thoughts or ourselves based on our thoughts. This judgment and attachment only serves to worsen the situation. Because if we judge our thoughts and ourselves for it, then this will cause us to spiral into deeper negative emotions like worthlessness, guilt, or shame.

Mindfulness helps us break free from this cycle by encouraging us to acknowledge our thoughts without judgment or attachment. We can learn to observe them, accept them, and then reframe or push away the ones that don't help us. This way we can measure how our thoughts influence our emotions and, ultimately, what actions we take.

Mindfulness isn't something you have to do for an hour a day or even 10 minutes every morning. It's bigger than just meditation—it's a skill, a practice, and ultimately a choice. You can practice mindfulness as often as you want or when needed—whether it's in the middle of classes, during break time, or even when feeling overwhelmed by your emotions. Just take a few moments to reflect on how you're feeling and make a conscious effort to be mindful of each moment.

Try to be gentle when observing your thoughts and feelings, being careful not to judge or attach too much significance to them. Be kind to yourself, understanding that it takes time and practice to get better at mindfulness. Remember, you're trying this out as an act of self-care—and that's something worth celebrating!

WHAT SKILLS

The mindfulness module has two skills for you to learn and practice in your daily life: WHAT and HOW skills. WHAT skills prompt you to focus on the present moment. The WHAT skills are:

Observe: Take time to notice what's happening inside your body, mind, and environment. Notice your thoughts, feelings, sensations, and surroundings without judgment.

Describe: Name what's happening inside your body, mind, and environment with words. This can include physical sensations, emotions, and thoughts.

Participate: Take part in the present moment without judgment or resistance. Even if it's uncomfortable or difficult, be willing to experience it fully.

WHAT DO THESE SKILLS LOOK LIKE IN ACTION?

You can practice these skills in your daily activities by being mindful of how you respond to situations and taking a pause before you react. For example, if you find yourself feeling overwhelmed with schoolwork or an argument with a friend, try taking some deep breaths and observe what emotions arise. Describe them without judgment and then participate in the present moment by talking to someone or taking a break. This will help you be more mindful and less reactive in your reactions.

By practicing these skills, you'll be able to become aware of how your thoughts and feelings affect your actions and make conscious decisions with a balanced perspective. DBT skills take time and dedication, but the rewards are worth it.

HOW SKILLS

Like I mentioned, the HOW skills of DBT are the skills that help you respond to the present moment in a healthy and mindful way. These include:

1. Non-judgmental stance: Remain open to the moment and accept your thoughts, feelings, and body sensations without judgment.

2. One-mindfully: Investing all of your focus into each activity that you do as if it's the only thing that matters.

3. Effectively: Make conscious decisions and take action in ways that best serve you and others involved.

WHAT DO THESE SKILLS LOOK LIKE IN ACTION?

For example, let's say you're feeling overwhelmed with a project at school. Instead of judging yourself for feeling anxious, you could take a non-judgmental stance and be open to the moment. You could try one-mindfully focusing on just the task at hand, instead of getting distracted by other things. And then, you could make effective decisions about how best to manage your workload in order to accomplish it without feeling overwhelmed.

By practicing these skills, you'll be able to manage difficult emotions more effectively and live in the present moment with a healthier perspective. With time and dedication, DBT HOW skills can help you make positive changes in your life.

THE WISE MIND

There's another integral part of mindfulness called the Wise Mind. This is the voice within us that has a balanced view toward our thoughts and feelings. It helps us to respond with wisdom instead of getting stuck in the negative emotion or judgment associated with it.

The wise mind is the balance of our emotional mind, which is subjective and driven by feelings and our logical or rational mind, which is objective and analytical. Rather than reacting impulsively to certain thoughts or emotions, the wise mind helps us take a step back and find insight in the situation. We can use this to make decisions that serve us best in the long-term, and that take into account the consequences of our actions.

You'll know you've embraced the wise mind if you feel a sense of clarity and peace—this is the essence of mindfulness. Other signs are that you're able to stay in the present moment, observe your thoughts and feelings without judgment, and respond with thoughtfulness.

Some ways to work on developing the Wise Mind are by being mindful of your thoughts and feelings, taking a pause before you react to those things and believing that everything will pass, eventually. Additionally, you can practice self-compassion, journaling your thoughts and feelings, or talking to someone you trust about how you're feeling.

Through mindfulness, we can learn to accept our thoughts and be open to all the possibilities that life offers. We can make conscious decisions based on a more balanced perspective and tap into more peace and joy in our lives. Mindfulness isn't something you do just once or twice, then forget about; it's an ongoing practice that takes time and dedication. It starts by becoming aware of how your mind works, observing how your thoughts and feelings affect your actions, and ultimately making the conscious effort to be mindful in each moment. So, start now—you've got this!

DBT MINDFULNESS EXERCISES

Now that we understand what mindfulness is and the benefits of it, let's look at some DBT mindfulness exercises that you can do to help practice this skill.

The body scan: This exercise helps us become aware of the physical sensations in our body by scanning from head to toe and focusing on each area for a few moments. As you scan, take note of areas where you feel tightness or tension and observe the sensations without judgment.

The five senses: This exercise involves engaging your five senses and noticing the physical sensations associated with each one. This can help us become more aware of the present moment and the unique experience that it brings. You can try this exercise by focusing on three objects you can see, two sounds you can hear, one scent you can smell, and one object you can touch.

Mindful breathing: You did this exercise at the beginning of the chapter. This exercise helps to relax the body by focusing on your breath. Take a few deep breaths, counting each one as you exhale. As you do this, notice how you feel in your body and be gentle with yourself.

Guided meditations: Guided meditations are an effective way to practice mindfulness. You can find a range of options online, from different lengths to varying topics.

These are just a few examples of DBT mindfulness exercises that you can try. Remember that there is no "right" or "wrong" way to be mindful—the most important thing is to be gentle and understanding with yourself as you practice this skill. It's not just a passing trend, but an important life skill to be cultivated over time. It takes practice and dedication for the results to start showing—so keep going and stay mindful!

MINDFUL ACTIVITIES FOR TEENS

Mindful activities are a great way for teens to get in touch with their feelings and provide an outlet to express themselves. Taking time out of your day to practice some mindful activities can be very beneficial in managing emotions, reducing stress and anxiety, and improving overall well-being. There are many different types of mindful activities that teens can do, such as:

Taking a mindful walk. This involves focusing on the sights, sounds, and smells of your environment while walking around your neighborhood or a local park.

Doing deep breathing exercises. Focusing on each breath can be calming and help reduce anxious thoughts. Try inhaling for four counts, holding for four counts, and exhaling for four counts.

Practicing yoga or stretching exercises. This helps to reduce tension in the body while also focusing on breathing and relaxation.

Writing down your thoughts and feelings. Journaling can be helpful in expressing difficult emotions and situations that are hard to talk about out loud.

Drawing or painting. Creating art can be a great way to express emotions without words.

Listening to music. Music can be an effective tool in calming down and resetting your mind during stressful times.

By trying out different mindful activities, teens will find the ones that work best for them and that can help them regulate their emotions in times of distress. Incorporating mindful activities into your daily routine can make an enormous difference in managing stress and anxiety.

BODY SCAN GUIDED MEDITATION FOR TEENS

Guided meditation is a great way for teens to learn how to relax and reduce stress. It can be done either in a group or alone. To get started, find a comfortable space where you won't be disturbed.

1. Start by closing your eyes and focusing on your breath.

2. Take a few deep breaths and bring your attention to your body.

3. Starting at the top of your head, focus on each part of your body in turn, paying close attention to any sensations or feelings you may experience throughout.

4. Once you reach the tips of your toes, focus on the breath again and take a few moments to notice how you're feeling.

5. Open your eyes and come back to the present moment.

VISUALIZATION GUIDED MEDITATION FOR TEENS

Visualization guided meditation is a great way to help teens relax and reduce stress. It involves using the mind's eye to create an image of a place or situation where they feel calm and relaxed. To get started, find a comfortable space where you won't be disturbed.

1. Close your eyes and begin by focusing on your breath, bringing attention to each inhalation and exhalation.

2. Imagine your body slowly relaxing and all the tension leaving it.

3. Bring to mind a place you find peaceful and calming. It can be a real or imagined setting.

4. Allow yourself to become fully immersed in the image, noticing all of its details such as the sounds, smells, and colors. Take some time to explore your surroundings before slowly returning your focus back to your breath.

5. Open your eyes and come back to the present moment.

Once you're finished with the meditation, take a few more moments to appreciate the stillness and relaxed feeling before slowly opening your eyes. Meditating can be helpful in providing clarity of thought, reducing stress levels, and improving overall mental well-being. Taking 15 minutes each day to relax and reset can make an enormous difference in how you feel!

Practicing these mindful activities regularly can help teens develop a sense of self-awareness and understanding of their emotions, while also helping them to manage stress in times of difficulty. Taking time out from everyday life to focus on the present moment is an important part of learning how to cope with our emotions.

MINDFUL RAIN

One of the most useful mindfulness tools is called RAIN. It's a useful tool to handle difficult emotions or situations with more emotional intelligence. This acronym stands for:

✓ Recognize: Acknowledge and recognize your thoughts, feelings, and physical sensations without judgment.

✓ Allow: Allow yourself to experience those emotions without trying to fight them or push them away.

✓ Investigate: Investigate what's happening in the present moment without judgment.

✓ Nurture: Nurture yourself and be kind to—and understanding of—yourself.

Practicing mindful RAIN can help teens to become more aware of their thoughts and feelings, as well as to take care of their emotional needs in a healthy and productive way.

WHAT DOES THIS SKILL LOOK LIKE IN ACTION?

When teens are feeling overwhelmed or stressed out, they can use RAIN to help them take a step back and process their emotions in a healthier way. For example, if someone is feeling angry or frustrated, they can first recognize what's happening inside of them without judgment. This could include paying attention to thoughts that may be running through the head, the physical sensations in the body, and any emotions that may be present. Maybe your jaw is tight and you feel a knot in your stomach—these are both physical sensations that can clue you in to the fact that you're feeling anger.

Then, you can allow yourself to experience those emotions without being judgmental. This doesn't mean that you have to act on them, but simply acknowledge that they're there.

After that, you can investigate why these feelings are present and what may have caused them—maybe someone said something to you or an event occurred that triggered the emotions. Lastly, nurture yourself in a kind and understanding way. This could mean taking deep breaths, walking away from the situation, or engaging in calming activities like reading or writing.

Mindful RAIN is an incredibly useful tool for teens to process their emotions in a healthy way, and it can help them become more emotionally intelligent as they learn to navigate difficult situations. Give it a try next time you're feeling overwhelmed or stressed out—you may be surprised at how much better you feel afterward!

RAIN WORKSHEET

If you want to practice mindful RAIN, here's a worksheet to help you. Fill in the blanks as best as you can and use it as a tool to become more aware of your emotions:

1. I'm feeling _____ (emotion).

2. My body is telling me _____ (physical sensation).

3. My thoughts are _____ (thoughts).

4. I'm going to allow myself to experience this emotion without trying to fight it away.

5. I'm going to investigate why I'm feeling this way and what may have caused it.

6. Finally, I'm going to nurture myself in a kind and understanding way by _____ (calming activity).

By using RAIN, you can gain greater awareness of your emotions and learn to process them in a healthier way. Give it a try today!

REFLECTION QUESTIONS

What are some of the mindful activities you can do?

How has your experience been with mindful breathing?

How does practicing mindful RAIN help you become more aware of your emotions and nurture yourself?

What do you find helpful in managing stress and anxiety?

What have been your experiences with mindful activities?

CHAPTER 5: HANDLING EMOTIONAL STRESSORS

Aside from embracing the moment and being mindful, DBT also teaches us skills to help manage our emotional stressors—challenges like big changes in life, arguments with loved ones, or tough conversations. When faced with these challenging situations, it's important to be aware of the impact they can have on us emotionally and to handle them better.

Take a moment to once again consider a problem that you're facing. What are some healthy and safe ways that you can cope with the emotions it's causing without making things worse? What's the best way to approach it? That's where DBT comes in.

Instead of trying to immediately solve or fix the problem, DBT teaches us to focus on managing our emotions around it and finding ways to cope. It offers several techniques to help us manage difficult situations or episodes of intense emotion, like when we feel overwhelmed or out of control. These techniques are called distress tolerance skills, and they can help us take a step back and accept the situation for what it is, instead of trying to change or escape it.

Distress tolerance skills are broken down into three categories: distraction, self-soothing, and improving the moment. Distraction techniques involve distracting yourself from your emotions by focusing on something else—this can be anything from playing a game to going for a walk. Self-soothing involves engaging all five senses—sight, sound, smell, taste, and touch—to help you take care of yourself in the moment.

Improving the moment techniques involves doing something different from your usual routine, like spending time with friends or listening to music. By using DBT distress tolerance skills, you can learn to respond in healthy ways when faced with difficult emotions. But it's important to remember that the goal isn't to change or fix the problem—it's simply to better manage your emotional reactions so you can function and cope one day at a time. By developing these skills, you'll be better equipped to face whatever life throws at you.

It's important to remember that distresses and crises are a normal part of life and that distress tolerance prepares you to tolerate them without making things worse. So, let's explore some of the DBT skills that can help you manage your emotional stressors.

THREE COMPONENTS OF DBT

There are three components of DBT designed to help you manage emotional stressors:

Radical acceptance:	Crisis survival:	Freedom:
This means accepting that life is what it is, rather than fighting it or wishing it were different. It's important not to judge yourself based on how you feel, but instead to acknowledge and accept whatever emotions come.	This is about managing the intense emotions that come with crises and major life events. It can involve simple self-care activities like taking a shower, going for a walk, or listening to calming music.	This is about learning to control your emotions and make better decisions. It involves understanding how our thoughts, feelings, and behavior are connected and using this knowledge to make changes in our lives.

CRISIS SURVIVAL

The purpose of crisis survival is to help you manage intense emotions and short-term crises. This can involve simple self-care activities. It also involves developing healthy coping skills, like problem-solving and positive self-talk. The idea is to be mindful of the moment and create psychological distance between yourself and the stressor. This can help to prevent a full-blown crisis or emotional outburst.

For example, let's say you're feeling overwhelmed after a big argument with your friend. Instead of lashing out or giving in to despair, you might take a few deep breaths and remind yourself that these feelings will pass. You could also focus on what you can control, like apologizing for any harsh words that were said and setting boundaries for the future.

Another example might be when your parents tell you that you can't go to a party. Instead of getting caught up in the feeling of disappointment, try to look at it objectively. Ask yourself why they said no and consider what the consequences might be if you attended, anyway. This will help give you clarity so that you can make an informed decision rather than simply reacting out of emotion.

Or, if you experience panic attacks or intrusive thoughts, crisis survival can help you stay grounded and in the present moment. You can try mindfulness exercises like focusing on your breath and counting to 10, or doing an activity that relaxes you such as drawing or reading.

FREEDOM

The freedom component of DBT focuses on comprehending how your thoughts, feelings, and behavior are intertwined. Then, you can use this knowledge to make changes in your life. It involves learning to recognize when you're making irrational decisions based on emotion, and replacing them with more rational choices.

RADICAL ACCEPTANCE

The last component of DBT is radical acceptance. This involves learning to accept yourself and situations for what they are—good, bad, or otherwise. This doesn't mean that you have to like it or agree with it, just that you acknowledge its existence and move forward from there.

For example, let's say your best friend is going through a tough time and you don't know how to help. Rather than trying to fix the situation or make it go away, radical acceptance means understanding that this is a part of life and that sometimes we can't control what happens. You could still offer your support by listening without judgment and doing whatever else you can to be there for them.

Overall, distress tolerance is an important skill to have in order to cope with life's challenges. It involves learning how to tolerate distress without making things worse and looking at situations from different perspectives in order to make informed decisions. Working on these skills can help you navigate difficult times with greater ease and resilience.

DIALECTICAL AND OPPOSING VIEWS

In DBT, you are encouraged to look at opposing views or perspectives in order to gain clarity and understanding. Trying to understand both sides of an argument can help you make more informed decisions and better handle hard conversations.

For instance, let's say you disagree with your parents about homework or going to a party on the weekend. Instead of rushing to make a decision, it's important to consider both sides. Rather than getting angry and screaming at them for "ruining your life," you can take a step back and consider the situation from their point of view. Why do they feel the way they do? How might this affect their decisions and behavior? Having an open dialogue with them may help resolve any underlying issues that are causing tension and ultimately create more harmony in your relationship.

Similarly, when presented with a tough decision in life, it's important to consider it from every angle. What are the potential benefits and risks of each option? Which ones might be more beneficial in the long run? Dialectical and opposing views can help you make the best decision for your life.

REALITY ACCEPTANCE SKILLS

Reality acceptance skills are the final component of DBT. This involves recognizing and accepting reality as it is, rather than trying to escape from it or wishing things were different. It means coming to terms with the fact that not all problems can be solved right away, and that some outcomes may be beyond our control.

One theory behind DBT is that pain plus non-acceptance equals suffering. This means that when we are in pain but resist accepting it, we become stuck and unable to move forward or grow. It is only when we accept the reality of our current situation that we can start to make meaningful changes and progress.

For example, let's say you recently failed a test. You could choose to accept the reality of your situation and learn from it. This might involve reflecting on what went wrong, apologizing if needed, and figuring out how to improve next time. Alternatively, you could try to deny or ignore the situation by avoiding thoughts about it or blaming someone else. But this won't lead to growth or problem-solving and could make you even more upset in the long run.

One way to reduce our suffering is through radical acceptance, as I mentioned in the above section. The other two ways are to turn the mind and practice willingness. Turning the mind means re-focusing our attention away from the problem and onto something more pleasant. It can be a helpful distraction that helps us gain perspective on what we are experiencing. For instance, if you are feeling overwhelmed by a difficult situation, you could take a few moments to go for a walk or listen to some calming music.

Practicing willingness is another way of dealing with unpleasant situations. This means that instead of resisting what's happening, we try to open up to it. We focus on the present moment and let go of our expectations, judgments, and demands. This can be challenging, but it's a helpful way to accept reality and move forward.

WHEN TO USE CRISIS SURVIVAL TOOLS?

Crisis survival tools can be used in times of distress when you're feeling overwhelmed and your emotions are running high. These crisis survival tools won't help you with every situation. However, they can be particularly useful in times of acute distress, when you're feeling overwhelmed, and when your emotions are running high. Here are a few signs that you're in a crisis:

- ✓ You feel immense pressure to solve the problem right now.

- ✓ The problem or situation is short-term.

- ✓ You are highly stressed from the concern.

- ✓ You are in danger of hurting yourself or someone else.

- ✓ Acting on your emotions will make the situation worse.

- ✓ You're overwhelmed but still have more work to do, or you can't remove yourself from the situation.

- ✓ You're feeling hurt but you won't heal quickly.

- ✓ Your emotions want to reveal themselves but you want to remain poised.

- ✓ The problem and feelings the crisis creates are intense, but you can't solve the problem quickly.

In times like these, it's important to take a step back and use crisis survival tools to cope with the distress. This will help you gain perspective and make decisions that are right for you.

By taking a step back and using crisis survival tools to cope with the distress, you can gain perspective and make rational decisions that are right for you. Through increased understanding of yourself, this process will also help build your resilience and increase your capacity to handle future crises.

DBT AND ADDICTIONS

Distress tolerance is an important skill for people in recovery from addictions. Oftentimes, addiction can be a way to cope with difficult emotions or situations—it can be hard to face them directly and so using substances as an escape may seem easier. However, this type of behavior often leads to more pain in the long run.

Distress tolerance can help people in addiction recovery to face their emotions and situations head-on, rather than using substances or other unhealthy coping behaviors. It also helps them gain perspective and make informed decisions about their life. By learning how to tolerate distress in a healthy way, individuals can learn to live a life free from addiction.

For example, tools like radical acceptance and distress tolerance can help an individual work through their emotions. It can also help them identify triggers for using substances, or other addictive behaviors, as well as how to deal with these triggers healthily.

Distress tolerance is an important skill to have. With practice, anyone can increase their distress tolerance and better handle difficult times. When used correctly, it can also be a powerful tool for people in recovery from addiction.

SIX DISTRESS TOLERANCE SKILLS AND EXAMPLES OF THEIR USES

SELF-SOOTHING

This simple and versatile tool can help you relax and stay grounded. This technique uses your five senses to help you focus on the present moment and take a break from stressful thoughts or feelings. Self-soothing is a great way to reduce distress. It involves engaging in activities that calm you down and help you relax. Unlike the other techniques that point you in a more specific direction, this skill requires that you know yourself well.

You know what calms you down and makes you feel better, so do that! For instance, maybe visualizing just isn't for you. Maybe you struggle to clear your mind of thoughts and you don't envision things easily. That's okay! Instead, you could do something tactile like knitting or playing with Play-Doh. The skill is all about doing something solely for yourself that soothes you. A popular grounding technique that uses all five senses is 5-4-3-2-1 (Mayo Clinic, 2020a). This involves naming 5 things you can see, 4 things you can hear, 3 things you feel, 2 things you can smell, and 1 thing you can taste. This will help calm your mind and body, so give it a try!

SCENARIO AND TOOL APPLICATION EXAMPLE

You just got into an argument with a family member, and you're feeling overwhelmed. Taking a few minutes for self-soothing can help you relax and gain perspective on the situation. You could listen to calming music, practice a deep breathing exercise, take a warm bath, or eat something comforting.

You're having a really rough day. Nothing seems to go your way and all you want is for things to get better. You decide to try self-soothing in order to bring yourself some peace of mind. For you, this means taking a hot bath with Epsom salts, listening to calming music, taking long walks, reading a book, getting a massage, going for a swim, etc.

SELF-SOOTHING WORKSHEET

This worksheet can help you narrow down your self-soothing options. Take a few moments to think about what activities could be beneficial for your current state of mind, and mark them with a checkmark in the box provided.

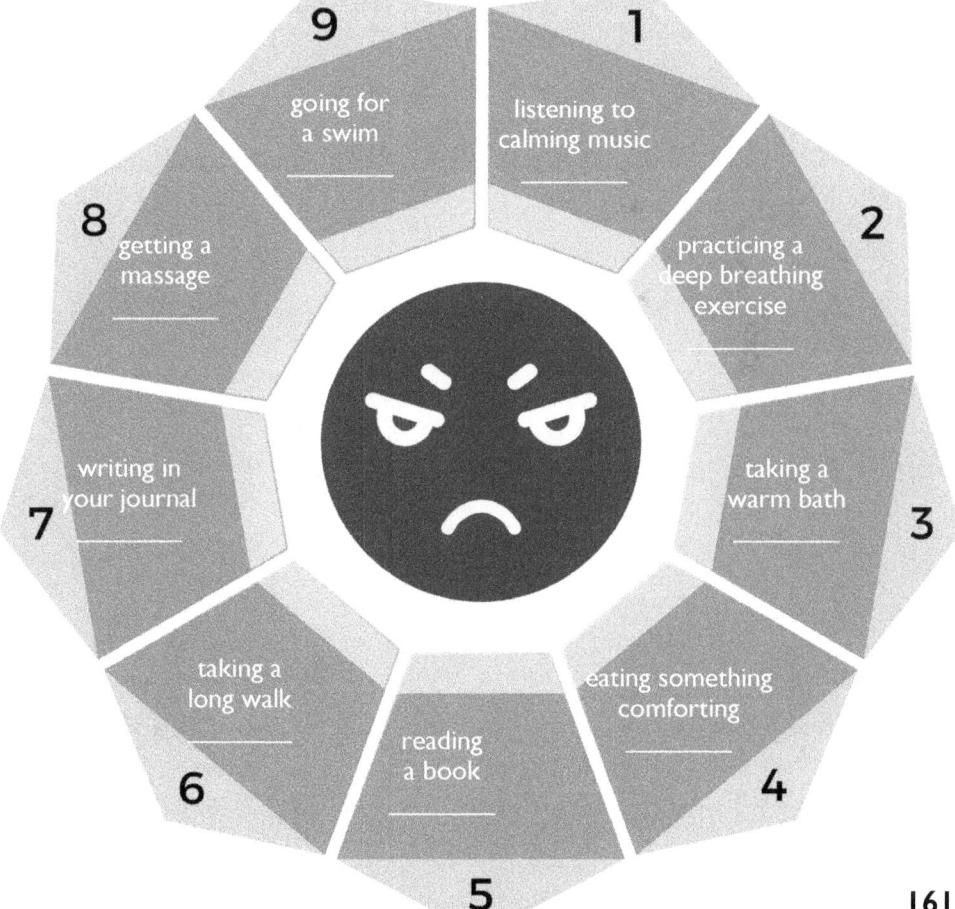

Once you have identified activities that could be beneficial, make sure to take the time to actually practice self-soothing and do one of these activities.

TIPP EXERCISE

This is an acronym standing for temperature, intense exercise, paced breathing, and paired muscle relaxation (Sunrisertc, 2017b). This skill is a great self-soothing technique that utilizes your senses.

✓ **Temperature:** When we are upset or angry, our body heat increases. To reduce this, try to cool your body temperature down with a cold drink or a bath or shower.

✓ **Intense exercise:** Move your body for at least five minutes by doing any physical activity that gets your heart rate up like running, jumping jacks, push-ups, etc.

✓ **Paced breathing:** Take deep breaths in and out in a slow and steady way. This will help to reduce your heart rate, lower blood pressure, and relax your muscles.

✓ **Paired muscle relaxation:** Tense up all of your muscles for five seconds and then relax them for fifteen seconds. Do this for at least two minutes.

SCENARIO AND TOOL APPLICATION EXAMPLE

You're feeling overwhelmed and can't seem to settle down. In order to calm yourself, you decide to try the TIPP exercise. You take some deep breaths, do five minutes of intense exercise, cool off with a cold drink or shower, and then finish with two minutes of muscle relaxation. Keep in mind that you don't have to use all the TIPP skills in one setting. If one or two tools help you relax, that's enough.

TIPP SKILLS WORKSHEET

If you are feeling overwhelmed, use this worksheet to help identify skills that could be beneficial in calming yourself down. You can also write down any additional self-soothing activities you would like to add.

Temperature: How can you alter your temperature? In what ways can you cool off?

....

....

Intense exercise: What type of physical activity can you do that will get your heart rate up?

....

....

Paced breathing: How long should you breathe in, and how long should you breathe out for? How do you know if you feel better? Which breathing exercises do you prefer?

....

....

Paired muscle relaxation: How long should you tense each muscle group for and how long should you relax them? Which muscle groups should you focus on?

....

....

Additional self-soothing techniques: What other activities can you do to help bring yourself peace of mind?

....

....

Taking a few minutes for yourself not only helps to calm your mind and body, but it can also improve your overall well-being.

IMPROVE

This acronym stands for imagery, meaning, prayer, relaxation, one thing in the moment, vacation, and encouragement (Sunrisertc, 2017b).

✓ **Imagery:** Visualize a peaceful image like a beach or a calming forest. This will help you relax and focus on the present moment. You could also visualize yourself solving the concern and cultivate those feelings.

✓ **Meaning:** Consider the meaning of what is causing you distress. Is there a higher purpose to this situation? Can something positive come out of it?

✓ **Prayer:** Pray for guidance and strength to help you through this time. If you're not religious, you don't have to pray. You can instead use this time for self-reflection, meditation, and positive thoughts.

✓ **Relaxation:** Take slow and deep breaths, practice progressive muscle relaxation, or simply close your eyes for a few minutes and imagine yourself in a quiet place.

✓ **One thing in the moment:** Focus on one thing around you that makes you feel relaxed or happy. You can look out the window and observe your surroundings or listen to calming music.

✓ **Vacation:** Take a mental break and do something that will momentarily distract you from the issue at hand. This could mean watching a movie, playing video games, listening to music, etc. You could also visualize yourself on a vacation to give your mind a break from reality.

✓ **Encouragement:** Talk to yourself as if you were talking to a friend in need of support. Encourage yourself and remind yourself that you can get through this. Remember, you don't have to seek acceptance or encouragement from outside sources—you can provide these things for yourself.

SCENARIO AND TOOL APPLICATION EXAMPLE

You're feeling overwhelmed by a lot of stress and cannot think clearly. You decide to try the IMPROVE exercise in order to cope with your distress. Think of the higher purpose behind this difficulty and imagine yourself in a happy place. Take a deep breath and talk to yourself in a positive way. Remember, you don't have to use all these skills at once. Use whichever one that works for you and helps you relax.

IMPROVE WORKSHEET

Consider a problem that you're having and use the prompts below to practice the IMPROVE exercise.

Describe your problem in detail:

....

....

....

....

....

Imagery: Visualize a peaceful image that relaxes you. Describe the image.

....

....

....

....

....

Meaning: Is there a higher purpose for this situation? What can you learn from it?

....

....

....

....

....

Prayer: What words of guidance or strength do you want to seek out and focus on?

....

....

....

....

....

Relaxation: Describe the relaxation techniques that you will use in order to cope with your distress. Maybe you will decide to close your eyes and focus on slow, deep breaths.

....

....

....

....

One thing in the moment: What is one thing that you can observe around you that will help bring you peace of mind?

....

....

....

....

Vacation: Choose an activity that can distract you from the issue at hand. This activity could be anything from listening to a podcast to playing video games.

....

....

....

....

Encouragement: Be your best friend. What words of encouragement are you giving yourself?

....

....

....

....

ACCEPTS

ACCEPTS is a popular skill used to cope with distress. It stands for: activities, contributing, comparisons, emotions, push away, thoughts and sensations (Sunrisertc, 2017b).

✓ **Activities:** Indulge in activities that you enjoy like playing sports or listening to music. It's important to find a healthy outlet to express your feelings and refocus your energy.

✓ **Contributing:** Find ways to contribute to something greater than yourself. This can be through volunteering, helping friends or family members in need, etc.

✓ **Comparisons:** Avoid comparing yourself to others and recognize the progress you've made so far. Additionally, you can also compare your situation to a worse experience and acknowledge how you overcame that challenge.

✓ **Emotions:** Acknowledge your emotions without judging them and allow yourself to feel whatever comes up without guilt or shame.

✓ **Push away thoughts:** Redirect your focus to something more positive and calming.

✓ **Thoughts:** Pay attention to the thoughts in your head and work on reframing negative thoughts into positive ones.

✓ **Sensations:** Notice any physical sensations you may have such as a racing heart or tense muscles, and try breathing or stretching exercises to help relax them.

SCENARIO AND TOOL APPLICATION EXAMPLE

You've been feeling down lately and can't seem to shake it off. Maybe you fail a test or your parents are arguing, and you feel like the world is against you. Or maybe it's a combination of all three! You decide to use the ACCEPTS exercise to cope with your negative thoughts and emotions.

You start by doing something that brings you joy, like drawing or playing some music. When you give a helping hand to a friend, you realize that there are people in worse situations than you. You acknowledge your feelings without judging them and then push away those negative thoughts by focusing on something that brings you peace, such as a happy memory or a beautiful sunset. Finally, you do some breathing exercises to relax any physical sensations of distress.

ACCEPTS WORKSHEET

Use the prompts below to practice the ACCEPTS exercise.

Describe your problem in detail:

....

....

....

....

Activities: What activities can you do that will bring you joy and help refocus your energy? For instance, you could go for a walk or paint. Make a list for yourself to review.

....

....

....

....

Contributing: What ways can you contribute to something greater than yourself? Maybe volunteering at an animal shelter or helping create a free library in your community?

....

....

....

....

Comparisons: In what ways do you compare yourself to others? What comparisons can you make instead?

....

....

....

....

Emotions: How can you acknowledge your emotions without judging them? What words of affirmation or encouragement can you give to yourself?

....

....

....

....

Push away thoughts: What are some healthy ways that you can redirect your focus to something more positive?

....

....

....

....

Thoughts: How can you reframe any negative thoughts into more positive ones?

....

....

....

....

Sensations: What physical sensations do you have and what exercises (e.g., breathing or stretching) can you do to relieve the sensations?

....

....

....

....

By using the ACCEPTS exercise it will help bring peace, comfort, and joy during times of distress. Remember that it's important to give yourself permission to feel whatever comes up without guilt or shame and recognize the progress you've made.

PROS AND CONS LIST

The benefits of creating a physical and visual list are not to be underestimated. This simple, yet effective tool helps you to process both positive and negative aspects of a situation or decision. It requires you to literally weigh the pros and cons, often resulting in a clearer understanding of which direction is best for you. Doing this on a paper or on the computer where you can physically see the list also helps to give an accurate representation of the situation.

SCENARIO AND TOOL APPLICATION EXAMPLE

You're trying to decide whether or not you should take that extra course this semester. To help you make your decision, you create a pros and cons list. On one side, you outline the benefits of taking it, such as gaining more knowledge and expanding your network. On the other side, you outline potential drawbacks such as taking up a lot of your time and possibly putting stress on your academic performance. By looking at both sides of the argument, you can make an informed decision about whether or not this is something that would benefit you in the long run.

PROS AND CONS WORKSHEET

Describe the challenge you're facing:

Pros	Cons

RADICAL ACCEPTANCE

Radical acceptance is about learning to accept reality for what it is—both the good and the bad (Sunrisertc, 2017b). It does not mean that you agree with or condone a particular situation, but rather that you acknowledge it and move on. This skill helps to reduce stress by allowing us to focus our attention on things we can control rather than getting stuck in unhelpful thoughts and emotions.

SCENARIO AND TOOL APPLICATION EXAMPLE

Your friend has just told you she's been cheating on her boyfriend. You don't agree with this behavior, but you accept it as reality and move on from the conversation. Instead of getting angry or frustrated, you let go of your expectations and focus on the things that are within your control.

RADICAL ACCEPTANCE WORKSHEET

This worksheet can help you practice this skill. Start by writing down a difficult situation or emotion that you're facing in the first column. Then, in the second column, write down how accepting this reality would make you feel. Finally, in the third column, write down any action steps that you can take to move forward.

Situation or emotion	Feelings of acceptance	Action steps

In conclusion, distress tolerance is an important skill to master as it helps us to deal with difficult situations without making them worse. There are various tools and techniques you can use to help manage distressing feelings, such as self-soothing, creating a pros and cons list, and radical acceptance. With practice and perseverance, you can learn to effectively cope with difficult emotions and manage distresses in healthy ways.

REFLECTION QUESTIONS

What types of distress tolerance skills have you used and how effective were they?

In what situations do you think using distress tolerance skills could be beneficial?

How can you practice self-compassion when it comes to distress tolerance?

What would you say are the most important aspects of developing distress tolerance skills?

How can you make sure that you are using distress tolerance in a healthy way?

What would be the best strategies to help someone else develop their own distress tolerance skills?

What sort of support system do you think is necessary when it comes to developing and maintaining your distress tolerance skills?

How can you make sure that your distress tolerance skills are up-to-date?

What tips would you give someone who is struggling with developing their own distress tolerance skills?

In what ways do you think distress tolerance can promote healing and growth in your life?

CHAPTER 6:
HOW TO ACTIVATE YOUR EMOTIONAL THERMOSTAT

Activating your emotional thermostat is a skill meant to help you regulate and manage your emotions healthily. It's all about understanding the intensity of your feelings and adjusting them accordingly.

Our emotions are powerful and can often overpower our rational thoughts. Therefore, it's important to learn how to adjust the intensity of your feelings so that they don't become overwhelming. For instance, if you're feeling anxious, those emotions can easily

escalate and cause a great deal of stress. But with emotional regulation skills, you can adjust that intensity and manage the emotions in a healthier way.

RECOGNIZING YOUR EMOTIONS

The first step of activating your emotional thermostat is to recognize the intensity of your feelings. This means being aware of how you are feeling and understanding why you feel that way. It's helpful to take a few moments to pause and reflect on what emotions you're experiencing, rather than just reacting without thinking. Relabeling your emotions can also be helpful. Instead of thinking "I'm panicked," you can change it to "I'm feeling anxious." This simple reframe can help put the emotion into perspective and allow you to more easily manage it. Pay attention to what triggers those feelings and how long they last. Also note any physical sensations that often accompany those emotions, such as racing heart rate or tightness in the chest.

MINDFULNESS AND EMOTIONAL REGULATION

Once you are aware of your emotions, the next step is to regulate them. Mindfulness can be a great tool for managing emotional intensities. This involves paying attention to the present moment and being mindful of your thoughts and feelings without judgment or attachment. When we become conscious of our emotional experience, it helps us adjust the intensity without going too high or too low.

EMOTION REGULATION AND WORRY, FEAR, AND ANXIETY

When it comes to regulating emotions, it's important to understand the difference between worry and fear. Worry refers to an ongoing cycle of worrying thoughts that can lead to feeling overwhelmed and out of control. Fear, on the other hand, is a natural response when faced with a potential threat or danger. Anxiety is a feeling of fear that is out of proportion to what's actually happening.

By understanding the differences among these three emotions, you can start to regulate and manage them in healthier ways. Aside from emotion regulation tools, mindfulness can also be beneficial for learning to identify and cope with fear and anxiety.

The key is to learn how to actively manage both fear and worry healthily. This includes recognizing when you're feeling overwhelmed by your emotions, addressing the underlying cause of your worries or fears, and engaging in activities that can help reduce your stress.

UNWANTED EMOTIONS

It's important to remember that all emotions, especially those that feel unpleasant, are not bad. In fact, they can be helpful in providing us with clues about our internal states and needs. For instance, sadness can be a signal that we're feeling disconnected or lonely, while anger may be an indicator of feeling powerless or frustrated. These feelings may seem uncomfortable initially, but 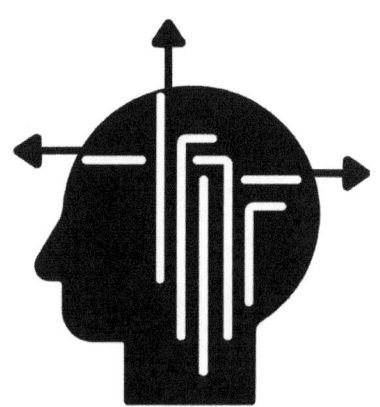 understanding why we are feeling them can help us gain insight and better manage our emotions.

Learning how to regulate unwanted emotions involves several strategies, such as recognizing when you're feeling overwhelmed, identifying the underlying cause of your emotions, and engaging in activities that can reduce stress. Additionally, it's important to practice self-care and create opportunities for connection with others.

The goal of regulating emotions is not to suppress or ignore them, but rather to recognize them, allow them to exist, and process them in a healthy way before they become overwhelming. The key to managing unwanted emotions is to accept them for what they are—natural reactions to particular situations—and then take action to address them healthily.

You can work on emotion regulation by identifying which emotions are unwanted, stopping unwanted emotions before they start, or changing unwanted emotions after they have started. To identify the unwanted emotions you can practice mindfulness, name the emotion, and understand what might be causing it.

To prevent unwanted emotions from getting out of hand, you can practice self-soothing, create a pros and cons list, or engage in radical acceptance—use the distress tolerance skills. And finally, to change your unwanted emotions after they have started, you can practice problem-solving or visualization.

By learning effective emotion regulation strategies, you can better manage your emotions and reduce the intensity of stress and anxiety. This can help you live a more balanced and emotionally healthy life.

PRACTICE SELF-COMPASSION AND NURTURING

It's important to be kind and nurturing to ourselves during difficult times. Talk to yourself like you would a friend—with understanding, encouragement, and positivity. Instead of getting overwhelmed by your emotions, try to accept them with understanding and compassion. The more self-compassionate you are, the easier it will be to regulate your emotions.

SETTING AND REACHING GOALS

Once you can recognize your emotions and the intensity of them, it's time to set goals. Before setting a goal, ask yourself: What do I want to achieve? For example, let's say you are feeling overwhelmed by an upcoming project. You could set a goal to complete the project in a certain amount of time or to take breaks in between tasks to manage your stress. By setting achievable goals, you can create a plan of action that will help you regulate your emotions and stay on track.

EMOTIONS AND PHYSICAL VULNERABILITY

Our emotions often manifest in physical ways, such as rapid heart rate, sweating, and shallow breathing. And sometimes these physical sensations can be more intense than the emotional feeling itself. When this happens, it's helpful to practice mindful breathing or grounding techniques. Focusing on your breath is a simple way to bring yourself back into the present and away from the intensity of the emotion. Taking deep breaths and focusing on your body can help calm you down and restore balance to your emotions.

Additionally, how we treat ourselves physically can have a big impact on our emotional well-being. Below is a list of habits for you to evaluate.

✓ **Food and diet:** Are you eating regularly and getting enough of the right nutrients?

✓ **Sleep:** Are you getting enough sleep each night?

✓ **Exercise:** Are you engaging in any physical activity throughout the week?

✓ **Stress management:** Do you have a good plan to manage daily stressors?

✓ **Physical illnesses:** Have you been feeling unwell or have any chronic ailments?

By engaging in healthy habits, you can promote better emotional regulation. Taking care of your physical body is just as important as taking care of your mental and emotional health.

EMOTIONS AND THOUGHTS

When we experience powerful emotions, it can be tempting to get lost in our thoughts. But sometimes these thoughts may not be based on reality or serve us well. It's important to recognize when this is happening and to challenge those negative thought patterns. Ask yourself: Is this thought true? Is there any evidence that supports this thought? Is it helpful to think this way?

By challenging your thoughts, you can help regulate your emotions and maintain a sense of control over them. It's also important to remember that feelings are transient and will pass with time. Instead of getting stuck in an emotional loop and ruminating on the same thoughts, try to focus on what is happening in the present moment.

Here are common thought distortions to be aware of:

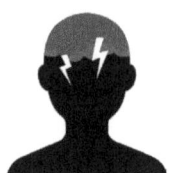

1. **All or nothing thinking:** Thinking in extreme terms like "always" or "never."

2. **Filtering:** Focusing only on the negative aspects of a situation and ignoring anything positive.

3. **Mind reading:** Assuming that you know what someone else is thinking or feeling.

4. **Jumping to conclusions:** Making assumptions about how others feel or will act without any evidence.

5. **Personalizing:** Taking things personally that are out of your control.

6. **Catastrophizing:** Assuming the worst possible scenario will happen in any given situation.

7. **Fortune telling:** Predicting the future and believing that it's predetermined.

This list isn't exhaustive, but can help guide your thoughts when faced with an emotional challenge. By recognizing these patterns, you can help manage your emotions more effectively. Remember, thoughts are not facts! Checking in with your emotions and thoughts can help you stay grounded and centered. With practice, you can learn how to navigate these complex emotions healthily.

EMOTION REGULATION AND THE REASONING MIND

Sometimes, the hardest part of emotion regulation is reframing our thoughts and feelings in a healthier way. This can be done by engaging your reasoning mind, which is the part of your brain that helps to analyze and process information logically. By understanding how emotions work, you can use cognitive behavioral strategies such as reframing or challenging negative thoughts, or engaging in positive self-talk. This can help you identify patterns of thinking linked with particular emotions and then work on replacing them with healthier, more helpful thoughts.

By regularly practicing emotion regulation skills, you are training your brain to respond differently when faced with certain situations or triggers. Over time, this helps to build emotional resilience and increase your capacity to effectively manage emotions.

EMOTIONAL REGULATION IS A SKILL YOU CAN LEARN

The exciting thing about emotion regulation is that it's a skill you can learn and practice over time, and with enough practice, you can become more confident in managing your emotions. It's important to remember that there is no one-size-fits all solution to emotional regulation, and that it may take some trial and error before you find the strategies that work best for you. Additionally, be patient with yourself, as learning how to regulate your emotions can take time.

MYTHS ABOUT EMOTIONS

It's important to recognize the myths and misconceptions about emotions that exist. Our culture often perpetuates certain beliefs about emotions, such as:

Emotions are bad.

You should never show your emotions.

It's not okay to ask for help when you're feeling overwhelmed.

Weakness is associated with showing emotions.

You should always be in control of your emotions.

These myths can lead to feelings of shame, guilt, and insecurity around our emotions. It's important to remember that all emotions are valid and don't make you weak or bad for feeling them. Emotions are a normal and healthy part of life that can reveal a lot about our internal experiences.

It's also important to realize that you don't have to manage your emotions alone. Surrounding yourself with supportive people can make the process easier, so don't be afraid to ask for help when needed. Reaching out to a trusted friend, family member, or mental health professional can make a tremendous difference in how you manage your emotions.

EMOTIONAL REGULATION STRATEGIES TO HELP ACTIVATE YOUR THERMOSTAT

There are several strategies that can help you regulate your emotions and activate your emotional thermostat. These include:

ABC PLEASE SKILL

ABC PLEASE: According to the Sunrise Residential Treatment Program, ABC PLESE helps to activate your emotional thermostat by redirecting attention away from negative emotions and onto your present experience (Sunrisertc, 2017c). This stands for:

✓ **A: accumulate positive experiences:** Treat your life like a bank account or a piggy bank and make tiny deposits of positive experiences. The more of these positive deposits you make, the easier it is to manage difficult emotions.

✓ **B: build mastery:** When you do something well, you increase your self-esteem and confidence. Doing something well gives us a feeling of control and power that can counterbalance the sense of helplessness when negative emotions take hold.

✓ **C: cope ahead:** This skill includes developing an action plan for difficult emotions so that when you experience them, you're already prepared with coping strategies.

✓ **PL: physical illness:** Understand the connection between physical health and emotional well-being. When you're feeling ill, it can make it hard to regulate emotions, so be sure to take care of your body.

✓ **E: eating:** Eating healthily can help to stabilize your mood and regulate emotions. When we're feeling low, junk food may temporarily make us feel better, but in the long run, it can actually worsen our emotional state.

✓ **A: avoid mood-altering drugs:** Although some drugs can temporarily reduce negative emotions, they can lead to more intense and frequent mood swings in the long run.

✓ **S: sleep:** Getting enough sleep is essential for emotional regulation; when we're tired, it can be harder to control our emotions.

✓ **E: exercise:** Exercise releases endorphins which have a positive effect on mood, and can help to regulate emotions.

ABC PLEASE WORKSHEET

Using the ABC PLEASE skill, write down how you can draw on each of these strategies to help regulate your emotions.

Accumulate positive experiences: What experiences can you have that will make you feel good? Try thinking of activities or experiences you can have throughout the day to bring a sense of joy and contentment.

....

....

....

....

Build mastery: Identify something that you are confident in doing, such as a hobby or task. Set yourself small goals for this activity and take time to appreciate your progress.

....

....

....

....

Cope ahead: Imagine a scenario where you might be feeling overwhelmed. What would your action plan be? Try to make it as specific as possible, visualizing what calming activities or self-care strategies you can use in that moment.

....

....

....

....

Physical illness: Are there any physical health needs that should be addressed? Make sure to get regular checkups and take time to nurture your physical health.

....

....

....

....

Eating: What nutritious foods can you incorporate into your diet? Take the time to plan meals that will fuel both your mind and body.

....

....

....

....

Avoid mood-altering drugs: Are there any mood-altering substances in your current life that could be disrupting emotional stability? If so, develop a plan to cut back or completely eliminate these substances.

....

....

....

....

Sleep: How many hours of sleep do you need each night in order to feel your best? Create an evening routine that helps you wind down and get the restful sleep you need.

....

....

....

....

Exercise: What physical activity can you engage in regularly that will help to improve your emotional state? Make sure to include fun activities that you genuinely enjoy.

....

....

....

....

By using the ABC PLEASE skill, you can learn how to regulate your emotions and build healthier coping strategies for difficult times. With practice, this skill can help you identify triggers and create a plan of action to manage intense feelings in healthy ways.

STOP SKILLS

The STOP skills are an acronym used to help you stay in control of your emotions (Sunrisertc, 2017c). STOP stands for:

- ✓ **S:** Stop and take a few deep breaths.

- ✓ **T:** Take a step back and think about the situation. Remember that taking a step back can help you gain perspective and make better decisions.

- ✓ **O:** Observe. Determine how you're feeling by labeling the feeling and pay attention to your body. Observe your surroundings and the other people involved in the situation.

- ✓ **P:** Proceed with intention. Now that you've taken a step back, you can decide on the best course of action. Think through your options and pick what is most appropriate for the given situation.

OPPOSITE ACTION SKILL

The opposite action skill (Sunrisertc, 2017c) can help you regulate your emotions by shifting your focus and behavior. This involves doing something that is the opposite of how you are feeling. For example, if you're feeling angry, instead of yelling or lashing out, take a few deep breaths and choose to do something calming, such as reading a book. Or, if you're feeling sad and want to isolate yourself from the world, instead take a walk or call a friend. By doing something that is the opposite of how you are feeling, it can help to reduce the intensity of your emotions and start to shift them into more positive ones.

Below are six common negative emotions, their characteristics, and examples of opposite actions that can help to reduce their intensity.

✓ **Anger:** Anger means we're feeling frustrated and have a lack of control. We might want to scream, attack, or defend.

> **Opposite Action:** Take slow, deep breaths, practice gratitude, or do a calming activity.

✓ **Shame:** Shame is feeling embarrassed or inadequate. We might want to hide and be alone.

> **Opposite Action:** Connect with someone you trust, practice positive self-talk, or do something that makes you feel proud.

✓ **Fear:** Fear means we're feeling threatened. We may want to avoid the challenging situation or run away.

> **Opposite Action:** Take small steps, be mindful of the present moment, or face your fears. Build courage by staying involved instead of retreating.

✓ **Sadness:** Sadness is feeling overwhelmed with emotion. We may want to cry uncontrollably or isolate ourselves from others.

> **Opposite Action:** Move your body, talk to someone about how you feel, or practice gratitude.

✓ **Guilt:** Guilt is feeling remorseful for a past action. We may want to punish ourselves or internalize our feelings.

> **Opposite Action:** Acknowledge your mistakes, practice self-compassion, and use it as an opportunity to learn and grow.

✓ **Anxiety:** Anxiety is feeling overwhelmed with worry or unease. We may want to freeze or overthink the situation.

> **Opposite Action:** Practice deep breathing, practice self-affirmations and focus on positive thoughts, or challenge negative thinking patterns.

OPPOSITE ACTION WORKSHEET

Describe the situation or challenge you're facing. How do you want to react?

What opposite actions could you take instead?

Remember that emotional regulation takes time, and it's okay to have setbacks. With practice, you can learn to regulate your emotions in a healthy way.

POSITIVE SELF-TALK SKILL

Positive self-talk is an important part of emotional regulation. This involves talking to yourself in a positive, encouraging way. Replace negative thoughts or patterns with more positive and realistic ones. When you're feeling down or overwhelmed, remind yourself that this too shall pass and things will eventually get better. Acknowledge your efforts and successes and be compassionate toward yourself.

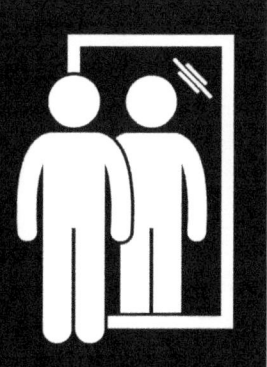

POSITIVE SELF-TALK WORKSHEET

Try this worksheet to help you practice positive self-talk.

Identify situations where negative thoughts tend to arise.

....

....

....

Challenge these thoughts by asking yourself if they are realistic and helpful.

....

....

....

Replace the negative thought with a more positive one that is realistic and supportive.

....

....

....

Take time each day to practice your positive self-talk.

....

....

....

Track your progress and celebrate your successes.

....

....

....

By consistently practicing these skills, you will gain control over your emotions and create healthy habits for managing difficult times. With self-awareness and practice, anyone can learn how to regulate their emotions in a healthy way.

MINDFUL BREATHING SKILL

Mindful breathing is another important skill for regulating emotions. This involves deep, intentional breaths that allow you to focus on the present. Sit or stand in a comfortable position, close your eyes, and take slow, deep breaths. Feel your body relax and notice how your breath flows in and out. With each breath, focus on how your body feels and let go of any tension. Mindful breathing can help to reduce stress and anxiety, and bring about a sense of calmness.

Overall, emotional regulation is an important skill for managing overwhelming emotions healthily. It takes practice and patience, but with the right tools, you can learn to regulate your emotions and lead a more balanced life.

REFLECTION QUESTION

What are some healthy ways I can manage difficult emotions?

How can positive self-talk help me regulate my emotions?

What techniques help me stay mindful and in the present moment?

How do I cultivate compassion toward myself?

What steps can I take to start regulating my emotions today?

What additional resources or strategies can I use to help me manage difficult emotions?

How can I hold myself accountable for emotional regulation goals?

What can I learn from my setbacks and successes when regulating my emotions?

CHAPTER 7: BECOMING BETTER AT FRIENDSHIPS

Making friends as a teenager is hard. When I was in high school, I felt like a complete outcast. I was the shy one who said nothing in class, and I had a hard time making friends. As a result, I kept to myself even more. I wouldn't attend parties or events, and instead I would stay in my room and watch movies.

What I didn't realize back then was that I was setting myself up for years of social anxiety and loneliness. I did not know how to build meaningful relationships and be confident in my interactions with others. One time, I ran into a classmate at a cafe and I was so embarrassed that I couldn't even look her in the eye. I left before I even received my drink.

Now, this was over 20 years ago and I'm no longer the same scaredy-cat I once was. But that doesn't mean I still don't feel uncomfortable in social situations today. What has changed is that I have developed a few different interpersonal skills that have helped me become more confident when talking with others.

Having good relationships can have a big impact on our well-being. We all need positive, supportive people in our lives to help us cope with challenges and share life's joys. That's why it's important to learn how to become better at friendships. There are several key skills that foster strong, healthy relationships, such as effective communication, respect, and empathy. In this chapter, we'll cover effective communication skills from dialectical behavioral therapy that can help you become better at friendships.

RELATIONSHIPS AND OUR EMOTIONAL HEALTH

Our relationships reflect our emotional health. When we have healthy relationships, we usually have higher levels of self-esteem and confidence. We also tend to be happier in general because it's easier to maintain positive outlooks when surrounded by people who lift us up and make us feel supported.

On the other hand, unhealthy relationships can damage our self-esteem and mental health. If we're constantly under the scrutiny of someone who doesn't understand us or our needs, it can make us feel worthless or trapped. As a result, we may become depressed, anxious, or develop other mental health issues.

That's why it's important to have healthy relationships and learn
how to become better at friendships.

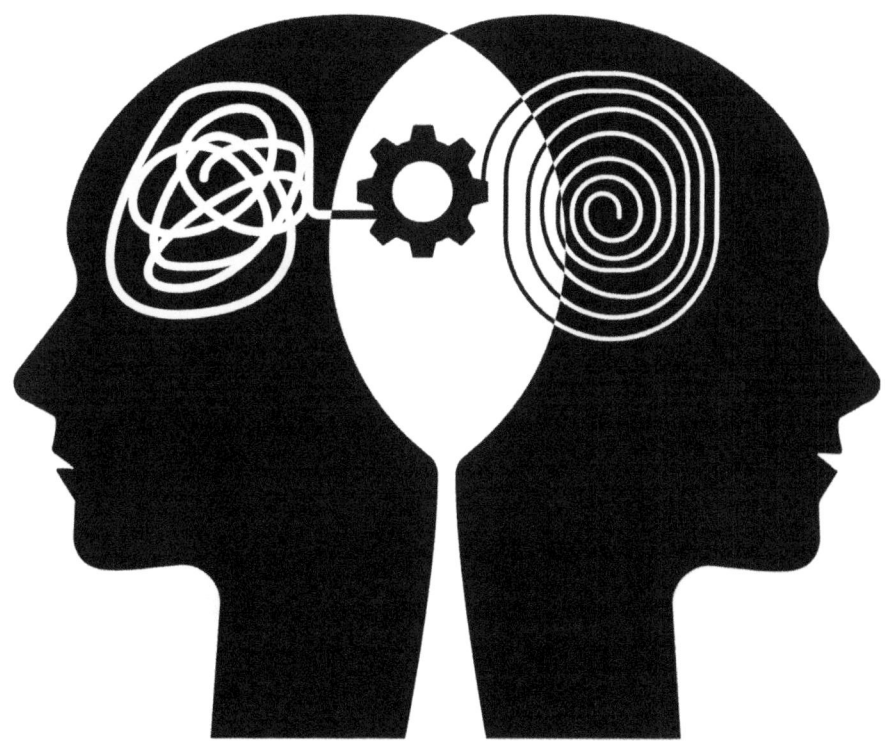

RELATIONSHIPS AND OUR MENTAL HEALTH

Our relationships also play a big role in our mental health. When we have positive, supportive relationships, it can significantly reduce our stress levels and help us cope with difficult emotions. This is because when we feel connected to someone, it sends signals to our brain that we are safe and supported. We then have more emotional capacity to process other things going on in our lives.

On the other hand, if we are constantly surrounded by people who are not supportive or don't understand us, it can increase our stress level and make it harder to manage difficult emotions. We may also become more prone to anxiety and depression.

Building strong relationships is essential for emotional and mental health. Our relationships play a big role in how we feel and how we interact with the world. And, more often than not, it's our relationships that are at the root of many of our emotional and mental issues. That's why having effective communication skills is key to fostering healthy relationships.

When we have good relationships with others, our overall sense of well-being increases. We gain a sense of connection, support, and belonging that can help us cope with difficult emotions or life challenges.

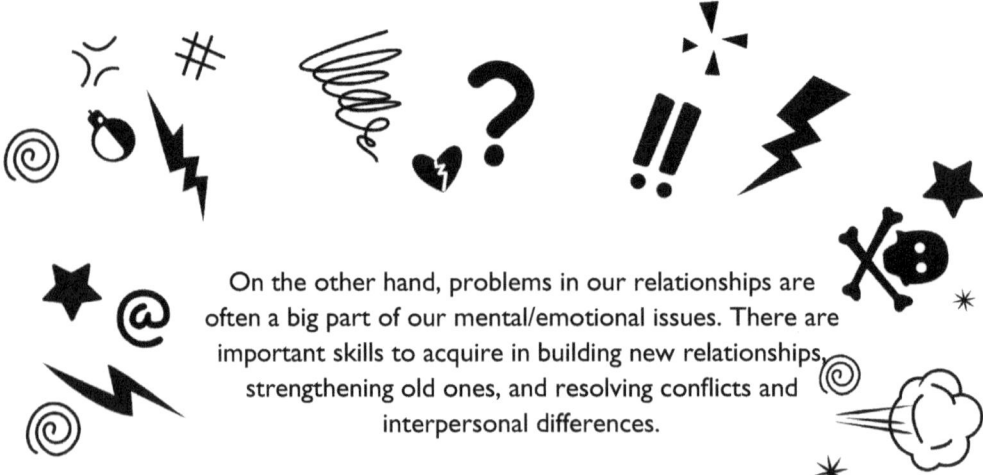

On the other hand, problems in our relationships are often a big part of our mental/emotional issues. There are important skills to acquire in building new relationships, strengthening old ones, and resolving conflicts and interpersonal differences.

THE LINK BETWEEN MENTAL AND EMOTIONAL HEALTH AND ISOLATION

When we feel isolated and alone, it can be hard to maintain good mental/emotional health. Without healthy relationships, we may lack the social support and connection needed to cope with life's challenges.

In addition, when our relationships are strained due to unresolved conflicts or interpersonal issues, it can cause us to retreat into further isolation. This can lead to further mental and emotional distress, such as depression or anxiety, which can make it even harder for us to maintain healthy relationships. If we remain isolated, it can be difficult to find the courage and strength needed to build new relationships or repair old ones. Isolation moves us away from sources of support, which can further our mental and emotional decline.

SKILLS NEEDED TO BUILD GOOD RELATIONSHIPS

We all need good relationships with others to stay mentally/emotionally healthy. That's why it's important to learn how to build strong and meaningful relationships. However, in order to do this, we must first understand how to maintain a relationship. This will help us learn which relationships are worth investing in and which ones should be avoided.

GIVE SKILLS

One way of learning how to build relationships is through effective communication. In dialectical behavioral therapy, there are four key skills known as GIVE (Sunrisertc, 2017a):

G: Gentleness	I: Interest	V: Validation	E: Empathy
Start by being gentle and kind in your conversations with others, rather than aggressive or confrontational. For instance, avoid using a harsh tone or strong body language when speaking with them.	Show genuine interest in the person you're talking to, their opinions and feelings, as well as what they have to say. Ask questions, listen attentively, and actively participate in the conversation.	Let the other person know that their feelings and opinions are valid, even if you don't agree with them. Letting someone else feel heard and understood can help to deepen your relationship.	Put yourself in the other person's shoes. This means understanding how they feel and responding to their feelings accordingly. Being able to empathize and relate to the other person helps build trust and strengthens your connection.

These skills can help us build strong relationships and become better at friendships. With practice, you can use these skills to maintain healthy relationships that promote well-being and emotional health.

GIVE WORKSHEET

Practicing GIVE skills can help you become better at communicating with others. Use this worksheet to reflect on how you can build relationships through effective communication.

What is a recent conversation that I had with someone?

How did I use gentleness in the conversation?

What could I have done differently to show more interest in the person I was talking to?

How did I validate the other person's feelings and opinions?

What could I have done to show empathy to the other person?

What are some ways that I can practice gentleness, interest, validation, and empathy in my conversations with others?

What are some ways that I can use GIVE skills to build and maintain relationships in the future?

By reflecting on your conversations and practicing GIVE skills, you can become better at communicating with others and building stronger relationships. With practice, you'll be able to develop healthier connections with people, which can help promote emotional well-being.

RELATIONSHIP MISTAKES TO AVOID

Relationships are important, but sometimes we can find ourselves in unhealthy or toxic ones. It's important to be aware of the signs of an inappropriate relationship, so you know when it's time to move on. Or we might give too much of ourselves to others, which can lead to burnout and exhaustion. Here are some potential relationship mistakes to avoid:

- **Failing to set boundaries:** It's important to give yourself permission to say "no" or put your own needs first. You should also be aware of boundaries other people establish and respect them.

- **Focusing on the negative:** Pay attention to the good things in a relationship and don't focus solely on problem areas.

- **Avoiding con ict:** Although it can be uncomfortable, addressing issues when they arise is key to resolving them and preserving your relationships. Ignoring problems won't make them go away.

- **Expecting the other person to change:** Trying to change someone leads to frustration and disappointment. Instead, accept and appreciate the other person for who they are.

- **Making goals together:** While working toward common goals can give you something positive to focus on, it can also cause people to force others to change or try to control them. Instead, make goals that focus on your wants and needs, and not what someone else wants.

- **Becoming dependent on friends, family, or a partner:** Too much reliance on someone else will lead to feelings of insecurity and a fear of abandonment. Instead, focus on building your own sense of self-worth.

- ✓ **Creating goals based on negative language:** Creating and working toward your goals is important. However, the language in which you specify your goals is also important. Steer away from negative language, such as "I must," "I can't," or "I should." Instead, use positive affirmations that focus on what you can do or want to do. Negative language can lead to feelings of shame and guilt, which can damage relationships.

- ✓ **Not committing to the relationship irst:** In many cases, people want to commit to any relationship after they've already invested time and energy into it—once they know it's "worth their while." However, without an initial commitment or genuinely "trying" in a relationship, there can be no true growth.

Not understanding your motives: Knowing why you want to be in a relationship is key to understanding how you'll approach it. If your motives are not clear, this can lead to confusion and misunderstandings later on down the line. Check in with yourself before entering into any kind of relationship and make sure that your intentions are positive and healthy.

Avoiding these mistakes can help you build successful relationships and maintain a healthy balance of give and take. It's important to practice DBT skills to better understand yourself, your feelings, and the other person in the relationship. With this knowledge, you will be able to create strong relationships that are beneficial for both parties. Relationships are key to our well-being. By developing healthy relationships, you can learn how to maintain them for a lifetime and avoid the pitfalls of unhealthy ones. With the right effort, you'll be able to build strong relationships that will last!

APPROPRIATE RELATIONSHIP GOALS

Now that we've reviewed some mistakes to avoid when it comes to relationships, let's talk about positive steps you can take in order to achieve healthy and successful relationships. When forming relationships, it's important to have appropriate goals and expectations in order to help the relationship grow and flourish.

Some positive goals you can set for yourself when it comes to relationships include the following:

✓ **Focus on communication:** It's essential to be honest, open, and clear with your thoughts and feelings when communicating with someone else. This is key to avoiding misunderstandings and creating trust.

✓ **Check in with yourself:** Learn how to recognize how you're feeling, why you're feeling that way, and what caused those feelings. This will help you express yourself better and also be more empathetic toward the other person in a relationship.

✓ **Accepting differences:** Remember that no two people are exactly alike. We all have our own unique personalities and backgrounds, and it's important to accept these differences in order to foster understanding between two individuals.

✓ **Reciprocity of effort:** It takes effort from both sides in order to make a relationship work. Learn how to balance your needs with those of the other person and maintain a sense of equality in the relationship.

✓ **Be yourself:** If you want a relationship to work out, it's important that you are being your authentic self. Don't try to be someone else or hide aspects of yourself that you think the other person won't like. Relationships are meant to be a safe space for both people to share and grow, so make sure you feel comfortable expressing your true self.

✓ **Search for positive friendship attributes:** In order to create healthy relationships, it's important to search for positive attributes in the people you want to be friends with. Look for qualities such as trustworthiness, kindness, empathy, and understanding. If people don't exhibit positive friendship qualities or if they do not meet your expectations, it's okay to politely walk away and find someone who does.

✓ **Know what you want from friendships:** It's important to identify what you need from a friendship in order to make sure that it is beneficial for both parties. Think about the type of relationship you want and decide if the other person is someone who can meet your needs. Doing this will help you form successful relationships that work for both of you.

✓ **Don't give up your values:** It's important to remember that you should never give up your values or change who you are to please someone else. If a friendship is causing you to compromise yourself, it might not be worth pursuing. Making sure that your values align with the other person's will help ensure that the relationship is healthy and positive.

✓ **Be picky:** It's okay to be picky about the people you let into your life. It's important to take the time to get to know someone before you start a relationship and make sure it's a good fit for both of you.

At the end of the day, it's up to you to decide which relationships are healthy and which ones should be avoided. By understanding the distinction between good relationships and bad ones, you can focus on positive ones.

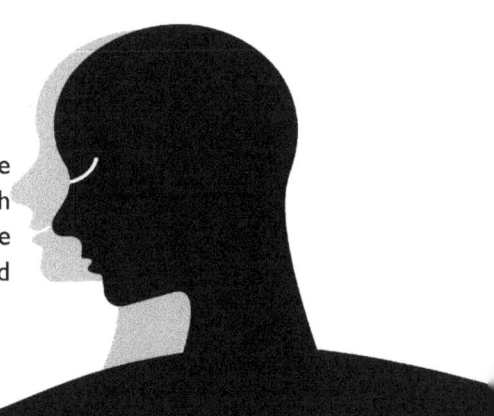

INTERPERSONAL EFFECTIVENESS TOOLS

Interpersonal effectiveness skills from dialectical behavior therapy can help you identify what is needed in a good relationship and learn to avoid any that don't provide these essential elements. These different tools help you understand and balance your needs, feelings, wishes, and objectives when interacting with others.

FAST SKILLS

Earlier in the chapter, we reviewed the GIVE tool, which encourages you to be gentle and kind while also speaking up for yourself. Another tool you can use is FAST, which stands for fairness, no apologies, stick to values, and truthful (Sunrisertc, 2017a).

Fairness: Take responsibility for your part in a situation and be willing to compromise when appropriate. Fairness also means being fair toward the other person in the situation. For instance, it might be easy to think that the other person is always the one who needs to make changes or adjustments, but that's not always true.

No apologies: You have a right to your feelings and opinions. You should also be able to share them. However, if you genuinely aren't intending to hurt someone and regret something you said, it's okay to apologize. Avoid excessive apologizing though, as it can make others think that you don't believe in yourself or your opinions and decisions. Don't apologize more than necessary and be cautious about what you choose to apologize for (your feelings, opinions, or needs are valid).

Stick to values: Stand up for yourself without being demanding or making threats. Don't change your core values to fit in with others. Respect the rights of other people and stay in control of your own emotions.

TRUTHFUL

Honesty is crucial in any relationship, so don't be afraid to speak your truth. Avoid exaggerating or misrepresenting the facts and don't lie or make excuses. Use truthful language to ensure that you're getting your point across without being overly critical or negative. Avoid exaggerating and don't lie in order to get what you want.

Using these skills can help you recognize good relationships, build stronger ones, and help you stay away from those that are not beneficial for your mental health. Remember, it's okay to set boundaries in the relationships you have with friends and family. You should also feel free to take time for yourself and be honest about your feelings.

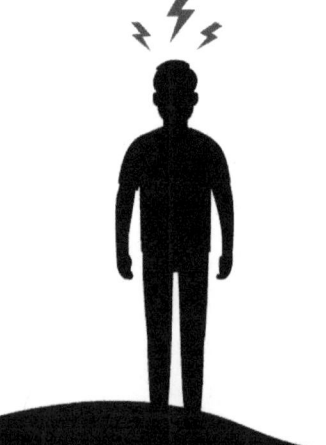

FAST SKILLS WORKSHEET

Use this worksheet to re lect on how you can use your FAST skills to build relationships.

How did I use fairness in a recent conversation?

....

....

....

Did I apologize more than necessary? If so, what could I have done differently to communicate better with others?

....

....

....

How did I stick to my values while still respecting the other person in the conversation?

....

....

....

Did I speak truthfully and honestly, without exaggerating or misrepresenting facts?

....

....

....

What are some ways that I can practice fairness, no apologies, sticking to values, and truthfulness in my conversations with others?

....

....

....

....

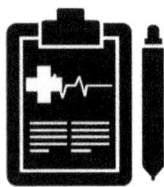

VITALS SKILLS

VITALS is another acronym that stands for validating, imagining, taking small steps, applauding yourself, lightening the load, and sweetening the pot (*Motivation Check Your V.I.T.A.L.S*, n.d.).

Validating: Affirm your own thoughts and feelings as valid, even if they seem irrational or wrong. Find comfort in knowing you have the right to feel a certain way and try not to downplay your emotions.

Imagine: Visualize how it would feel if you accomplished something difficult or overcame an obstacle. Really see yourself succeeding, and use the vision to stay motivated.

Take small steps: Break down your goals into small, manageable steps and work toward them one at a time. Trying to complete long-term objectives in one go can be overwhelming, so take it easy!

Applaud yourself: Celebrate your successes no matter how small they may seem. Acknowledge that you're doing the best you can and reward yourself for milestones along the way.

Lighten the load: It's okay to ask for help when needed. Don't be afraid to lean on others if it helps make things easier or more bearable. On the other hand, you can also lighten the load by considering the benefits you'll receive when things are complete.

Sweeten the pot: Offer yourself rewards for completing difficult tasks. This could be something like a night out or a special treat—whatever will help to motivate you!

These skills will help you build confidence, self-compassion, and strengthen your relationships with others. With practice, you will be able to better manage your emotions and stay on track toward achieving your goals.

VITALS WORKSHEET

Use this worksheet to reflect on how you can use your VITALS skills to build relationships.

Consider a challenge you're facing with a friend or acquaintance. How can you validate your thoughts and feelings?

....

....

....

....

What steps can you take to imagine yourself succeeding? What goal do you want to visualize?

....

....

....

....

What small steps can you break the challenge into that will make it more manageable? How will you reward yourself for completing milestones or goals associated with the challenge?

....

....

....

....

How can you lighten the load by asking for help or considering the benefits of completion? What reward could sweeten the pot and motivate you?

....

....

....

....

....

THINK SKILLS

The THINK skills are another set of interpersonal effectiveness tools that can help you build good relationships and keep bad ones at bay. THINK stands for think, have empathy, interpretations, notice, and kindness (Sunrisertc, 2017a).

Think: Take a moment to review the situation and consider your options. Think of what's most important to you, how best to achieve it, and which course of action is the most reasonable one. Consider the problem or situation from the other person's perspective. Maybe they feel as equally frustrated or confused as you do.

Have empathy: Listen carefully to the other person and try to understand their perspective. Put yourself in their shoes so that you can better understand why they are feeling, thinking, or reacting the way they are. This will help you determine if your expectations of them are reasonable or not.

Interpretations: Be aware of your own interpretations and perceptions. Reflect on what the other person is saying and try to assess if your interpretation of it matches theirs. If not, ask for clarification or further explanation so that you can better understand the situation from their point of view.

Notice: Notice the other person. Are they being kind, mean, or communicative? Pay attention to their nonverbal communication and body language, which can provide additional insight into how they're feeling and thinking. If they're being nice, take note of that.

Kindness: Speak to the other person with kindness and respect. This doesn't mean that you have to agree with everything they say, but it does mean showing them compassion and understanding. Showing kindness can go a long way in resolving conflicts and building positive relationships.

Using these skills can help you maintain positive relationships and avoid unhealthy ones. Remember that both your feelings and needs are valid, so be honest with yourself and others while respecting their rights as well.

THINK SKILLS WORKSHEET

Use this worksheet to re lect on how you can use your THINK skills to build relationships.

Consider a challenge you are facing with a friend or acquaintance. What do you think about the situation? What other perspectives should you consider?

....

....

How can you have empathy for the other person and better understand their perspective? What do you believe they are feeling, thinking, or reacting to?

....

....

What interpretations are you making about the situation and the other person's intentions? Are your interpretations matching theirs? If not, what can you do to better understand their point of view?

....

....

What cues are you noticing from the other person in terms of body language and nonverbal communication? How can you use these cues to better understand them?

....

....

Finally, how can you show kindness and respect while communicating your needs? How can this help resolve the challenge or conflict?

....

....

....

By breaking down the challenge into manageable pieces and rewarding yourself along the way, you'll stay motivated and dedicated toward achieving success in all of your relationships. Practice using the THINK skills and you'll be sure to see positive results.

DEAR MAN SKILLS

The DEAR MAN skills are also an important tool for building good relationships and avoiding bad ones. This acronym stands for describe, express, assert, reinforce, mindful, appear confident, and negotiate (Sunrisertc, 2017a).

✓ **Describe:** Start by honestly describing the situation so that the other person can understand why you're feeling upset or anxious. Explain the problem without being too critical or blaming them. Try to keep it short, sweet, and simple.

✓ **Express:** Express how you feel in a clear, assertive, but non-confrontational way. Don't be afraid to express your emotions as they can help you better understand the situation and yourself.

✓ **Assert:** Be assertive in your communication style so that you can effectively get your point across without appearing aggressive or passive. Make sure that your body language, facial expressions, and tone of voice all match the message you're trying to convey.

✓ **Reinforce:** Reinforce the positive aspects of the relationship, such as shared interests and values. Explain the benefits of solving the problem your way. This will help you foster a better understanding between you and the other person.

✓ **Mindful:** Be mindful of your own thoughts, feelings, and behaviors in order to stay grounded during challenging conversations. Remember that it's okay to take a break if it gets too overwhelming or you need time to collect your thoughts.

✓ **Appear con dent:** Act confidently so that the other person will respect you and take your opinion seriously. Even if you don't feel confident, try to project an air of self-assurance so that the other person will take you more seriously.

✓ **Negotiate:** Negotiate a compromise or solution for both parties. Be open to their ideas and opinions and try to come up with a win-win situation. This will help you maintain a healthy relationship and build trust between both parties.

Overall, having strong communication skills is essential for building good relationships and avoiding bad ones. Taking the time to use these DBT skills can go a long way in helping you establish positive connections with others and create a better understanding between both parties involved.

DEAR MAN WORKSHEET

Use the prompts below to brainstorm how you can use the DEAR MAN skills in a challenging conflict or situation with a friend or acquaintance.

How can I accurately and briefly describe the situation so that my friend/ acquaintance understands why I'm feeling anxious or upset?

....

....

....

....

How can I express how I'm feeling in an assertive but non-confrontational manner?

....

....

....

....

What body language, facial expressions, and tone of voice can I use to effectively convey my message?

....

....

....

....

How can I reinforce the positive aspects of our relationship, such as shared interests and values? What benefits can come from our friendship?

....

....

....

....

How can I stay grounded and mindful of my thoughts, feelings, and behaviors during this conversation?

....

....

....

....

....

....

How can I project an air of self-assurance even if I don't feel particularly confident in the situation?

....

....

....

....

....

....

How can I negotiate a compromise or solution that works for both of us? What actionable steps can I take to resolve the conflict and move forward in a positive direction?

....

....

....

....

....

....

By taking the time to use these DBT skills, you can create strong connections with others and master healthy communication strategies. Use this DEAR MAN worksheet as a guide when practicing your communication skills, and you'll be able to navigate tricky conversations with confidence.

REFLECTION QUESTIONS

What are some things that I can do to demonstrate kindness and respect when communicating with someone?

How can I use assertive communication skills to effectively get my point across without appearing aggressive or passive?

How can using the DEAR MAN skills help me foster a better understanding between me and another person?

How can I negotiate a win-win situation when both parties are in disagreement?

How can having strong communication skills help me build and maintain healthy relationships?

What other strategies can be used to build trust between two people?

In what ways have I seen the DEAR MAN skills positively affect my relationships with others?

What have I learned from using the DEAR MAN skills in my interpersonal relationships?

What can I do to create a better understanding between both parties involved when communicating?

PART THREE

CONCLUSION
AND DISCLAIMER

CHAPTER 8: A NOTE TO PARENTS, TEACHERS, AND THERAPISTS

It's important to remember that the strategies discussed in this book are meant to be used as part of a holistic approach toward teen stress management. While these techniques may offer some relief, it's also important to seek professional help when needed. Parents and guardians should pay attention to their teens' behavior and watch out for signs of distress or depression.

If your teen is struggling, it's important to find a professional who can help them learn how to cope with and manage their anxious thoughts and

feelings in healthy ways. Therapy can be an effective tool for teens' mental health, and many therapists have specific training in helping teenagers work through stress, anxiety, and other mental health issues. Counseling can help teens build self-esteem, improve communication skills, learn healthier coping strategies, and explore difficult emotions in a safe and supportive environment.

DIALECTICAL BEHAVIORAL THERAPY CAN HELP PARENTS GET BETTER AT PARENTING

DBT isn't only for teens or the people who work with them. It can help parents too! DBT helps to foster a supportive and mutually respectful relationship between you and your teen. Parental involvement in DBT is crucial, but not only to support their child. It teaches them how to be more effective and positive in their relationships with their teens. It also teaches them how to be more understanding, supportive, and predictable in their interactions with the teen.

By using DBT, you can learn the skills needed to better parent your child in a constructive way. You will also have an improved understanding of how your child thinks and reacts, enabling you to provide better guidance.

Parents, teachers, and therapists can become a team to help your teen with DBT. Therapists are often there to listen, provide support, and teach your teen the skills they need. Teachers can provide insight into what challenges your child is facing at school. And as a parent, you know your child better than anyone else.

By working together, you can provide a better support system to help your teen lead a successful life. It's important for the entire team to agree on goals and strategies to best help your teen. With DBT, everyone involved will be able to understand the struggles and successes of your teen more clearly and effectively.

The goal of DBT is to create a balanced and cooperative relationship between the team, your teen, and yourself. By understanding each other's roles better, you can work together in harmony to help your child reach their potential.

> So, don't forget: Include everyone in the process—parents, teachers, therapists—so that your teen can get the most out of DBT.
> Working together is the key to success!

WISE MIND VERSUS ADULT ROLE MODELS

The wise mind is a popular concept in the world of DBT. It's a way to help your teen make decisions by considering both their emotional side and logical side. However, this is a concept that would benefit many adults well beyond their teenage years.

As parents, teachers, or simply adults, we are role models for children, even if we don't realize it. By practicing and exhibiting the wise mind in our everyday lives, we can serve as examples for children and set a positive example of how to handle difficult situations.

The goal is not only to help teens, but also adults to become aware of their feelings and make rational decisions when emotions are running high. By demonstrating wise minds ourselves, we can teach our teens the value of considering both sides of the equation in order to make sound decisions.

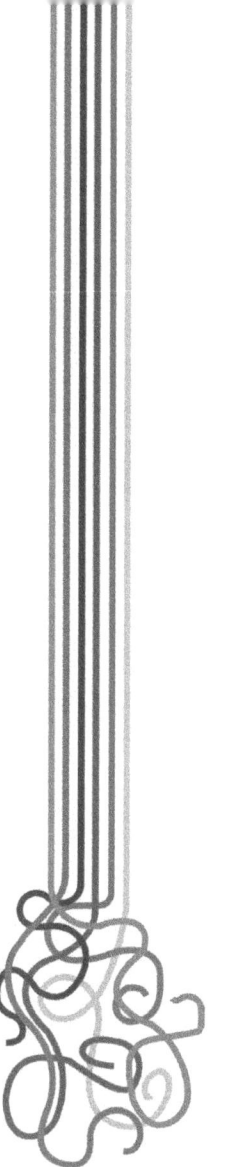

We can also teach our teens that they don't always have to rely solely on their own wisdom. We can be a source of wisdom and advice, helping them to make better informed decisions. That way, as adults, we can help our children develop into more mature individuals with the skills they need to succeed in life.

To practice the wise mind, you can start by recognizing when there is a conflict between your head and your heart. Then, try to identify the pros and cons of each side objectively in order to better understand the situation. This will allow you to work out the most beneficial solution for all involved parties.

WALKING THE MIDDLE PATH

DBT aims to help you and your teen find a "middle path" in difficult situations. This means that it teaches teens to respond from a place of emotional regulation, rather than responding immediately with an emotional outburst. The middle path is about finding a balance between emotions and logic. It requires us to accept our feelings and be mindful of them, while still being able to think objectively about the situation and make logical decisions.

By teaching our teens the concept of "walking the middle path," we can help them become more balanced people. We can teach them how to better understand their emotions and use logic to inform their decisions. This will give them the tools they need to make positive changes in their lives. We can show them how to accept their feelings of anger, sadness, or frustration without being overwhelmed by them. We can teach them how to take a step back and recognize that although these emotions are real, they don't define us. By walking the middle path, we can help our teens gain control over their emotions and live a more balanced life.

THERAPISTS AND FAMILIES MUST WORK TOGETHER

DBT is most effective when both the therapist and family work together to foster a therapeutic alliance. For the most part, your teen will be the one to make decisions about their treatment. However, family involvement is essential for success.

When it comes to DBT, the therapist and parents must create a cohesive team. The goal of this should be to put your teen in the best position possible for recovery and long-term success.

Parents can help by doing things such as providing emotional support and reinforcing skills. They can also provide insight into the things that their teen struggles with in order to better inform the therapist's treatment plan.

The therapist, on the other hand, can provide support and instruction to both the teen and family members. They will also be able to recommend resources or activities to help your teen practice their skills in the real world.

However, in some cases, this can lead to your teen feeling threatened by the relationship with their therapist. They may feel like it is a partnership between the two of you and that there is no room for their opinions. Or they may worry about their privacy being invaded.

In order to prevent this, it's important to make sure your teen feels included and has a say in the treatment process. Do this by asking them questions, making sure they understand why certain decisions are being made, and encouraging their input throughout the process. This will help to create a trusting relationship between you, your teen, and the therapist, so that all involved can work together for the benefit of your teen's well-being.

It is important to remember that your teen must feel comfortable and safe in the therapeutic environment, and that they have a voice in their treatment plan. Talk to them openly about these concerns so they feel listened to and respected.

Ultimately, it's up to both parties—family and therapist—to work together to get the best outcome for your teen. With the right support, patience, and hard work, a strong therapeutic alliance can be formed that will help your teen become their best self.

TEACHERS CAN USE DBT SKILLS TO PROVIDE A SAFE SPACE

Teachers can also play an important role in helping teens gain access to DBT skills. By creating a safe climate where students feel accepted and respected, teachers can provide an environment that is conducive to learning.

They can also encourage their students to practice mindfulness techniques and use positive communication strategies when discussing difficult topics or emotions. This will help to create an atmosphere that is more conducive to open and honest conversations and will ensure students feel respected and supported.

Teachers can use distress tolerance skills to help students manage difficult emotions and situations. They can also provide guidance and support to help students understand the difference between helpful and unhelpful coping strategies, such as using drugs or alcohol to self-medicate.

Finally, teachers can use validation skills to help teens learn how to be respectful of each other's opinions while still engaging in constructive dialogue. This is especially important for teens who may not feel like their voice is heard or respected.

By creating an environment that is safe and supportive, teachers can help teens access the skills they need to be successful in life. They can also provide them with a place to process difficult emotions, learn new coping strategies, and make positive changes in their lives.

In conclusion, building a therapeutic alliance with your teen is essential for helping them access the skills they need in order to become emotionally healthy and successful. It's important that both family members and therapists work together to provide support and understanding while respecting your teen's autonomy. With the right kind of support, you can help your teen access the tools they need to become their best self.

CHAPTER 9: STAYING THE COURSE

Now that you've made a plan, the most important part is to stay the course. It can be tempting to give up when things don't go as planned or when it seems like you aren't making progress fast enough. But remember that every step forward counts! If your goal requires long-term commitment, focus on making small changes each day. The best way to stay motivated is to celebrate your successes and recognize how far you've come!

Celebrate the little victories, like checking off a task or completing a project. It's important to take time for yourself to reflect and appreciate the progress you've made. Another way to stay on track is to find an accountability partner, someone who will help you stay focused and on task. Knowing that you have someone else invested in your success can be a great motivator! Don't forget to have fun as well—find activities that make the process enjoyable, so you don't burn out. If you stick with it and stay the course, you're sure to reach your goal!

GROWTH VERSUS FIXED MINDSET

Remember, it's all about having a growth mindset. With a fixed mindset, you believe that your talents and abilities are set in stone—you can't change them or improve them. However, with a growth mindset, you understand that you can always learn new things and get better at something if you put in the work. Remind yourself that you can always learn more and do better—that's the key to staying the course.

HOW TO DEVELOP A GROWTH MINDSET

If you want to develop a growth mindset, here are some tips:

1. **Celebrate small successes:** Remind yourself that even small steps forward count and make progress over time.

2. **Acknowledge your mistakes:** Accept responsibility for your mistakes and look at them as learning opportunities rather than setbacks.

3. **Set challenging goals:** Push yourself to do more than the minimum and challenge yourself with bigger goals.

4. **Use positive self-talk:** Remind yourself of your strengths and focus on what you can do rather than what you can't.

5. **Celebrate others' success:** Recognize when someone else achieves something and celebrate their hard work!

So, no matter where you're headed, remember to stay the course and trust the process! Achieving your goals is possible if you stick with it.

DBT TAKES TIME

In a traditional setting, DBT can take up to one year or more to complete. This is because it is a long-term program that requires dedication and patience. During this time, it's important to remain consistent in order to see the most success.

The first step of DBT involves identifying skills and behaviors that need to be addressed. This can take up to six months or longer, depending on the individual and the complexity of their issues.

The second step involves practicing the skills regularly and making consistent progress toward goals. This will help you become more comfortable with the skills as you start to form healthy habits. You'll also start to notice the positive changes in your life as you continue to apply the skills.

The third step involves consolidating your progress and maintaining your gains. This is an important part of DBT because it will help ensure that any skills learned during treatment are not forgotten or neglected. It's also important to remain mindful of any triggers or situations that can lead to a relapse and use the DBT skills to effectively manage emotions and behavior.

Finally, it's important to remember that progress may be slow or there may be setbacks along the way. This is normal with any type of therapy and should not discourage you from continuing. Just remember to stay focused on your goals, remain patient, and be consistent in your efforts. With dedication and perseverance, you can achieve success with DBT!

VISUALIZE IT

Visualization is a great tool for helping you stay focused on your goals. Find a quiet place and take some time to close your eyes and visualize what it would look like when you have achieved success. Imagine how it would feel, and the emotions you will experience. Connecting with these feelings can help you stay motivated and inspired enough to keep going, even when it gets hard.

DBT SKILLS VARY AND ARE MULTIFACETED

It is important to understand that the skills used in DBT vary depending on the individual and their needs. It's also important to remember that the skills are multifaceted, meaning they can be used in different situations and contexts.

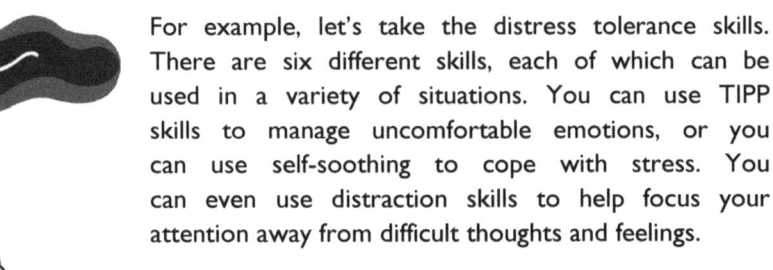

For example, let's take the distress tolerance skills. There are six different skills, each of which can be used in a variety of situations. You can use TIPP skills to manage uncomfortable emotions, or you can use self-soothing to cope with stress. You can even use distraction skills to help focus your attention away from difficult thoughts and feelings.

In addition, the mindfulness skills can also be used in different ways. While they are often taught in a formal setting, such as mindfulness meditation, you can also practice mindfulness in everyday activities. For example, you can practice mindful eating by focusing on each bite or practicing mindful walking by noticing the sights and sounds around you.

On the other hand, if your emotions aren't your primary concern, then you have several other tools, like interpersonal effectiveness skills, to help with communication and assertive negotiation.

These multifaceted skills are essential in helping you manage your emotions, thoughts, and behaviors in different situations. Finally, it's important to remember that DBT is a journey and not a destination. Of course, our goal is to gain emotional regulation and healthy coping skills, but the key is to find what works best for you. The important thing is to keep practicing and stay consistent in your efforts so that you can make progress. With time, patience, and practice, you can use DBT skills to transform your life!

 # TIPS FOR IMPLEMENTING THESE TECHNIQUES

When you start to look at each DBT pillar and realize how many skills there are, it can be overwhelming. Here are some tips to help you implement these skills in your daily life:

Start small and make sure to focus on one skill at a time. Taking baby steps might seem like it will take you longer to complete your goals, but it will actually help you stay consistent and motivated. This will help you become more comfortable with the different techniques and allow you to gradually build up your skill set. As you gain proficiency in one skill, you can move onto the next.

Find different ways to practice your skills. Consistency is the key to successful implementation, so make sure you find creative and meaningful ways to use the skills in your daily life. This could be something as simple as setting reminders on your phone or writing notes in a journal. You can also practice skills with a friend or family member, seek out support groups, or join an online DBT community.

Stay open-minded and don't give up. Every journey has its ups and downs, but it's important to stay focused on your goals and remember that progress often takes time. Be patient with yourself and focus on the progress you've made, rather than comparing it to where you want to be.

DBT INCLUDE NEW HABITS AND UNLEARNING OLD ONES

We don't always realize it, but our habits play a crucial role in how we feel. If we regularly engage in unhealthy habits like unhealthy eating or holding onto negative thoughts, it can contribute negatively to our emotional and mental well-being.

That's why it can be helpful to practice new habits while unlearning old ones, which is the purpose of DBT. When we focus on developing healthier habits, such as taking time for self-care or engaging in positive self-talk, it helps us feel better in the long run.

On top of that, by unlearning old habits, it creates more space for new ones to take root. DBT helps you determine which habits you need to work on and how to replace them with healthier ones. DBT is not just about learning new skills, but also integrating them into your life and unlearning old habits. Once you've become comfortable with using DBT skills in one context, you can start to incorporate those same techniques in other areas of your life.

For example, if you've been able to use distress tolerance skills when you're feeling overwhelmed, you can then use those same techniques when faced with other difficult situations. If you've been using mindfulness to become more aware of your emotions, you can then use those same practices to improve your relationships and interactions with others.

By applying DBT skills in different contexts, it helps us develop healthier habits that will benefit our emotional and mental well-being. By taking the time to practice DBT skills and be mindful of our habits, we can learn to take better care of ourselves and develop a more positive outlook on life. So, even if you find yourself struggling to make progress with DBT, don't give up! With time and practice, you can develop healthier habits that will ultimately help improve your emotional regulation and overall well-being.

DBT HELPS WITH EVERYDAY LIFE

While DBT significantly helps with challenges or life changes, it can also be a valuable tool in our everyday lives. We all have stressful moments and difficult days, but with DBT skills, we can learn how to manage those experiences and respond in healthier ways. You don't have to be facing a problem or feeling overwhelmed to start using DBT skills.

You can use DBT techniques like mindfulness and distress tolerance in everyday life, such as when you're feeling frustrated, anxious, or overwhelmed—or even if you're happy. Here are five instances throughout life that you can use DBT skills:

1. **Eating:** You can use mindfulness skills to be more aware of when and why you're eating. You can also apply mindful techniques to the whole shopping process. Practice being mindful at the supermarket and as you cook. While you eat, focus on the taste, texture, and temperature of your food.

2. **Walking:** Use walking as an opportunity to practice mindfulness and distress tolerance. Use it to connect with your surroundings, be aware of the sounds and feelings around you, or simply take time for yourself.

3. **Experimenting:** Experimenting with new activities and hobbies can help you learn more mindful practices. For instance, by engaging in art or music, you can become more aware of your surroundings, as well as your own inner world.

4. **Appreciation:** Take time to be mindful of what you have and show appreciation for yourself, your family, or friends. You can practice mindfulness by being grateful for the small things in life, such as a good conversation with a friend or a sunny day.

5. **Breathing:** If you're feeling overwhelmed or anxious, it's important to practice breathing exercises. Focusing on your breath for a few minutes can help you relax and regain focus.

By taking the time to practice DBT skills in our everyday lives, we can learn how to better manage our emotions and live with more balance.

CONCLUSION

Congratulations, you have completed *DBT Skills and Mindfulness for Teen Anxiety*! How do you feel? Have you tried any of the skills yet? DBT has been an invaluable tool for me in managing my mental health and emotions, and I hope it can help you, too. It takes dedication and practice to master these skills, but the results are worth it! If you feel ready to take control of your life and make positive changes, DBT is here to help.

You have come a long way on your journey toward mastering DBT skills. I'm sure you're feeling a sense of accomplishment for all the hard work you have put in. This book has been a great foundation for getting to know your emotions, building healthy relationships, and living life according to your values. I hope you can use this knowledge to gain control of your emotions and take ownership of your mental health.

When I first started practicing DBT, I could not have imagined the transformation that it would bring to my life. At first, I was resistant. I hated having to confront my feelings and learn about myself.

I struggled to stay consistent and practice the skills every day. I avoided these skills because I was afraid of facing my emotions and learning to manage them. And yet, I persisted and kept trying until slowly but surely the skills became second nature. With time and dedication, I learned to accept myself and my emotions. I found peace within the struggle and developed resilience through understanding how to better manage my mental health. But over time, I saw the beauty of how DBT helped me grow and become a better version of myself.

I realized that DBT is more than just a set of skills; it's about learning to own your mental health and taking control. Over the years, I have developed a strong relationship with myself and feel that I can confidently navigate life's challenges. I hope that by reading this book, you have been inspired to take control of your mental health journey as well. DBT is an invaluable tool for anyone who wants to build resilience and cultivate inner peace. It may at first appear daunting, but with the right mindset and dedication, you can learn to master these skills.

I'm so grateful that I stuck with it and made the effort to learn and practice these skills. I can communicate with others more effectively, stay present in the moment, and manage difficult emotions. And now that you have mastered all four modules, I hope it will do the same for you. I am confident that if you stick with it, you can gain control of your mental health and life, too.

Here's a brief reminder of what you've learned throughout the book:

- ✓ DBT is an effective and powerful way to manage intense emotions, difficult behaviors, and mental health struggles.

- ✓ There are four modules that make up the core of DBT: mindfulness, distress tolerance, emotional regulation, and interpersonal effectiveness.

- ✓ Mindfulness teaches you to stay present in the moment, as well as be aware of your thoughts and feelings without judgment or resistance.

- ✓ Some common mindful techniques are meditation, deep breathing, and writing.

- ✓ Distress tolerance is all about coping with difficult emotions in a healthy way. Techniques such as self-soothing, distraction, and radical acceptance can be helpful in managing distressing situations.

- ✓ Emotional regulation involves learning how to identify, understand, and control your emotions. Practicing emotional regulation can help you to become aware of your triggers and manage emotions before they become too overwhelming. Some emotional regulation techniques are self-reflection and relaxation techniques.

- ✓ Interpersonal Effectiveness is all about communicating with others in healthy and respectful ways. It includes skills such as assertiveness, empathy, and problem-solving. Some popular acronyms for interpersonal effectiveness are DEAR MAN and GIVE.

Now that you have completed the book, go out there and use your newfound skills to live a life free of intense emotions and mental health struggles!

I hope this guide has been impactful in helping you explore the power of DBT skills and mindfulness for managing anxiety. The way forward is up to you—you have all the tools and support you need to keep growing and mastering DBT techniques. With these tools, you can become an expert in managing your emotions and mental health.

Whether you use them for yourself or to help someone else, DBT will be a great asset in your life. With practice, you will be able to look back at this book and feel proud of the journey that you've taken. Thank you for reading and good luck. If you enjoyed this book, please share it with a friend or leave a review!

GLOSSARY

ABC PLEASE:

ABC PLEASE is an emotion regulation skill acronym that stands for accumulating positive experiences, building mastery, coping ahead, (treating) physical illness, eating, avoiding mood-altering drugs, sleep, and exercise.

ACCEPTS:

ACCEPTS is a distress tolerance skill acronym that stands for activities, contributing, comparisons, emotions, push away, thoughts, and sensations

BORDERLINE PERSONALITY DISORDER (BPD):

BPD is a mental disorder characterized by difficulty with emotion regulation, interpersonal functioning, and the stability of behavior. People with BPD may experience intense emotions, fear of abandonment, impulsive behaviors, and unstable relationships. DBT is an evidence-based form of treatment for BPD.

DEAR MAN:

DEAR MAN is a dialectical behavior therapy skill that stands for describe, express, assert, reinforce, mindful, appear confident, and negotiate. It is used to help people learn how to be assertive in their communication with others.

DIALECTICS

Dialectics is a philosophical concept that seeks to reconcile opposing ideas or forces into a unified whole. It looks at both sides of the issue, then works to combine those two sides in order to find balance. In DBT, the dialectic emphasizes the balance between acceptance and change.

DISTRESS TOLERANCE:

Distress tolerance refers to the ability to tolerate distressful emotions and experiences without making them worse. This includes learning how to control your reactions when faced with a difficult situation and developing the ability to ride out the storm until it passes.

EMOTION DYSREGULATION:

Emotion dysregulation is a term used to describe difficulty managing emotions. It often involves intense emotions lasting longer than expected or out of proportion to the situation, resulting in difficulty functioning and/or making decisions. In DBT, emotion regulation skills are used to help manage emotion dysregulation.

EMOTION REGULATION:

Emotion regulation refers to the ability to recognize, manage, and respond to emotions in a constructive way. It involves understanding your triggers, learning how to identify and label different emotions, and developing strategies for managing them. In DBT, emotion regulation is one of the four core skills.

FAST:

FAST is an interpersonal effectiveness skill acronym that stands for fair, apology, stick to values and facts, and truth. It can be used to help you stay focused on the important issues in a conversation and speak your truth in a respectful way.

GIVE:

GIVE is an interpersonal effectiveness skill acronym that stands for gentle, interested, validating, and easy manner. It can help you communicate effectively in difficult situations.

IMPROVE:

IMPROVE is a skill acronym that stands for imagery, meaning, prayer, relaxation, one thing in the moment, vacation, and encouragement

INTERPERSONAL EFFECTIVENESS:

Interpersonal effectiveness refers to the ability to get what you want while maintaining, or even improving, relationships. It is a set of skills designed to help you communicate effectively and navigate social situations with ease.

MINDFULNESS:

Mindfulness is a practice of focusing on the present moment without judgment or analysis. It involves cultivating an awareness of your thoughts, feelings, and environment in order to gain insight into how you interact with your world. In DBT, mindfulness is one of the four core skills and is used to increase acceptance of oneself and others.

MODULE:

A DBT module is a set of skills that build upon each other to help you better manage your emotions, cope with distress, communicate effectively, and improve relationships. Modules typically include an overview of the concept, an explanation of how to practice it, and exercises to help you apply the skill in real life situations.

OPPOSITE ACTION:

This is an emotion regulation skill used to help you shift your emotional state in a way that is helpful and adaptive. It involves taking action that is the opposite of what your current emotion might suggest, such as forcing yourself to act cheerful when feeling sad.

PROS AND CONS:

Pros and Cons is a skill used to help you make decisions. It involves listing the advantages and disadvantages of each option, weighing them against each other, and making an informed decision.

RADICAL ACCEPTANCE:

Radical acceptance is a practice of embracing and accepting the present moment without judgment or resistance. It allows you to acknowledge your feelings and experiences without getting caught up in the need to change them. In DBT, radical acceptance is one of the four core skills and can increase self-compassion.

SELF-SOOTHING:

Self-soothing is a skill used to help you manage difficult emotions. It involves using calming activities, such as deep breathing or reading, to help you relax and cope in the moment.

STOP SKILLS:

STOP is an emotion regulation skill acronym that stands for stop, take a step back, observe the situation objectively, and proceed mindfully. It can help you stay mindful in difficult moments and make decisions based on what is best for you.

THINK:

THINK is an interpersonal effectiveness skill acronym that stands for think, have empathy, interpretations, notice, and kindness. It can help you communicate effectively in difficult conversations.

TIPP:

TIPP is a distress tolerance skill acronym that stands for temperature, intense exercise, paced breathing, and progressive muscle relaxation. It can help you cope with difficult emotions in a healthy way.

VALIDATION:

Validation is the process of recognizing and understanding another person's feelings and experiences without judgment or criticism. It can build relationships and foster greater empathy, understanding, and compassion between people. In DBT, validation is a core skill that can help you better understand yourself and others.

WISE MIND:

The Wise Mind is a concept that combines the logical and emotional aspects of the self. It encourages you to use both your rational and intuitive sides to make decisions, rather than relying on one or the other. In DBT, the Wise Mind serves as a guiding principle for making mindful, balanced decisions.

THE DBT SKILLS WORKBOOK FOR

TEENS

ADHD

Essential Coping Strategies to Develop
Distress Tolerance Skills, Effective Emotional
Regulation Habits, and Strong, Resilient
Interpersonal Relationships

M.A. MARTINE

INTRODUCTION

Hi Reader,

'm glad to finally get through to you on this subject. I've helped a lot of young people with this, but I don't think I am done yet because we haven't met. Now that you have my book in front of you, I'm hoping we can have some interesting interactions as we go through each page.

I've been longing to ask a crucial question as I prepared to write to you: "Why?" Yes, why do you need this therapy? Why do you need this book to educate you about this therapy? Will this therapy make you a better human being? Will this therapy alleviate emotional symptoms partially or completely?

Aren't those the questions you've been asking, too? I know, right? And I know it's the reason you picked this book.

The same question that made you select this book, among many others, motivated me to write it. It's to let you know that this book is for *you*. I put my expertise and years of experience into writing this book with you in mind.

Now, to answer our mutual question, let's get this straight first. Do you need dialectical behavior therapy (DBT)?

You need this therapy if:

✓ You're hyperactive; that is, you have lots of energy or move and talk too much. Or you have difficulty paying attention. Or you act without thinking it through. These are symptoms of a disorder in teens and young adults known as attention deficit hyperactivity disorder (ADHD).

✓ You fidget a lot and barely sit still.

✓ You avoid tasks that require a lot of mental effort like schoolwork or homework.

✓ You don't pay close attention to the details and make "careless" mistakes.

✓ You have trouble following instructions and finishing tasks like chores or homework.

✓ Small things like sosound outside the window often distract you.

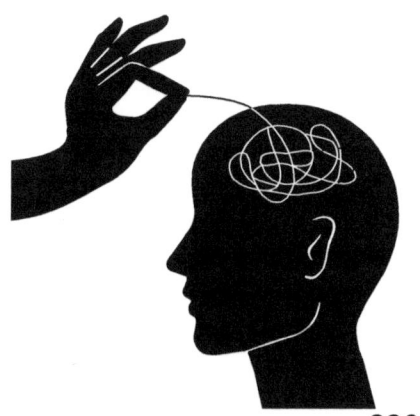

✓ You have trouble remembering everyday hings. You constantly experience extreme mood swings and uncontrollable emotions. Such experiences are related to a disorder known as Borderline personality disorder (BPD).

✓ To cope with emotional pain, you harm your body by cutting your skin.

✓ You have a mental health issue that may have developed after a scary, shocking, dangerous, or life-threatening event. This mental health issue is usually termed Post-traumatic stress disorder (PTSD).

✓ Your eating pattern is abnormal, like eating large amounts of food when you're not hungry or you eat in large quantities to get rid of it later. It could also be that you eat way faster than every other person, or you eat till you feel uncomfortable. That's known as a binge eating pattern.

✓ You're always anxious.

If you fall into any of the categories above, don't drop this book. But if you don't belong to any of those, don't drop it just yet. You're about to become a solution provider for someone who needs this book.

If the list above is any indication, you could benefit from some assistance in overcoming these abnormalities. On a scale of 1 to 10, this therapeutic option I'm about to share with you rates a 9 in its effectiveness in transforming you into a happier kid, a healthy young adult, and a loving human.

Here is a stat to support my claim:

✓ BMC Psychiatry found that after finishing the group treatment, 88% of the participants reported that they could better control symptoms of ADHD.

Note that in my years of working with ADHD patients and other disorders using dialectical behavioral therapy, I discovered that this therapeutic option works best for those committed to the process.

So, I'd like to know before we continue:

✓ Do you like your current state or want to be a better, healthy person?

✓ How many resources can you commit to becoming the better, healthier, and more organized person you've been dreaming of?

So, if you desire,

✓ to learn life-long coping skills

✓ how to calmly interact with people in your life – in a good way

✓ to feel and live happier

- ✓ to be more productive
- ✓ to improve chronic stress
- ✓ to stop negative habits
- ✓ to be healthier

I recommend that you make a firm commitment to practice every piece of information I uncover in the chapters of this book as they apply to you.

WHAT'S MORE?

I've only introduced the theme of this book here, but there's a whole lot more you can learn in this book. You'll get to know more about DBT and its benefits to you. You'll also get to know why this therapeutic option works. You'll learn how it works and how to apply it to your context.

You won't be the last person I take on this transformational journey, but you're one of the most important people I'm glad to have along for the ride. I'm not done in this spatiotemporal realm until I've seen you become the best version of yourself. This book is just a step in that direction.

Finally, I know what it means to have one of those behavioral, mental, or emotional disorders. I've seen and experienced it. Nothing is more implausible than when these disorders persist, they make you believe that's just how you were born and there's nothing you can do about it. However, that's just a partial fact. There's a flip side. There's a flip side to those disorders.

The good news is that I've seen both sides. And I can tell which of the sides looks good. Right now, you've experienced just one side of that fact. You've seen how ugly and frustrating it could be.

Don't quit just yet. My objective in writing this to you is to take you on an adventure that will help you cross from the side you're on to the other side. On arriving at the other side, what you'll discover will amaze you.

Your current situation doesn't accurately reflect who you really are. There is more to you than you initially realized. These disorders cloud your judgment about your identity and essence. As a result, the images you have been seeing are distorted. Yes, before you ask, I am more aware of who you are and what you are made of. This book aims not only to tell you how lovely you are but also to demonstrate how you can change into what you see.

Now, I know we've only just met, but I have a simple favor to ask of you:

Pick up a blank piece of paper. Boldly write on it two things you hope to accomplish after this journey.

Stick the paper in a visible location at all times. Whenever you pick this book up, take a quick look at what you wrote to keep your goals in mind.

Oh wow, that's three favors I've already asked for. Thank you!

I'm ready to come with you on this adventure. The question is, are you ready?

Best wishes,
Teen Advance

CHAPTER 1: DIALECTICAL BEHAVIOR THERAPY FOR LAYMEN

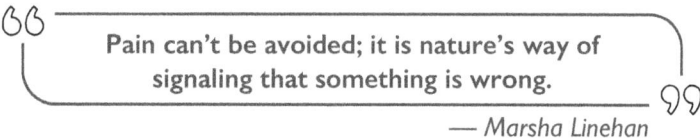

> Pain can't be avoided; it is nature's way of signaling that something is wrong.

— *Marsha Linehan*

In an interview, Annie, a female Caucasian, described her 20-year-old life as a "living hell." She was referred from one specialist to another. To alleviate her troubles, she was given psychotropic medications. Instead of helping her get better, the medications only increased her level of depression. Annie began self-medicating to relieve her pain to help herself. But she eventually got addicted to those pain medications.

As a result of the severity of her mental health challenge, Annie was placed on mental health treatment over three years in outpatient and intensive outpatient programs. Although she got a lot of support from her family, they felt helpless at a certain point because Annie continued to struggle with her addiction. Annie's depression level shot up, and as a result, she began to withdraw from her family.

Annie's relationship with her parents was marked by conflict. She became defiant, and it made her parents irritable and concerned. Her condition didn't get any better. She degenerated into constantly yelling at her parents. This was partly because she was in despair. But her parents didn't quit on her. They kept researching an inpatient program that could offer evidence-based treatments. Their search led them to DBT.

Here's the interesting part: after going through four DBT treatment stages, Annie abstained from using pain medication. She had returned to school. Also, she had decided to take a degree in English. She discovered her unique gift for writing poetry, so she decided to take a creative writing class.

Well, therapy could be the last word you want to hear right now. You might even think therapy is only for adults going through a really difficult moment in their lives. Actually, contrary to that, therapies are designed to help every patient—young and old—improve their total well-being. There's no age limit to it. Dialectical behavior therapy (DBT) isn't an exception. With the rising rates of mental stress and behavioral disorders in our society, we could use a lot more therapy.

DBT may be the answer to your behavioral disorder.

Let's bring you up to speed on what DBT is.

INTRODUCTION: UNDERSTANDING DIALECTICAL BEHAVIOR THERAPY

DBT is a type of therapy for people who have trouble controlling their emotions and actions. This could indicate that they experience emotions with greater intensity than other people, which makes them difficult to tolerate. For instance, some teens get angry at the slightest provocation. Usually, they fiercely yell at everyone when angry, and there's nothing anyone can do to appease them. Some kids might go as far as destroying things around them when enraged.

Not everyone with trouble controlling their emotions and actions loves to behave uncontrollably. The kids feel helpless and sometimes sober after their disruptive behavior. To cope with the pain of their emotions, some go as far as cutting their skin, substance abuse, or unhealthy eating.

Those are the kinds of people DBT is designed to help.

When Dr. Marsha Linehan, a suicide researcher, designed this therapy in the late 1970s, she didn't know it would also be effective for helping people with a neurodevelopmental disorder like ADHD until later.

Ever since the evolution of DBT, it has become a well-known method for dealing with emotions and behavior problems. It helps people feel and control their feelings without necessarily acting on them. As an evidence-based treatment, it has been shown through research to be an effective method for treating a wide range of issues.

This treatment isn't just for adults alone; adolescents and pre-teen children with severe emotional difficulties could greatly benefit from this treatment as well.

DBT is an alternative treatment for problems that cognitive-behavioral therapy (CBT) alone can't solve. DBT is tailored to treat the more complex issues of self-harm and emotion dysregulation, drawing heavily on these behavioral treatments.

DBT'S APPROACH

The approach of DBT to treating patients is deeply rooted in the definition of the word "dialectic." It means combining opposing ideas to come up with a positive resolution. In this case, the contrasting ideas are acceptance and change.

On the surface, these two concepts don't seem to mix. But when used together, they can help people improve their lives. Teenage issues like depression, self-harm, and suicidal ideation may be magnified by adolescent therapists' efforts to help them change their thought, emotion, and behavior patterns and their ability to tolerate distress, validate emotions, and accept things as they are. In a comprehensive DBT program, these ideas are incorporated into each component and emphasized throughout treatment.

So, the therapist focuses on helping the patient accept the realities of their current state and then helps them explore ways they'd like to change those negative behaviors. Therefore, in DBT, you accept the reality of your life and behaviors. And as an active participant in the process, you get to learn ways to change your life.

WHAT! HOW COULD I HAVE A DISORDER?

That's the kind of response we get after diagnosing our patients' emotional and/or behavioral disorders. Though they know things are not right with them, accepting the results of the diagnosis to determine what types of treatment they'll get is usually hard for many people.

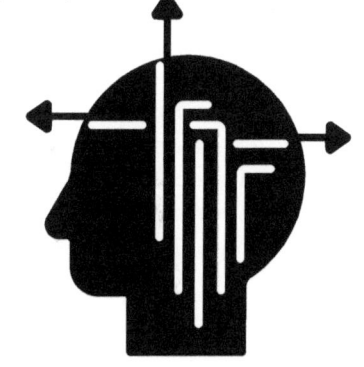

This is to validate the acceptance of the condition as a valid aspect of treatment. For instance, Catelyn had tried different change-focused therapies, but to no avail. On opting for DBT, she realized DBT skills have a unique feature absent in other therapies she had tried. She referred to it as a "dynamic dance" with acceptance and change. She understood that she wouldn't have gotten much from DBT without the acceptance skills.

According to the *Child Mind Institute*, children, teens, and young adults who struggle with any or all of the following have benefited from DBT:

- ✓ Behaviors that are impulsive or disruptive
- ✓ Frequent mood swings
- ✓ Self-harming and suicidal thoughts and actions
- ✓ Depression and anxiety
- ✓ Conflict with family and friends

- ✓ Outbursts of anger
- ✓ Eating disorders
- ✓ Drug or alcohol abuse
- ✓ Poor coping skills

DOES DBT HAVE A GOAL?

Yes! DBT aims to help people understand the connections between their thoughts, feelings, and actions and how changing negative thought and action patterns can improve their feelings.

WHAT DBT ISN'T

✓ **DBT isn't a quick-fix therapy.** It was after about six months into DBT that Dephanee only felt a tinge benefit of the treatment he began six months ago. He felt discouraged and hopeless during those periods of no change. But he held on, and he kept trusting the process.

I guarantee that DBT has an answer to your question. But don't think that you'll immediately begin to experience transformation once you get started. *Nah.* Patience is a virtue you need to adorn to get the full benefits of DBT.

Just before you conclude that DBT isn't for you, give it a little more time. And don't forget to check those goals you wrote down on the sheet constantly. It could be of great help.

✓ **DBT isn't a cure.** When you think of a cure for something, you think of a medicine that can rid you of certain sickness or disease symptoms. You know you're healed when you no longer feel those symptoms. DBT won't do that for you.

DBT won't rid you of your emotions. It'll teach you skills that will give you control over your emotions.

For instance, you won't suddenly stop getting angry, but how you react when you get angry after learning DBT skills will be different from how you used to behave before. When you suddenly feel like gulping down large quantities of uncontrollable food, you'll know how to curb that feeling after learning DBT skills.

So, you see, it would be unjust for DBT to take away your emotions. That's what makes you human, isn't it?

✓ **DBT isn't an escape from reality.** In fact, it's an acceptance of reality. Self-harm, substance use, excessive eating, and the like are all ways of escaping reality. But you'll discover that after these escape mediums have taken their full effect and you're now calm, what you tried to escape from hasn't left. It's still present with you. So, what those mediums do is just suppress your reality.

But DBT teaches you first to accept your reality instead of running in futility from it or, worse, suppressing it. Haven't you done more harm to yourself by trying to suppress your reality?

✓ **DBT isn't a one-time fix.** Catelyn accepted that the DBT program was incorporated into her daily life. It's not a one-time change program she could check off her to-do list and move on with her life. She woke up daily to dance with acceptance and change.

Another success story with DBT, Vikkie, said that DBT was a life kit to stay afloat as she continued to evolve into a better version of herself. She said skills like mindfulness and tools like the crisis tool from DBT were things she could take away with her and keep practicing every waking moment.

You're in for a lifelong transformational journey, friend. And just like Alvin Toffler rightly said, learning, unlearning, and relearning are the goals of the 21st century's education program. And those three processes take time.

Regardless of how long it'll take, you're up for it.

I'd advise you not to focus on how long it'll take you to change but rather focus on the process. Your transformation and emergence are in the process.

COMPONENTS OF DBT

A comprehensive DBT program has four result-oriented components. They consist of the following: group skills training, one-on-one therapy, DBT phone coaching, and team consultation.

1. DBT SKILLS TRAINING GROUP

This technique focuses on teaching clients behavioral skills to improve their capabilities. The group is run like a class, with the leader teaching the skills and giving clients homework to do so they can practice using the skills in their daily lives. The full skills curriculum is typically repeated to create a one-year program, and groups meet for approximately 2.5 hours each week. It takes 24 weeks to complete the curriculum, which is repeated.

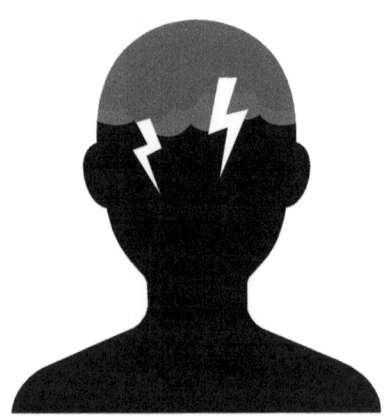

That's just a glimpse of what to expect in a DBT skills training group. Vaughn (2022) took it further. She created a template we can adopt to run a group session. For effectiveness, she suggested that:

✓ A DBT Skills Group should have a leader and a co-leader

✓ Group should last up to 1.5-2.5 hours

✓ Group members who are unable to contain their open hostility toward others are not permitted.

She also suggested these rules to keep the program highly disciplined and efficient.

✓ A member is out of the group if they miss four sessions in a row.

✓ Members of the group must support one another.

✓ Members of the group must contact the leader if they'll be late or absent.

✓ Members of the group mustn't tempt one another.

✓ Members of the group mustn't form confidential or sexual relationships with one another.

✓ Members of the group have an individual therapist if they are suicidal or have

2. INDIVIDUAL DBT THERAPY

This focuses on motivating clients and assisting them in applying the skills to specific life challenges and events. Individual therapy takes place once a week for approximately 60 minutes under the standard DBT model, concurrent with skills groups.

This will foster a strong connection between the guide/specialist and client through week-after-week meetings. Individual treatment assists a client with remaining on track and inspired all through treatment. Additionally, individual treatment gives down-to-earth solutions to specific issues.

3. PHONE COACHING

DBT phone coaching aims to give clients coaching on how to use skills to deal with difficult situations in their daily lives effectively. Between sessions, clients can call their individual therapist to get coaching when they need it most.

4. DBT THERAPIST CONSULTATION TEAM

This is meant to be therapy for the therapists and to help DBT providers work with people who frequently have severe, complicated, and hard-to-treat disorders. The purpose of the consultation team is to assist therapists in maintaining their competence and motivation to provide the best possible treatment. Teams consist of individual therapists and group leaders who share responsibility for each client's care and typically meet weekly.

Coordinating these DBT components gives the specialist a superior method for interacting with a client regularly and during emergencies.

BENEFITS OF DIALECTICAL BEHAVIOR THERAPY

1. YOU'LL FIND YOURSELF

The primary focus of this therapy is you. Every activity, task, assignment, tool, and medium is designed to work for your good. Throughout the process, the specialist who guides you through it will focus on an image of you. It's the picture of you as a beautiful, loving, emotionally stable, and healthy human being that he keeps in mind.

Therefore, every session he has with you is to help you find yourself. DBT hasn't done its job completely until you discover your real essence.

2. YOUR RELATIONSHIPS WILL IMPROVE

Having a strong support system is essential when dealing with mental health issues. This is overlooked by many types of therapy, which assume that you'll handle things on your own. However, DBT emphasizes the significance of your social relationships in overcoming obstacles.

Building healthy relationships with trust, respectful boundaries, and respect for one another greatly impacts your health and well-being.

You'll notice that you can better manage your relationships as you participate in DBT therapy. This means that you can begin to heal your relationships. You can recover from your addiction, learn how to be more effective in personal interactions, and realize that the people in your life want to help you recover.

3. THE QUALITY OF YOUR LIFE INCREASES

One of DBT's primary goals is to enhance your quality of life. We can't always control what happens to us, but we can control how we respond to it. Our response to it is what determines the quality of our lives.

One of the things you'll enjoy in DBT is the acceptance of the fact that mental health issues are a part of life for some people. Knowing this is essential to moving forward. But that's not all. DBT gently assists patients in making changes that will move them in the right direction and let them know that it's okay to find things challenging.

DBT will help you cope with difficult or negative situations. In addition to putting you on the road to recovery, DBT teaches you how to be your best self no matter what happens.

4. YOUR UNDERSTANDING OF YOUR FEELINGS AND THOUGHTS INCREASES

DBT is a form of cognitive behavioral therapy that focuses on "dialectics," or the use of dialogue to work through current symptoms and past traumas. You become aware of the complex emotions and thought structures that influence your behavior and choices as a result of DBT treatment.

You can make healthy choices when fully comprehending your feelings and mental assumptions. DBT enhances mindfulness, allowing you to remain rooted in the present and focus fully and calmly on your surroundings as well as the situation at hand. Learn ways to keep your thoughts and actions positive. DBT improves your interpersonal effectiveness, communication skills, and ability to handle conflict and distress.

You'll build a comprehensive set of methods you can use in everyday life and difficult situations.

5. YOU'LL BE ABLE TO DEAL WITH POTENTIAL TRIGGERS IN A HEALTHY WAY

You will learn how to deal with painful emotional triggers. When you learn the principles of DBT, you can control the inner triggers that threaten your serenity. You can let go of anger, fear, anxiety, loss, stress, and even trauma.

6. THE SKILLS GO BEYOND MENTAL ILLNESS

DBT's goal is to alleviate the symptoms of mental illness, but it doesn't stop there. The DBT therapist teaches skills useful in many other areas of life. For instance, numerous other facets of health and well-being are linked by research to mindfulness. This ability can be beneficial in various settings, including at work, at home, and while having fun.

You can enhance other areas of your life. Even though you're taking DBT to help you recover, you'll find it applicable to many different aspects of your mental health and that what you learn will benefit your wholeness. Your mental health is central to your functionality.

ADDITIONAL BENEFITS OF DBT INCLUDE THE FOLLOWING:

- ✓ It'll guide you to change unhealthy patterns of behavior into healthy ones

- ✓ It'll help you recognize your strengths and put them to use in all aspects of your life.

- ✓ It'll teach you to improve your communication skills

- ✓ It'll assist you in gaining a stronger sense of control over your relationships, life, and emotions.

- ✓ It'll show you how to change your negative thought processes, so you don't act impulsively.

- ✓ It'll teach you to prioritize—say no and ask for what you want.

- ✓ It'll improve emotional regulation and self-care through the application of mindfulness techniques. You'll get better at paying attention to what's happening inside and around you. You'll be able to make rational decisions instead of impulsive ones with the assistance of this therapy.

- ✓ Understanding your distress tolerance can assist you in determining what you can and cannot change. Instead of making decisions based on how you feel or think about a situation, you make decisions based on facts and logic.

THE PROS AND CONS OF DIALECTICAL BEHAVIORAL THERAPY

While DBT can be highly effective for some individuals, it may be ineffective for others. Thus, DBT also has its advantages and disadvantages. What's advantageous to you might not be to another.

Here are some of the advantages of DBT you need to know:

- ✓ It is thorough: DBT is an intensive type of therapy focusing on getting results quickly from the first day.

- ✓ Reduces hospitalizations, self-injury, and the seriousness of borderline personality disorder (BPD) symptoms significantly.

- ✓ Boosts self-esteem and respect.

- ✓ Improves emotion control.

- ✓ Reduces avoidance through experience.

- ✓ Reduces assertive rage.

- ✓ Tools for Managing Stress: The patient in DBT is taught techniques for managing stress, such as mindfulness. This is especially helpful because it teaches the patient to remain calm and grounded in the present moment during challenging times.

- ✓ Low rate of dropouts: In contrast to many other types of therapy, DBT appears to have a low dropout rate, indicating that the majority of patients will complete treatment. This suggests that DBT works very well.

- ✓ Therapy and medication together: Medication is often used to treat borderline personality disorder. Therapy and medication can be used together to great effect.

- ✓ Zen Buddhist mindfulness techniques are incorporated into DBT, which may pique the interest of spiritual seekers.

- ✓ Through the phone coaching component, participants have access to their clinician round-the-clock in the event of a crisis or for immediate guidance during difficult times as an additional layer of support.

- ✓ Participants in the weekly DBT skills training group therapy sessions have access to an emotionally secure setting in which they can begin to apply the DBT skills alongside others working on issues similar to their own.

- ✓ DBT, an evidence-based treatment, improves people's quality of life and goes beyond mental illness.

THE DISADVANTAGES OF DBT INCLUDE:

- ✓ It's not a quick fix: Changing deeply ingrained emotions and thoughts takes time. Even though change can occur almost immediately, DBT won't give you all the benefits right away.

- ✓ It requires commitment: DBT necessitates a strong commitment to therapy. A person is expected to commit to the entire duration of the therapy, which can last up to 30 sessions. The number of sessions may vary, though.

- ✓ Because mindfulness practice based on Zen Buddhist teachings forms the basis of DBT, some clients (such as conservative Jews, Christians, Muslims, and so on) may be opposed to DBT's elements based on Eastern religious philosophies.

- ✓ Assignments corresponding to the DBT skills taught or visited during each session are essential to the weekly DBT skills training group therapy sessions, which some may find burdensome.

- ✓ Problems with group settings: As previously stated, receiving DBT in a group setting may be beneficial but may not be appropriate for all individuals. Additionally, it means that the patient does not receive the individual attention that one-on-one sessions do.

- ✓ It can bring back memories: DBT focuses on the present in some areas but also on past events in others. This could be traumatizing, but a therapist will ensure you feel at ease.

- ✓ The numerous DBT skills may appear overwhelming and discouraging. As a result, some people who would benefit greatly from dialectical behavior therapy consider it too complicated and are reluctant to try it.

These are the basic things I consider important for you to know about DBT.

Have you started taking notes yet? Here's a quick recap of what you've read in this chapter: I introduced you to the creator of DBT, Dr. Marsha Linehan, and the reason DBT was created. You've got to know that DBT isn't for everyone; it's just for a specific group who need extra help controlling their emotions and injurious behavior patterns. DBT isn't a person; it's just a handy tool set you can take along anywhere you go. Don't fret; DBT isn't a burden you need to include in your daily routine; in fact, it'll help you ease the stress you've been bearing. And this comes with some other amazing benefits, too.

Remember that I told you not to think of DBT as a fix-it-all tool because it's not.

Now, let's take a quick look at what you've got:

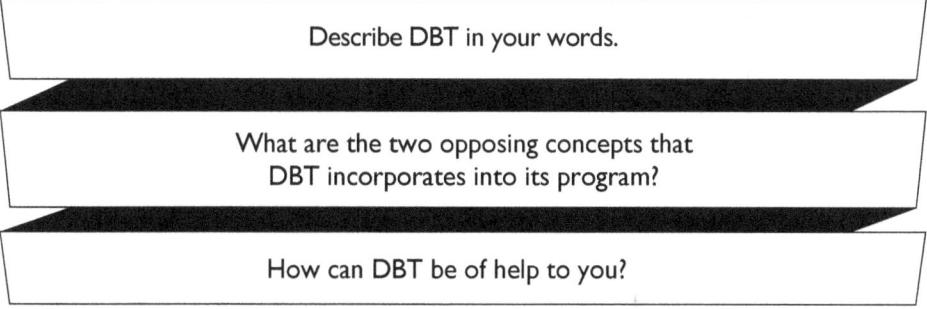

Describe DBT in your words.

What are the two opposing concepts that DBT incorporates into its program?

How can DBT be of help to you?

CHAPTER 2: WHY DIALECTICAL BEHAVIOR THERAPY WORKS

> 66 Live the actual moment. Only this actual moment is life. 99
>
> — *Thích Nhất Hạnh*

In my semi-short note, I listed categories of people who need DBT. You'll notice that I didn't write an extensive explanation for any of those mental or behavioral patterns. I just highlighted them. In this chapter, I'll narrow it down to a particular behavioral pattern evident in several children and teenagers. Young adults are not excluded anyway.

Rosa, from Wellington, New Zealand, shared her struggles as a young girl diagnosed with attention deficit hyperactivity disorder (ADHD). Before she was diagnosed with this disorder, she was perceived as a loud, unbearable, and genuinely indifferent child. Her sports coaches had issues with her. They frequently complained about how difficult it was to coach her. The same was true for her instructors.

She experienced similar difficulties at home, too. Every time she tried to discuss essays and tests with her dad, he would get angry when she lost focus or started staring at other things. She frequently misplaced her laptop, her school lunch box, and sports practice equipment. She was constantly blamed for losing things and getting them back.

Rosa exhibited symptoms of a disorder known as attention deficit hyperactivity disorder (ADHD). We'll just stick to the acronym hereafter.

Let's drive this home. Before we go into how DBT can be used to correct ADHD, let's talk about some of the *ADHD symptoms* that ADHD Ireland highlighted:

✓ **Self-centered behavior.** An inability to recognize the wants and needs of other people is a common symptom of ADHD. This could be displayed when you're having trouble waiting for your turn and/or you impatiently interrupt a procedure, a conversation, or a game you weren't part of. You're focused on your interest alone.

✓ **Mood swings.** Teens with ADHD might have trouble controlling their emotions. They might become annoyed at inappropriate times. Younger children may throw tantrums.

✓ **Fidgeting.** ADHD teens frequently have trouble staying still. When forced to sit, they might try to get up and run around, fidget, or squirm in their chair. When they fidget, playing quietly or relaxing during leisure activities becomes difficult.

✓ **Unfinished tasks.** Teens with ADHD may be interested in various things but have difficulty finishing them. For instance, they can begin assignments, chores, or projects but move on to the next thing that interests them before completing them. Even when someone is speaking directly to them, a teenager with ADHD may have trouble paying attention. They will claim to have heard you, but they won't be able to repeat what you said.

✓ **Avoidance of tasks requiring a sustained mental effort.** This same lack of focus can lead to a teenager avoiding tasks like paying attention in class or doing homework that requires a sustained mental effort.

✓ **Difficulty adhering to instructions.** Teens with ADHD may have difficulty adhering to instructions that necessitate planning or carrying out a plan. This may result in careless errors but does not indicate laziness or intelligence deficit.

✓ **Escape from reality.** Teens with ADHD who daydream (introverts are found doing this mostly) are not always boisterous and loud. Being quieter and less involved than other kids is another sign of ADHD. A teenager with ADHD may avoid paying attention to the world around them. They daydream or stare into space.

✓ **Disorganized.** An ADHD teen may have trouble keeping track of activities and tasks. They may have difficulty setting priorities for homework, school projects, and other assignments. This could land them in trouble at school.

✓ **Forgetting Things.** Teenagers with ADHD may forget things in their daily lives. They might neglect their chores or homework. They might also frequently misplace things.

NOTE: A teenager with ADHD will exhibit symptoms in multiple contexts. For instance, they might appear distracted at home and in school.

Every child, teenager, or young adult has exhibited one or two of these symptoms at some point. However, it becomes something to act on if those symptoms become regular or affect school performance and/or relationships with others.

DBT FOR ATTENTION DEFICIT HYPERACTIVITY DISORDER

The DBT Center of Marin stated that 9.4% of children aged 17 and younger had been diagnosed with ADHD. Fascinating, right? The good thing about this is that ADHD can be treated.

Many conditions with such features as an inability to control emotions, such as ADHD, mood and anxiety disorders, etc., can be successfully treated with DBT.

Wasn't DBT designed to treat borderline personality disorder? Yes, so it seemed. Before it was adapted to treat ADHD, DBT was used to treat various mental illnesses.

Do you remember Marsha Linehan? The brain behind DBT? Yes, that's right. When she created DBT, it was designed for individuals diagnosed with Borderline personality disorder (BPD). DBT was created to help people recover from emotional outbursts, such as self-harming behaviors.

But do you also remember that the main feature of BPD is emotional dysregulation? DBT has been demonstrated to be a successful treatment for all the illnesses since they are all characterized by an inability to manage emotions, including attention deficit disorder (ADHD or ADD), mood and anxiety disorders, and substance use disorders. It is now a standard treatment for ADHD.

HOW DOES DBT HELP WITH ADHD?

A dialectical approach to things leads to a balanced view of things. When your thoughts, feelings, and life situations are not all running agog, DBT employs a dialectical approach to help you have a more balanced perspective.

I told you about those two odd approaches DBT employs—acceptance and change. Accepting uncomfortable feelings and situations before attempting to change them is a central belief of DBT. This approach is effective in helping ADHD patients agree with their therapists to develop a recovery strategy by accepting the existence of troubling thoughts and feelings.

For instance, an ADHD patient who struggles to concentrate while studying can be taught to adapt her thinking style and change her study routine. So let's say she wants to study for one hour. She can't concentrate for that period. She has to accept that reality first. But instead of forcing her to try harder, a dialectical approach will encourage her to change her studying routine. So, instead of studying for one hour non-stop, she would study for 30 minutes. She'll take a 10-minute break and then continue studying for another 30 minutes.

She'll discover that she'll accomplish significantly more in two shorter periods than in one full stretch.

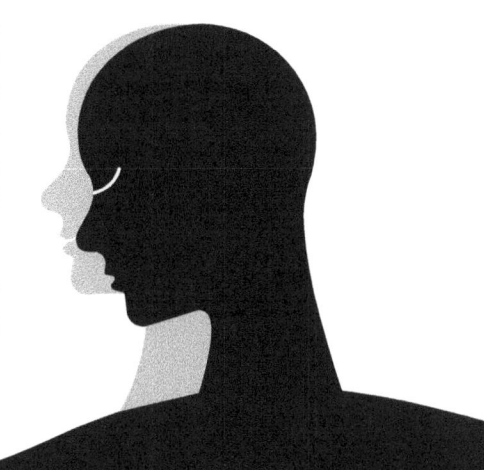

DIALECTICAL BEHAVIOR THERAPY FOR TEENS AND YOUNG ADULTS

According to Brillante (2020), DBT's main objective is to assist young people in creating a worthwhile life. Teenagers who experience depression, severe family conflict, or trouble controlling their emotions may occasionally believe that their life is not worth living, especially if these issues have persisted for a long time.

There are primary areas of challenge that adolescent DBT seeks to address. Addressing them could help young people decide in what direction they want their lives to go.

Can you relate to any of the issues below? The list below summarizes the major issues resulting from disordered mental and behavioral patterns in teens and young adults. These and many more are why we have distraught young people in our communities today.

A CONFUSED SELF

You could get stuck in the past when you're unsure about your emotions and don't understand your thoughts. This could also rack up a lot of fear about what the future holds for you.

With those thought patterns, it'll be difficult for you to ever appreciate your present moment, not to talk of focusing on it.

This could also make teens lose a sense of their individual values and goals.

CONFUSED SELF IMAGE

It's difficult to identify who you really are if you have unstable emotions you don't have any control over. Before people identify you by your emotional reaction, you will have convinced yourself that your emotional and mental behavioral patterns are just who you are.

The question is, can you see the beauty of a stream when it's troubled? If you answered no, it implies that your beauty and true identity aren't in your troubled state. Your negative behavioral pattern gives you a false view of your image.

ABNORMAL EMOTIONAL DISPLAY

This is otherwise known as emotional dysregulation. This happens when a person experiences intense emotions but has limited control over how they are managed and how they behave as a result. This could be a sudden, intense change in mood or a negative emotional state that lasts for a long time, like depression.

THOUGHTLESS ACTIONS

I've worked with young adults who are highly impulsive. I feel compassion for them whenever I realize their helplessness. Looking past their emotional outburst will show how vulnerable they are inside. As a matter of fact, some of those actions are borne out of frustration.

Acting impulsively means acting on an urge or emotion without thinking about what might happen or what might happen next. Substance use, self-harm, impulsive eating, and verbal or physical outbursts fueled by anger are examples of impulsive actions. These actions may be taken to avoid or escape difficult emotional situations.

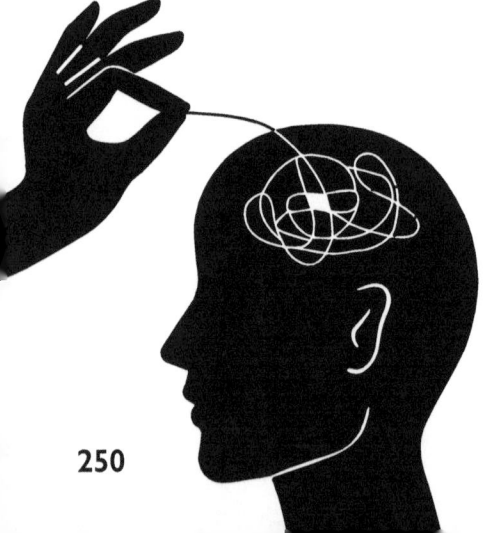

TOXIC RELATIONSHIPS

You can't expect an impulsive teenager to have a healthy relationship, can you? There will always be one issue after another with one's peers. Due to how relationships have been negatively impacted, interpersonal challenges may result in difficulty maintaining healthy relationships, a lot of conflict in relationships, and potential loneliness.

This could result in difficulty maintaining self-respect under peer pressure, expressing one's needs, and saying no to others.

PROBLEMS FOR FAMILIES AND TEENS

Virtually every normal child has disagreements with their parents at some point when they are growing up. Teens' disagreements with parents or other family members are common. However, when it becomes a serious disagreement, it's something to be concerned about.

This could result from trouble comprehending each other's feelings, behaviors, or points of view. And just like in other relationships, it could cause relationships with people who should be the first circle of support to go so wrong.

HOW CAN DBT WORK FOR TEENS AND YOUNG ADULTS?

Science is always advancing. And it might interest you to know that researchers see teens' needs, including yours, as distinct from adults.' Therefore, treatments for both age groups should differ.

Here's the good news: Pieper (2020) announced a program validated by research to address the key differences between DBT for adults and DBT for adolescents, DBT-A (DBT for Adolescents). Including caregivers is the most significant distinction between DBT for adolescents and DBT for adults. Caregivers are frequently a part of skills training sessions or may participate in their own sessions.

So, when you're having individual or one-on-one therapy, it'll occasionally include caregivers, as will additional family sessions. Also, you won't be the only one to go through the phone coaching; your caregiver will as well.

Your adolescent stage development is also something to consider in your program. Naturally, most teens have a shorter attention span compared to adults. Therefore, your group sessions will be shortened compared to adults.'

Another consideration is that since people in your age group learn quicker with learning aids like pictures, examples, and metaphors, DBT for teens has been designed to include those elements in your individual and group therapy.

Additionally, skilled therapists will know the distinction between adolescent and adult developmental tasks. This knowledge will be incorporated into the issues being treated for utmost effectiveness.

Some of the methods, which you could also call "skills," employed in DBT to treat teens and young adults include:

✓ **Mindfulness**

This skill teaches you to understand the peculiar symptoms of uncontrolled emotions. It also encourages you to be present and rooted in the moment, not some warped past or a future you don't have access to yet.

You'll learn more about mindfulness in a later chapter.

✓ **Self-acceptance**

Acceptance, as I've stated before, is paramount to your transformation. Self-acceptance is an offshoot of mindfulness. It teaches you to fully accept what is happening or has happened. This does not mean you're okay with what has been happening to you; it just means that you're no longer living in self-denial of your reality. You accept that it's a disorder. And it's simply a disorder that can be reorganized. This method can free you from fighting reality.

Before you go further, can you take a moment to reflect on those injurious behavioral patterns? Don't deny their existence because they do exist, and you've been exhibiting them.

Confront yourself with the truth, like "It's true I get angry excessively." "And I yell when I'm really angry."

EMOTION REGULATION SKILLS

Emanuele (cited by Garey, 2022) said that emotion regulation places a significant emphasis on the physical body. Eating right, getting enough sleep, taking medication, and not using drugs are all important. They all have a way of boosting your emotional well-being.

This skill helps you comprehend how emotions work, the urge to act attached to each emotion, and whether to act on these urges.

Note that every feeling you experience serves a particular purpose. You can learn more about your current situation from these emotions.

Don't judge yourself quickly when you notice that you're feeling something. Just observe it. Each emotion has value, even if some are more pleasant than others. Consider what this feeling might be trying to tell you about your situation and identify the emotion you're experiencing. After that, you can respond to the emotion or let it go.

✓ Opposite Action

This skill falls under the category of emotion regulation. Teens who struggle with trauma, depression, anxiety, low self-esteem, anger management issues, and other issues can benefit from this skill.

Use the opposite action when you're going through a painful emotion that doesn't fit your particular circumstance or isn't working for you at the moment. Let's say, for instance, that a teen experiences an increased sense of shame each time she enters the class. There was no reason for her to be ashamed because she had done nothing wrong to her teachers or peers. However, her current reality is that each time she enters that class, she experiences feelings of shame, worthlessness, and low self-esteem. As a result, she rarely speaks up or raises her hand in class.

At this time, the opposite action should be taken.

✓ Walking the Middle Path

Miller (cited by Garey, 2022) stated that this has to do with acknowledging multiple truths in the worldview of the teenagers and their parents rather than saying, "I'm right, and you're wrong." Through this skill, you and your parents will learn to validate one another, negotiate and compromise, and see things from the other person's perspective.

This skill employs other skills such as dialectics, validation, and behavioral change

DIALECTICS

This method focuses on finding common ground between opposing viewpoints, meaning you value and acknowledge the other person's view instead of castigating them. For instance, someone may be doing their best but still need improvement. Acknowledging their best effort before telling them how they need to improve will inject positive energy into them.

VALIDATION

Recognizing the significance of both your own experience and that of another person is validation. Validation acknowledges one's actions, feelings, and thoughts, regardless of disagreement.

CHANGE IN BEHAVIOR

This is a collection of strategies for motivating, implementing, and sustaining desired behavior changes.

WHAT AGE IS DBT APPROPRIATE FOR?

The DBT program has evolved from treating only adults with mental and behavioral disorders. It can now be used to treat other age groups.

Pieper stated that DBT now has an adapted program for adolescents, DBT-A (DBT for Adolescents). *The Child Mind Institute* has also announced that it has a DBT-adapted program for children and preadolescents. They call it DBT-C. DBT-C is a practical version of DBT for children and preadolescents between 6 and 12. It's an extensive DBT program tailored to meet the requirements of children in this age range.

THE FOUR PILLARS OF DBT

I've touched on these previously. I'll elaborate a little more here. The four pillars of DBT are what Dr. Marsha Linehan, the creator of DBT, also referred to as the "modules" of DBT.

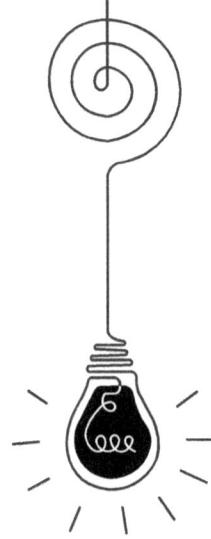

They are:

1. Mindfulness
2. Distress tolerance
3. Interpersonal effectiveness
4. Emotional regulation

Let's have a brief discussion on each of these pillars:

MINDFULNESS

You'll learn more about this pillar in the next chapter. However, let's have a look at what mindfulness is. It's a tool and a skill. This implies that you can learn it.

Mindfulness is a powerful tool designed to make you worry less about the past and future and help you live in the moment.

So, basically, mindfulness will help you to:

- ✓ Learn to control one's emotions and thoughts.
- ✓ Acquire the ability to be more aware and to live in the now.
- ✓ Gain a sense of identity.

DISTRESS TOLERANCE

Even though some of us experience emotional highs and lows that are more frequent and intense, we all have times when they feel big and overwhelming. Distress tolerance skills aim to teach how to get through difficult times without making things worse by providing alternative and proactive responses to situations.

This module helps you accept certain circumstances, thoughts, and feelings that cannot be changed.

Summarily, the distress tolerance module does the following:

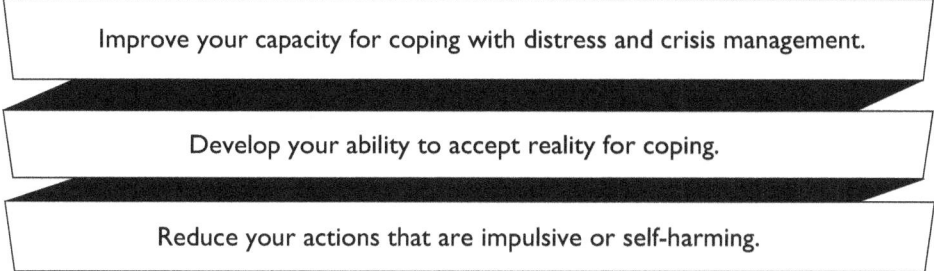

Improve your capacity for coping with distress and crisis management.

Develop your ability to accept reality for coping.

Reduce your actions that are impulsive or self-harming.

INTERPERSONAL EFFECTIVENESS

Every human on the planet has an innate desire for social interaction. But what happens when, in your own way, you've tried several times to establish a connection with someone, yet you continue to feel rejected, hurt, and disappointed?

Naturally, you might observe that you begin to get into more arguments, avoid this individual, or just feel like giving up.

The interpersonal effectiveness module aims to teach how to interact effectively with others, formulate requests that increase your chances of satisfying your needs, and consider your self-respect.

EMOTIONAL REGULATION

The fourth module, emotional regulation, teaches you how to control your emotions rather than let them control you. In this module, you'll learn acceptance of your emotions through reality-checking, opposite actions and behaviors associated with particular emotions, etc.

In summary, you'll

 Figure out ways to feel more secure.

Gain the ability to feel more cheerful.

FOUR STAGES AND TARGETS OF DBT

STAGE ONE

Most clients' reactions in Stage One are frequently negative. They start with seemingly out-of-control behaviors like suicide attempts, self-harm, excessive alcohol and drug use, and other kinds of self-destructive behavior.

Now, moving the client from being out of control to being in control is the primary objective of this stage.

At this stage, you'll work with your therapist or specialist to begin to gain behavioral control and view treatment as a means of improving your mental, physical, and spiritual well-being.

STAGE TWO

At this stage, most clients may experience a sense of quiet desperation. They report still having the impression that they have failed in life, despite the fact that a behavioral approach has controlled their life-threatening behavior. Stage two aims to assist you in transitioning from quiet desperation to a full emotional experience.

Stage two also entails reducing any symptoms related to trauma, such as formal PTSD diagnoses and other traumatic emotional experiences. At this stage, the client's traumatic past is being investigated. This invariably leads to heightened emotion.

Here, you'll need to start finding the inner strength you lost. You will learn to recognize, comprehend, and appropriately manage your emotions.

However, an expert in this program will try to avoid intensifying your emotional experiences from the beginning. That will not make things more difficult for you.

STAGE THREE

The objective of this stage is to learn to live life, trust oneself, develop self-respect and self-worth, develop interpersonal skills, set and reach life goals and find contentment and happiness.

This stage builds on the previous stage.

This is the stage where you'll get to learn how to cope without substances and other harmful behaviors. You'll be encouraged to focus on living the life you were created for. Your creative passions, strength, dreams, and desire for meaningful living all come to the fore at this stage. You'll learn to trust, validate, and be empathic here.

The skill of mindfulness is one of the skills you'll learn at this stage.

STAGE FOUR

Dr. Marsha Linehan designed this stage for those seeking deeper meaning through spiritual existence.

This stage aims to help clients overcome a sense of incompleteness and establish a life with an ongoing capacity for unconditional love, joy, and freedom.

DBT was designed to be complete in helping patients recover completely. If you can be committed to the six-month program of DBT, you'll cross to the other side, where everything is beautiful.

Let's review your objectives for this adventure again to see if you're still on track. *Go check now. ...*

While you're on that, here are a few things you should remember about this chapter:

| DBT is effective for treating ADHD. | ADHD has several symptoms that are not peculiar to children or teens alone. | DBT has practicable tools like mindfulness, distress tolerance, and emotional regulation that can help you surmount the challenges of managing your emotions. | DBT offers every ADHD patient an opportunity to alter the course of their life and choose to be better individuals. |

CAN YOU ATTEMPT THESE QUESTIONS?

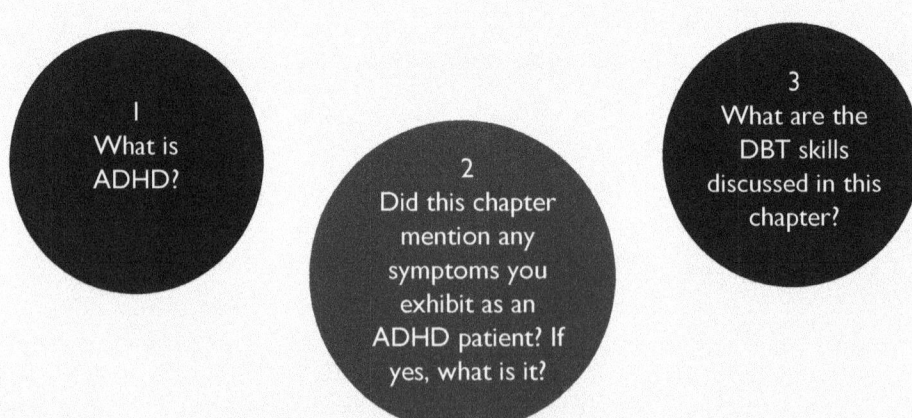

1
What is ADHD?

2
Did this chapter mention any symptoms you exhibit as an ADHD patient? If yes, what is it?

3
What are the DBT skills discussed in this chapter?

CHAPTER 3: PUTTING MINDFULNESS SKILL TO USE

66

Emotions are not good, bad, right, or wrong. The first step to changing our relationship to feelings is to be curious about them and the messages they send to us.

99

—Lane Pederson

You're not new to *mindfulness,* are you? I know you're not if you haven't skipped any part of this book.

Here's a quick story of Katie and her application of this skill. Katie was surprised to find out that mindfulness, a practice her boyfriend, Tal, had encouraged her to learn, was at the heart of DBT when she first heard about it at the beginning of 2019.

Katie experienced such unbearable anxiety that she just wanted a quick fix or a 60-minute meeting with a therapist who would tell her what to do and she would be fine. She suffered from severe anxiety so much that mindfulness sounded nonsense then.

When she sought the assistance of a therapist specializing in Borderline personality disorder (BPD), her self-diagnosis of anxiety matched the symptoms of BPD.

Guess what her therapist recommended …

WHAT IS MINDFULNESS?

Partington (2021) said that the practice of paying attention where and when you want to pay attention is known as "mindfulness." And she said that mindfulness is a practice like swimming or any other sport. By deliberately and repeatedly focusing on the present moment, you strengthen your mindfulness muscles.

The Hope Therapy and Wellness team (2019) also agreed that being present in the present moment is mindfulness. And being mindful means paying attention to everything that is going on around you: where you are, how you feel, what you see, and what you hear right now.

It's easy to know you're mindful with this simple exercise:

Look around you and feel exactly what is happening right now. What did you see?

If you were overthinking, judging, or worrying about what would happen next, you're not being mindful. Because mindfulness is accepting the present in its entirety without judging, worrying, or feeling anxious about it. You are mindful if you can confirm your current experience.

Doesn't that sound simple?

Well, maybe. Our society shows how much time people spend being mindful and fully present in the now. A lot of people are suffering from stress and anxiety. Here are some statistics to show that:

A stress statistic carried out by the *Single Care* team:

✓ Over three-quarters of adults report experiencing signs of stress, such as headaches, tiredness, or trouble sleeping.

✓ Eighty percent of American workers report experiencing stress at work.

✓ Nearly half of all adults in the United States (49%) claim that stress has had a negative impact on their behavior.

✓ Nearly one in five adults in the United States report declining mental health over the past year.

✓ In a 2020 survey, adults in the United States reported that increased stress had:

Affected their behavior in a negative way (49%)	Caused them to feel more tension in their bodies (21%)
Caused them to "snap" out of anger (20%)	Caused them to have unexpected mood swings (20%).

The American Institute of Stress also reported this:

- ✓ 77% of people experience stress that has an impact on their physical health
- ✓ 73% of people experience stress that has an impact on their mental health
- ✓ 48% of people have trouble sleeping as a result of stress
- ✓ 33% of people report feeling extremely stressed.

Sadly, the levels of stress experienced by approximately half of all Americans are increasing rather than decreasing.

A lot of people "tune out" from what is actually going on, becoming instead distracted by how they see it, what it means, or what it might mean for them in the future. People are unable to truly live in the present, and as a result, they become perplexed and irritated as to why nothing seems to be under their control.

The skill of mindfulness might sound like an easy option; however, it's a practice that can be applied to any activity you're engaged in. Keep your attention on the task at hand, and if it wanders, stop it and bring it back. That capacity for mindfulness can be developed through practice.

Being completely present in the moment without judging is the essence of mindfulness.

 SO WHAT HAS MINDFULNESS GOT TO DO WITH DBT?

Since DBT is about regulating and reordering emotional patterns, mindfulness can help to achieve that easily. This makes mindfulness an essential component of DBT because it helps overcome emotional dysregulation.

Whenever we're not mindful of the present moment, we tend to become overwhelmed by things that other people may find insignificant—even though it may seem like the sky is falling on us. It is essential to acknowledge that when we are not mindful, it is typically not due to the actual event but rather to our interpretation of it.

Here's a clear example:

Diana recently started working for a new company. On her first day at work, she accidentally deleted a file she believed her boss would find useful. Diana became overwhelmed with fear right away.

Different thoughts began to run through her mind. Thoughts like:

> "Oh! I'm going to be fired."

> "I will be viewed as stupid and useless by everyone."
> "This is such a shame."

> "There is still $200 in my bank account."

> "I won't be able to find a new job right away because I will be fired today."
> "This is a small town, and everyone hears everything." "I may not find another job, and no one will hire me after this."

> "This is awful." "I won't be able to pay the rent."

> "I don't like anyone in the family because of this." "This is why I'm still single."

"I'm worthless."

Can you relate to Diana's case? Maybe yours was that your mother's tumbler mistakenly fell off your hand. And while you were there, lots of negative thoughts began to run through your mind. You became sweaty and panicky in a jiffy.

Well, you're not alone. You've got a company spread across the globe.

I'm not sure about this, but it sounds like that's how humans naturally respond to things like that. Does that mean we all need a DBT session? Maybe not. DBT becomes required when this behavioral pattern becomes intense and regular.

Just imagine how Diana conjured an entire scenario in her mind from a single incident. She spiraled into panic by assuming she knew what other people thought of her and what the future held.

YOU MIGHT BE WONDERING ... SO, HOW DOES MINDFULNESS WORK?

The first place to start is, "How does your mind work?"

Badcock et al. (2019) believed that the brain (or the mind) is where human thoughts, feelings, and actions originate. There, a complex network of cells receives information from both the inside and outside of the body and transforms it into how we experience ourselves, the world around us, and our relationships with it.

It's obvious from that scientific discovery, although it's still ongoing, that our minds and activities there affect our entire being.

If our thoughts and feelings affect our behavior and how we relate to ourselves and the world around us, isn't it worthwhile to pay close attention to what goes on in our minds?

This is the essence of mindfulness. This skill will teach you to be aware of your thoughts and feelings. This also implies paying attention to your actions, reactions, and surroundings.

Practicing mindfulness puts you in charge of your feelings. You'll be free from being dragged around by your feelings and tortured by thoughts when you practice mindfulness.

It's a fact that there will always be thoughts in your mind. You can't control that. OK, it looks like you don't believe that. Is it because you read an article about how to control your thoughts?

Well, if anyone had succeeded in trying, no one would be having those "Aha!" moments—an excited reaction to a spontaneous, genius idea that flowed in when you weren't thinking about it.

No one has succeeded in controlling their thoughts. What you can do is direct your awareness in the direction you desire. That's the essence of mindfulness.

You can decide where you want your mind to be and how you want to act by being aware. To accomplish that, you must strengthen your mindfulness muscles through practice.

EXAMPLES OF MINDFULNESS EXERCISES

To practice mindfulness, you don't need any special equipment. You just need you, a little space, and some time.

DETAILED APPRECIATION

I'm starting with this exercise because it's something a lot of us—young and old—do less often. You don't know how significant a thing is until you pay attention to it. Think of the smallest thing that contributes to your daily activities. Pay attention to the benefits you get from that little thing. You'll realize that you've not given it the credit it deserves.

Most times, because we're used to seeing things work, we don't realize that some things or people make those things work.

The point of this exercise is to simply express gratitude for the seemingly insignificant things in life—those things that sustain your existence but rarely receive any consideration amid our desire for greater and better things.

For instance, electricity powers your iron; the postman delivers your mail. Your mouth allows you to take in food while your nose takes in the air, and your clothes keep you warm. However, do you know how these things and processes came to be or how they actually function? If they stop working, what do you think will happen?

Have you ever considered how life would be different without these things?

Have you ever stopped to consider the tiniest, tiniest details they have?

Have you ever taken some time to reflect on the connections that exist between these things and how, taken together, they contribute to the earth's overall operation?

To practice mindful appreciation,

> Identify three things you appreciate less yet are significant to your existence.

> Pay attention to their modalities and how they function. Your perspective about them will change.

CONSCIOUS WALKING

Mindful walking is the practice of becoming aware of your surroundings and how your body and mind feel while moving. Moving around can help some people become more aware of their bodies, minds, and the present moment.

Pick a route that lets you walk without interruption for at least ten minutes, preferably outside. Spend the time just walking. Don't do this when you're headed to a destination or running an errand.

1. Focus on your breathing while standing still for a few moments prior to beginning your walk. Keep track of how every part of your body is feeling.

2. Pay full attention to your body's movements and sensations as you begin to walk.

3. Pay attention to the sensations in your feet, legs, arms, chest, and head as you carry your body.

4. Start paying attention to the sights around you once you have connected with the sensations in your body.

5. Take note of how you feel when you are finished. Do you feel more focused, energized, or calm?

In Daphne's experience with mindful walking, it wasn't until about six months into the treatment that she personally believed the practice was beneficial. But before that, she almost gave up until one summer day when she was walking. During that walk, she naturally noticed that the trees around her were dropping leaves. She felt the warm sun on his face. When she realized this for the first time in years, she realized she had a life worth living. That was her Eureka moment.

INTENTIONAL EATING

When you eat intentionally, you use all your physical and emotional senses to enjoy and experience the foods you choose. This contributes to an increase in appreciation for food, which may enhance the eating experience as a whole.

You're encouraged to make choices about food that will satisfy and nourish the body through mindful eating. However, because eating experiences vary, it discourages judging your eating habits.

Therefore, mindful eating focuses on your eating experiences, body-related sensations, and thoughts and feelings about food with heightened awareness and without judgment.

Here's a simple model Fung et al. (2016) created to guide your mindfulness when eating:

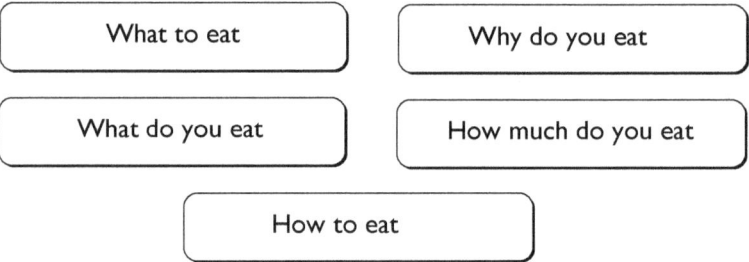

What to eat	Why do you eat
What do you eat	How much do you eat
How to eat	

Hanh & Cheung (2010) suggest seven practices of mindful eating:

✓ **Respect the food.** Recognize who cooked the meal and where the food was grown. Eat without distractions to enhance the experience of eating.

✓ **Use every sense.** Take note of how you feel while eating as well as the sounds, colors, smells, tastes, and textures of the food. Take a break from time to time to use these senses.

✓ **Serve in small servings.** This may assist in preventing food waste and overeating. Fill only one dinner plate that is no bigger than nine inches across.

✓ **Enjoy each bite slowly and thoroughly.** The meal can be slowed down and the flavors of the food can be fully appreciated with these practices.

✓ **Eat slowly to avoid eating too much.** When you eat slowly, you are more likely to know when you are full and can stop eating, which is about 80% of the time.

✓ **Avoid skipping meals.** When you go too long without eating, you run the risk of feeling a lot of hunger, which may cause you to choose the quickest and easiest food option, which isn't always healthy. These dangers can be reduced by planning meals for the same time each day and giving yourself enough time to eat or snack.

✓ **Eat a diet based on plants for your health and the environment.** Take into account the effects that certain foods have over time. Saturated fat and processed meat are linked to increased heart disease and colon cancer risk. The production of plant-based foods is less harmful to the environment than that of animal-based foods like meat and dairy.

Other mindful exercises you can practice include:

✓ Mindful Breathing

✓ Deliberate Listening

✓ Mindful Observation

✓ Mindful meditation

THE PURPOSE OF MINDFULNESS

Mindfulness serves a lot of purpose ...

FREEDOM FROM ANXIETY

One of the reasons we get worried is because we try to control something we don't have the power to—the future. Through mindfulness, you'll stop worrying about what will happen tomorrow or in years to come.

You'll begin to appreciate the blessings of today and now, and you'll live them to the fullest. A bright day today guarantees a bright future. Your "future" is a product of how you respond to today. Begin living in the present moment with awareness.

A TRANSITION FROM RESTLESSNESS TO REST

Restlessness isn't a good thing for a young mind. It could lead to some health challenges. Now, I'm sure you won't want to be a regular at the hospital.

Just like anxiety, restlessness takes away your peace. That's not good. You can only be happy and effective at what you do when you're at peace. Rest is a state of being at peace within, despite the situation outside.

Mindfulness brings you to the point where you're in the eye of a storm, unmoved and at peace. That's rest.

AN INCREASE IN RESILIENCE

Resilience is the capacity to overcome obstacles in one's life and grow emotionally, psychologically, and academically as a result. Training in mindfulness has been shown to help people build resilience and cultivate positive emotions and attitudes. Mindfulness-Based Cognitive Therapy is a specific therapy that aims to improve your social and emotional resilience while helping you identify and reduce "problem behaviors," attention issues, and anxiety.

REDUCED PAIN AND STRESS

This training teaches you to let go of pain and release stress. This is a scientifically proven method for reducing stress. The brain learns to accept and tolerate pain through mindfulness practice. You learn to treat pain as something that cannot be avoided rather than as a sign of danger.

It has been demonstrated that mindfulness-based stress reduction (MBSR) is just as effective as taking painkillers. In addition, the effect appears to last longer. Instead of using chemicals to combat pain, mindfulness teaches the brain to be more open to it.

BOOSTS PERFORMANCE

Are you into any sports? I've read many athletes vouch for mindfulness. The practice enhances their ability to focus and prevents distraction. Instead of stressing about the outcome, these athletes focus on the game's process and let the results take care of themselves.

Even if you are not an athlete, this mindfulness will enhance every part of your life, academics, and relationships.

A REDUCTION IN SYMPTOMS OF DEPRESSION

Mindfulness has long been regarded as a successful treatment for depression. By assisting practitioners in identifying and taking a step back from intense negative emotions and feelings, it has been found to reduce depressive symptoms, anxiety, and stress levels. This idea of observing and letting go of thoughts and feelings rather than fighting them is the foundation of mindfulness.

1. NON-JUDGMENTAL

As you begin your mindfulness practice, you may begin to pay close attention to your thoughts. Avoid getting caught up in ideas, opinions, and preferences. Recognize that your mind has wandered and return it to your breath as soon as you notice it without judging yourself for not paying attention.

2. PATIENCE

Recognize and accept that things will unfold over time. Be open to each moment and patient with yourself. Instead of rushing to get somewhere else or better, give yourself permission to take the time you need for mindfulness and observe what is happening right now.

3. BEGINNER'S MIND

Try to see things clearly and without clutter. Too frequently, we allow our expectations, beliefs, and past experiences to prevent us from seeing things in the here and now.

As if you were experiencing something for the first time or seeing it through the eyes of a child, try opening yourself up to new possibilities.

4. TRUST

Trusting oneself and one's feelings is an essential component of meditation training. Despite the possibility of making mistakes along the way, trust your instincts and look within for direction. Learn to listen to and trust yourself while also being open to what you learn from others.

5. **NON-STRIVING**

Most of what you do in life probably has a goal or purpose. Mindfulness meditation, on the other hand, entails "non-doing" and concentrating on seeing and accepting things as they are right now. Try not to react or enter goal-setting mode. Embrace the present moment and maintain awareness.

6. **ACCEPTANCE**

Allowing things to be as they are without trying to change them is called acceptance. You can be more aware of what you are experiencing when you accept your current circumstance without wishing it were different or attempting to change it.

7. **LETTING GO**

As you begin to pay attention to your inner experiences during meditation, you may discover that your mind may want to hold onto particular thoughts or experiences. Try to let your experiences or thoughts be what they are. Try not to focus on how each experience should be judged. Simply allow it to be and let it go.

FINALLY ... PRACTICE! PRACTICE! PRACTICE!

Theresa practiced and internalized mindfulness to the point that she concluded she was in charge of her life, with herself in the driver's seat. She concluded that she didn't need to wait until her next treatment appointment to feel better. She had the resources she needed to deal with her emotions.

Just as lifting weights is necessary for weight training and picking up an instrument to play is important to learning it, practicing mindfulness is important to learning it.

Standing at the edge of a swimming pool to receive lessons on the techniques of swimming won't make you a swimmer. You have to get into the water and practice. So also, reading about mindfulness or listening to a podcast about it won't teach you any new skills. You must practice it.

Here's how I'll summarize everything I said in this chapter: to live a happy and fulfilling life, worry less about the past you can't alter and the future you can't control. Appreciate the present moment and live it to the fullest. You could do this while eating or walking mindfully.

Here's a simple question for you:

How relevant is mindfulness to your experience?

CHAPTER 4: BUILDING RESILIENCE WITH DISTRESS TOLERANCE SKILLS

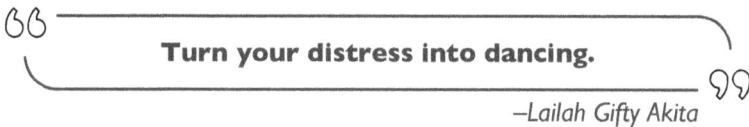

Turn your distress into dancing.

—*Lailah Gifty Akita*

Alice confessed that she regretted not seeking an ADHD diagnosis early enough and not confronting all her difficulties as a child. She couldn't blame herself for that because she knew nothing about it then. She was afraid of getting diagnosed because she didn't want to be judged. In her view, people tend to judge you when you're different. As a result, she had to internalize every emotion and endure every hardship until she could no longer bear it.

She was in her late 20s when she received a late diagnosis of ADHD during a session with a mental health professional. She knew she had those ADHD symptoms, but she didn't know that's what it was. She wished she had dealt with it earlier.

It can be challenging to control emotional stress, whether it's real or imagined. It's even worse if you don't know what you're dealing with. It'll result in more frustrations. And most ADHD patients have a short life span for frustration.

A person's capacity to manage actual or perceived emotional distress is known as *distress tolerance*. Every day, we all face various emotional challenges, ranging from minor irritations to high-stress situations. If you have distress tolerance, you can experience unpleasant and uncomfortable feelings without engaging in unhealthy behavior or worsening the situation.

In stressful situations, people with a low distress tolerance become overwhelmed and are more likely to use unhealthy coping mechanisms or have angry outbursts or meltdowns. This chapter aims to show you how one of the DBT skills—distress tolerance—can be used to curtail the emotional side of ADHD.

INTRODUCTION TO DISTRESS TOLERANCE SKILLS

Certain emotions may be brought on by attention deficit hyperactivity disorder (ADHD). For instance, you can feel guilty or humiliated about how you believe others view you. If your loved ones accuse you of not listening and you believe you have let them down in some manner, you could get anxious. Some other issues on the list below could also trigger intense emotions in ADHD patients:

- ✓ Having parents get divorced
- ✓ Getting into an argument with classmates,
- ✓ Receiving bullying,
- ✓ Not being cast in the role they desired for the school play
- ✓ High academic demands
- ✓ Failing an exam, etc.

But I want you to know that everyone else experiences the same feelings as you do. The only difference is that you could experience them longer or more powerfully due to ADHD, though. That doesn't make you a *weirdo*.

ADHD can indeed make you struggle to control your emotions, especially when it comes to strong emotions like anger, impatience, or sadness.

You're not from some extraterrestrial world, and you don't need some time on the lab table to understand yourself. Because I know that it hurts to feel intensely negative and have so little control over your responses. But *how bad could it be?* When others feel these emotions, emotional responsiveness can harm your social relationships.

Most teens with ADHD are impulsive people who just react depending on how urgent the circumstance is. If it's then coupled with adolescent shenanigans, it becomes unbearable. Does that apply to you?

However, did you know that by being able to wait before responding, you may respond more logically and somewhat detach yourself from your emotions? Sadly, I know this capacity to delay responding can occasionally be quite difficult for those with ADHD, at least the ones I've worked with.

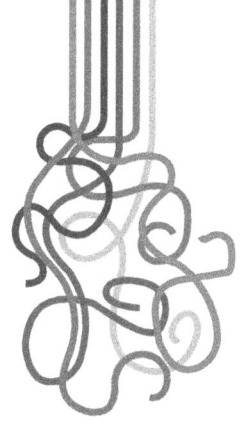

I also know that some people with ADHD may just be more sensitive to criticism, recommendations, or even mild suggestions than others who didn't have ADHD growing up.

You can control those ADHD symptoms and emotions with the appropriate counseling and treatment. You can acquire new coping mechanisms and improve how you feel about living with ADHD.

The good news is that this is not an entirely hopeless situation. The frustration you feel as a result of your inability to control these emotional outbursts may lead you to believe you've reached a dead end, but this is not the case. Dr. Marsha Linehan came up with something learnable to put you in charge of your emotions instead of being at their mercy.

Linehan (cited by Compitus, 2020) believes that you can endure a sudden emotional crisis by having the ability to handle it without making it worse. That's one of the skills you'll learn in distress tolerance. When you feel out of control and powerless to change the circumstance, the distress tolerance skill will also assist you in accepting the truth of the scenario.

Another thing you'll learn through distress tolerance is how to manage your emotions when you're not sure what you need.

Emotional stress could pose a real-time crisis, but this DBT skill is up to the task. It's designed to help you survive this crisis.

WHAT ELSE DO YOU NEED TO KNOW ABOUT DISTRESS TOLERANCE?

Generally, the founding principle in DBT is acceptance and change. Do you remember this from the previous chapters?

Now, one of the first orientations you'll get when learning distress tolerance skills is that it's not only acceptable to experience feelings of sadness or anxiety but that it's also crucial to acquire the ability to accept them. Then you'll learn how to tolerate pain and distress skillfully. Therefore, you'll learn to recognize and accept emotions in a non-judgmental way rather than becoming overwhelmed by them or hiding from them, avoiding unhealthy or self-destructive choices.

Don't think that with these skills, your emotions will change. No, you'll still get angry, you'll still feel sad, and you'll still feel disappointed even after learning this skill. The only difference you'll notice after acquiring distress tolerance skills is how to respond better to your emotions. Your response is what will, essentially, make the difference. Therefore, don't struggle to change your emotions because that's not the objective of this skill.

WHAT ARE THE DISTRESS TOLERANCE SKILLS THAT WE CAN LEARN?

The following distress tolerance skills are taught most frequently:

- Self-Soothe
- TIPP
- IMPROVE the moment
- ACCEPTS

These skills are often tagged "*crisis survival skills*" because they assist a person in traversing a perceived or actual crisis. The fact about human beings is that none of us really finds it pleasurable to go through pain or anything that causes discomfort. We often try to find ways to avoid those pains or get rid of them. That is what drives us to seek ways to alleviate the pain.

Mckay et al. (cited by Compitus, 2020) said that self-harm behaviors—cutting, burning, etc.—are examples of ways some people numb pain. Using alcohol or drugs, running away from the situation, or denying that the pain exists are other options some people choose. According to Mckay and his colleagues, numbing emotional pain doesn't eventually take the pain away; rather, it causes more harmful behavioral patterns with serious long-term consequences.

However, the crisis survival skills I listed above are short-term coping mechanisms that can help you better manage your emotional pains and prevent destructive behavioral patterns. You'll get to learn more about these skills in the next session. You're in safe hands (smile).

HOW TO BUILD DISTRESS TOLERANCE SKILLS AND HOW TO USE THEM

Before I start to show you more about each of these distress tolerance skills, I need you to understand this. You're unique and different from everyone else. These skills don't work the same for everyone because of our uniqueness. Therefore, I'll need you to do two things in this session:

✓ Pay rapt attention to how each skill works

✓ Test to see which skills are best suited to you.

Are we cool with that?

1. SELF-SOOTHE

It is generally believed that the capacity to self-soothe develops during early childhood through the internalization of reassuring experiences. Have you ever seen a child sucking their thumb or stroking a stuffed animal? Those are examples of self-soothing techniques some children naturally develop.

But if you didn't, you can still learn these skills through deliberate strategies. Learning these strategies could be difficult for some people, though. Those natural self-soothing abilities children develop can also be adapted for teens and young adults.

ARE YOU WONDERING HOW THOSE SELF-SOOTHING SKILLS CAN BE ADAPTED FOR TEENS?

Well, that's the whole point of learning.

Here's an explanation of why self-soothing should be adapted to help you control your emotions. Usually, our (human beings') emotional brain takes over when we're emotionally stimulated. When this happens, our natural instinct is to do something that could be harmful to ourselves or others. During those times, the rational part of the brain is offline.

In order to regain control over your actions at that moment, you must first calm your emotional brain. Self-soothing can help accomplish this. Instead of doing something harmful or likely to worsen things, you can do something else that brings you joy and comfort.

According to Schwartz (2022), engaging in activities that are relaxing, reassuring, and centered on the five senses to relieve stress is known as "self-soothing." Below are examples of how you can engage your five senses:

SIGHT

- ✓ If you're close to a park during the emotional distress, focus on the beautiful way the sky, trees, grass, benches, and people create a collage of colors and life in nature. If you're not, just focus on the scenery around you.

- ✓ Go for art or pictures!

- ✓ You could turn your attention to a movie that helps you relax.

- ✓ For subsequent occurrences, you could create a collection of pictures that make you happy and help you relax. Whenever you feel emotionally distressed, you can flip through those pictures.

HEARING

- ✓ Instead of expressing your emotional stress immediately, you could turn to someone you like and whose voice makes you happy. This could be through a phone call or a social media platform.

- ✓ Music—good and calm music—could also do the trick. Listening to one could calm you. So instead of an outburst of rage, take out your mobile device, plug your ear pod into your ears, and play the music.

- ✓ You could also turn your attention to the lively sounds around you—birds, wind, and people talking. One of the best places to get this combo is at a park.

- ✓ If you play a musical instrument, that's even better. Pour out your emotions while you play alone.

- ✓ Listening to your favorite audiobook or podcast at that time isn't a bad option either.

SMELL

- ✓ Before leaving your room, you could put on a cologne or perfume you like to smell.

- ✓ You could transfer your energy into preparing a meal that smells good.

  Flowers! If you love them, you could purchase and keep them fresh in your room.

- ✓ You could sneak to a place to enjoy the scent of a bakery, flower shop, perfume shop, or restaurant.

TASTE

- ✓ You could escape to an eatery to buy your favorite meal at your favorite restaurant. Or even order it online.

- ✓ You could choose to buy some snacks or comfort foods. A caution here: eat moderately.

- ✓ Make yourself a cup of cocoa, coffee, tea, or any other beverage you like. Alcohol is a no!

- ✓ You could chew or blow some gum while chewing.

TOUCH

- ✓ Hold your pet in your lap and pet it.

- ✓ You could wrap yourself in your favorite clothes. Take pleasure in the way they feel on your skin.

- ✓ You could take a shower and relax in the warm, calming water. If that suits you better, you can also take a cold shower.

- ✓ You can go for a massage or massage yourself, as the case may be.

- ✓ Touch something silky, supple, or fluffy.

Rather than remaining in a crisis, opt for self-soothing. It is less stressful. You can choose which of the senses works best for you.

 NB: You're not restricted to the suggestions under each sense. You're free to choose yours. The goal is to achieve calmness.

2. TIPP

TIPP is another distress tolerance skill. It's an acronym for:

T – Temperature

I – Intense exercise,

P – Paced breathing

P – Paired muscle relaxation.

TEMPERATURE

Our bodies frequently become hot when we are upset. Altering your body temperature could help you change your mood quickly and keep you from doing something rash. To combat this, you could:

Splash some cold water on your face

Put a cold ice pack on your face or hold an ice cube

Turn on air conditioning in your room or an alternative to blow on your face.

INTENSE EXERCISE

Stress levels go down when oxygen flow is increased, and it's hard to hold on to explosive emotions when you're physically exhausted and out of breath. So,

✓ Run! Sprint to the end of the street

✓ Punch some punchbag hard. Or exercise hard to match your intense feelings.

✓ Jump in the pool for a few laps or do jumping jacks until you get tired

Additionally, when you're tired, it's hard to stay dangerously upset.

RHYTHMIC BREATHING

In case you didn't know, breathing exercises can reduce stress levels. It reduces emotional pain. You can try these breathing exercises:

Box/square breathing:	Nose-mouth breathing:	4-4-8 breathing:
While tracing the four lines of a square, hold your breath for four counts and let go of your breath for four counts. Repeat until you feel more at ease.	Try inhaling through your nose for seven seconds and exhaling through your mouth for ten.	First inhale through your nose for four counts, hold your breath for another four counts, then exhale for eight counts. When you exhale, purse your lips to hear your breath coming out.

This type of breathing manipulation causes your heart rate to slow.

PAIRED MUSCLE RELAXATION

Teens with ADHD are usually tense, sometimes without knowing it. Paired muscle relaxation works like this:

✓ First, tighten a single muscle or group of muscles very strongly.

✓ Hold that position for ten seconds.

✓ Then, relax the muscle.

Your heart rate and breathing will slow down as your muscles relax and require less oxygen.

Sokya (2021) suggested that to practice paired muscle relaxation, any of the following muscle groups can be targeted:

✓ Make fists with your hands and arms,

✓ Make fists and tense your biceps and triceps,

✓ Wrinkle your forehead,

✓ Close your eyelids tightly.

✓ Push your chin down toward your chest.

✓ Take a deep breath and hold it – this is for your chest.

✓ Tense your stomach muscles.

✓ Squeeze your buttocks and gluts together.

✓ Point your toes down.

3. IMPROVE THE MOMENT

Greene (2020) said that improving the moment helps us get through emotionally challenging situations when a technique like self-soothing isn't working. The DBT IMPROVE the Moment skills are meant to provide you with options you can choose from when faced with an emotionally challenging circumstance. You don't need to practice them all.

The goal of the IMPROVE skill is to make the moment more pleasant and bearable by substituting a more positive action for the immediate event that sparked negative feelings.

IMPROVE is an acronym for

I – Imagery
M – Meaning
P – Prayer
R – Relaxation
O – One thing right now
V – Vacation
E – Encouragement

IMAGERY

This technique requires you to put your mind to work to achieve emotional de-stress. There are a few applications for this ability:

✓ Picture yourself in a completely secure location with everything you require.

✓ Picture yourself overcoming the difficult situation you're in right now.

✓ Imagine that you are releasing hurtful feelings.

Engage your mind to create an emotionally stable world for yourself.

MEANING

Have you realized that, sometimes, certain things just happen to you that aren't your fault? The truth is that some painful situations can sometimes have a deeper meaning for us if we look beyond the pain. Try to find meaning in difficult circumstances. What can that experience teach you? You might become more sympathetic. You might form new relationships. You might begin your healing journey with this. Find a reason because there's one.

PRAYER

This is not about a specific religion. Everyone prays, in a way. But prayer has a different outlook for different people. It could be giving things over to a higher power or connecting with a wise mind. This approach takes you beyond yourself to seek help from someone or something greater than yourself.

RELAXATION

Our instinct to fight or flight makes us tense up in stressful situations. To alleviate the mental pain, try engaging in activities that can calm you. As an example, consider:

- ✓ Yoga
- ✓ Hot/cold bath
- ✓ Taking a long walk
- ✓ Deep breathing, etc.

ONE THING IN THE MOMENT

Did you remember the skill of mindfulness? This technique is similar to it. Let go of the future and the past to stay in the present. To solve the issue, it will not be helpful to bring up old issues or to speculate about what might happen in the future. Concentrate entirely on completing a single task. Emotions are less overwhelming when the mind is focused in one direction.

VACATION

C'mon! You need a break! We all take breaks from time to time. This technique says you should give yourself a break, provided it doesn't lead to additional issues. The "vacation" shouldn't be long, just a few hours. This may require you to go back to bed or turn off your phone for a day. Sometimes you just need to watch a show on TV for a few hours. You should determine how your vacation will look.

ENCOURAGEMENT

I love this the most. This technique asks you to assume a new role—that of a cheerleader. For which team? Team You! You need to learn to cheer yourself on more often. If you tend to be critical of yourself, it's time to begin to see that you're worth more. Tell yourself,

> "I can get through this."

> "I'm trying my hardest."

> "This is difficult, but it will pass."

> It may be difficult initially, but you need to. You want to hear *you*.

4. ACCEPTS

ACCEPTS is a distraction skill. It's designed to distract you from difficult emotional situations and help you get through those emotional situations one moment at a time.

ACCEPTS is a set of skills that are part of the DBT distress tolerance model to help you tolerate negative emotions until you can address and ultimately resolve the situation. So, while you're in emotional distress, and you don't want to act based on how you feel, ACCEPTS says you should:

> **A** – engage in some productive **ACTIVITIES** like volunteering.

> **C** – **CONTRIBUTE** to the well-being of someone else, or to a cause. You could contribute to a project or cook with someone. Help a friend or family member.

> **C** – **COMPARE** your present situation with a worse situation you've experienced before or with someone else's situation. You could read about people going through difficult times.

> **E** – switch your **EMOTIONS**. Watch a comic animation, listen to music, or watch a funny clip.

> **P** – **PUSH AWAY** the situation from your mind by leaving it for a while.

> **T** – redirect your **THOUGHTS**. You could play a game, count something, read a book, or just do anything that takes your thoughts somewhere, but the emotional situation is different.

> **S** – as in "self-soothe," means to create positive **SENSATIONS** using your five senses to relieve you of stress.

Some other distress tolerance skills include:

PROS AND CONS

Most times when we're overwhelmed by emotions, we become impulsive, and our logical side goes offline. Such impulsiveness is heightened in people with ADHD. However, the essence of this skill is to help you put logic over emotions. Pros and Cons simply teaches you to consider the good and bad sides of the action you're about to take before you act on it. Ask yourself:

- ✓ What is the effectiveness of the behavior now and in the future?
- ✓ Is the behavior harmful or incompatible with your objectives?
- ✓ What are the benefits and drawbacks of engaging in crisis behavior or acting on your impulses?
- ✓ Before a recurring impulsive reaction occurs, you can answer these questions beforehand, write them on a plain sheet of paper or in your journal, and take it with you as a reminder.

RADICAL ACCEPTANCE

The complete and utter acceptance of reality is radical acceptance. This indicates that your mind, heart, and body accept the situation as it is. You accept reality instead of fighting against it.

DBT distress tolerance skills focus on tolerating one's emotions during painful events, reducing impulsive behavior in a crisis, and accepting the situation as it is without trying to change it.

WHAT ELSE CAN YOU DO TO COPE WITH STRESS?

Don't forget that no one skill fits all here. Because of our uniqueness, there are specific skills that suit each of us. You deserve to have lots of options you could try before settling on a few you know will work for you.

After you've learned and practiced those distress skills, here are three things you can do to cope with emotional stress:

REDEFINE WHO YOU ARE

Who do you want to be known as? An impulsive individual with no emotional control? Will you continue to allow your emotions to define who you are? You're better than your emotions.

Redefine who you are, and then let your emotions align with that definition. If your emotions attempt to run wild, use any coping skills to control them. Ultimately, knowing who you are can help you tolerate emotional distress.

RECOVER YOUR IMAGE

Wouldn't it be nice to hear someone say, "I thought you would yell at me, but you didn't?" That's new ..." It sounds like someone is recovering their image. No one should label you based on your negative emotional reactions. There's a better version of you.

You won't want to ruin an image you're trying to build with another act of emotional outburst, would you?

REDISCOVER YOUR CORE VALUES

Your values are the norms, morals, principles, and ideals that give your life meaning, value, and significance. Those are the things that give you reasons to get out of bed in the morning and the drive to keep going. You can begin to build a life that is worth living by discovering or rediscovering your values. This will help you tolerate emotional distress.

A recap of the lessons in this chapter: you'll handle issues better if you can learn to manage distress. This skill gives you various tools you can adopt to achieve this. You can engage your human senses to distract you from an annoying situation. You could IMPROVE, and you can also burn your anger through intense exercise.

Most importantly, redefining who you are, what you want to be known for, and what you stand for could also shape your responses to situations.

There are still more things to learn in this book on how to cope with ADHD using DBT. But before you proceed, attempt these questions:

How can you apply any of the distress tolerance skills to a practical issue you've faced before?

Which of the skills is most fitting for you?

CHAPTER 5: EMOTIONAL REGULATION SKILLS: PAYING ATTENTION TO YOUR FEELINGS

> In between every action and reaction, there is a space. Usually the space is extremely small because we react so quickly, but take notice of that space and expand it. Be aware in that space that you have a choice to make. You can choose how to respond ...
>
> — *Rebecca Eanes*

INTRODUCTION TO EMOTIONAL REGULATION SKILLS

Theo was a fifth-grader when he started to receive his behavioral healthcare at school. His mother realized that Theo had been through a lot, including losing a loved one. Those events began to wear on him emotionally. He struggled emotionally and with some behaviors. Theo got angry and anxious more often.

When Theo was diagnosed, it was discovered that ADHD was the cause of his anger outbursts and impulsiveness. By applying emotional regulation skills, Theo began to learn self-control. He became aware of his anger and how to feel it healthily. Whenever he noticed difficulty sitting still or paying attention in class, he spoke with his teacher about it.

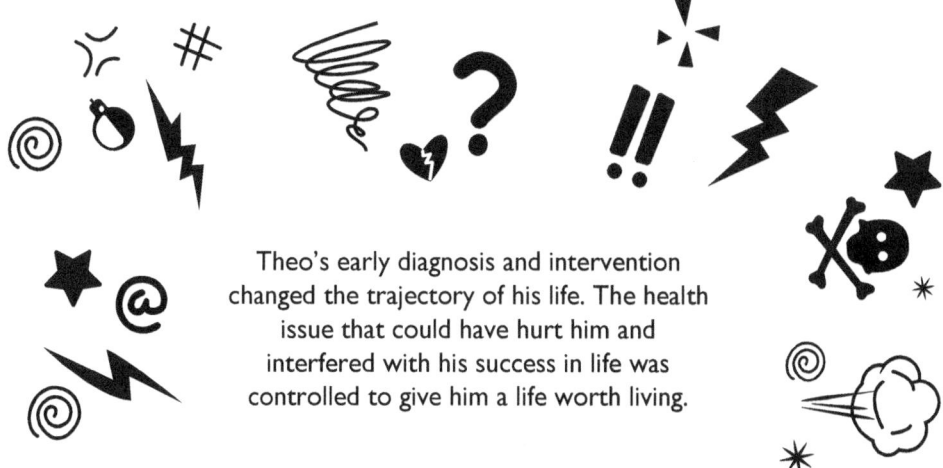

Theo's early diagnosis and intervention changed the trajectory of his life. The health issue that could have hurt him and interfered with his success in life was controlled to give him a life worth living.

EMOTIONS AND THE PECULIARITY OF YOUR AGE

Adolescents have a harder time controlling their emotions because they frequently get into fights with their parents and peers. Adolescents with ADHD are especially vulnerable to this.

Teens with ADHD have a lot of trouble controlling their negative emotions, but many also have trouble controlling their positive emotions. Specifically, adolescents with ADHD frequently exhibit age-inappropriate levels of enthusiasm or exuberance when they are happy or excited. When they hear good news, they might scream, jump up and down, and invade other people's personal space. As a result, these teenagers are frequently viewed as immature and brash by peers, teachers, and family.

Breaux (2020) said that people in your age group who have ADHD exhibit rapid and drastic emotional shifts, stronger responses to stress or frustration, and intense displays of both positive and negative emotions.

Also, Littman (2022) said that a significant and overwhelming period of change occurs when you're a preteen or a teen. Teens with ADHD have trouble navigating the following:

✓ A need for sensitivity to peer acceptance, a growing social life, questions about identity, and a desire for independence.

✓ Changes in the body and the development of sexuality which frequently cause embarrassment and confusion.

✓ Mood swings and more emotionality which are caused by hormonal changes. Girls' ADHD symptoms are intensified by monthly drops in estrogen levels during puberty.

✓ Stress is caused by increased academic demands and frequently decreased parental support.

BUT HAVE YOU EVER WONDERED WHAT EMOTIONS ARE?

Dr. Bruce Lipton (cited by DBT Tools, n.d.) said that emotions arise in response to a stimulus. A thought, a sound, a smell, or a sight can all act as triggers. Emotions and thoughts result from triggers. We are motivated to take action as soon as the emotion occurs.

> Good news! We can learn to regulate our emotions and how we react to things.

SO, WHAT IS EMOTION REGULATION?

Emotional regulation is one of the skills you'll learn under dialectical behavior therapy (DBT). I mentioned this to you in a previous chapter.

Taking any action that changes the intensity of an emotional experience is what emotional regulation is. This skill doesn't teach you to avoid or suppress what you feel. Rather, it teaches you to control it. Thus, you can control the emotions you experience and how you express them.

The goal of the emotional regulation skill is to enable you to:

- ✓ Comprehend the function of emotions

- ✓ Understand the urge that goes along with each emotion

- ✓ Make the decision to heed or resist these urges.

- ✓ Reduce vulnerability

- ✓ Build resilience against negative emotions

- ✓ Improve your mental health as a whole.

The emotional regulation skills you need to learn are:

- ✓ STOP
- ✓ PLEASE
- ✓ Opposite Action
- ✓ Build Mastery
- ✓ ABC
- ✓ Positive Self-Talk

We'll talk more about this later in this chapter.

WHY IS EMOTIONAL REGULATION IMPORTANT?

You can better deal with stress, interact with others, and focus on learning when you learn how to control your emotions. Instead of suppressing your emotions, many experts believe it's essential for teens to learn how to manage their feelings.

Learning how to control your emotions has lots of benefits. A teen with ADHD will benefit more from it.

MORE DELIBERATE IN DECISION-MAKING

Think about coming home after a challenging day at school to spend time with your family. It's so easy to enter the house or the next room and lash out at others, but you can't. Do you know why? It's like you have no control over it since it simply happens.

Life doesn't have to seem chaotic. Instead of letting your emotions control your conduct, you may choose how you want to act on purpose. Once you have improved your emotional regulation, you can make deliberate decisions in situations rather than simply reacting. This can help you feel less out of control and more in control of your life.

FREEDOM TO MAKE HEALTHY CHOICES

The worst moment to make a decision is when we're emotionally unbalanced. During that time, we make some poor decisions. Some young adults make bad decisions on food, leisure time, or interpersonal relationships during such moments. And instead of getting better, a feeling of emptiness and dissatisfaction follows. It further intensifies the emotional distress.

The ability to control your emotions doesn't guarantee you won't make the same choices or decisions. What it really implies is that you'll have a choice between what is good and bad for you. You're free to decide what's healthy for you and what isn't.

HEALTHY COMMUNICATION

Did you know that communication is the soul of any relationship? Have you tried talking back to someone when you're upset? What happened to your relationship with that person afterward?

You will not express your wants or desires to others intelligently if you are emotionally unbalanced. It'll result in a breakdown in your relationship with others.

Your relationships with others will be better if you learn to regulate your emotions. You'll be able to listen properly and convey your messages better with your emotions under control.

PEACEFUL RELATIONSHIP

Healthy communication will produce a peaceful relationship. It's only when you're calm that you can express concern for someone else.

When you speak with your peers and colleagues at school with controlled emotion, you will be at ease with them. People keep their distance from anyone who speaks to them rashly.

A SENSE OF FULFILLMENT

When you're able to develop a healthy relationship that gives you peace and you can make healthy, wise choices for yourself, it gives you a sense of satisfaction and fulfillment. You'll be pleased with yourself for doing the right thing for yourself.

IMPROVED SELF-ESTEEM

An emotionally distressed teen will always think less of themselves. They'll not see anything good about themselves, so it'll be difficult to speak confidently with others without looking down.

They're usually critical of themselves. Emotional regulation skills will help you accept and embrace yourself without being critical of your flaws. Overall, it'll boost your self-esteem and confidence. You'll learn to appreciate yourself more and acknowledge your worth and strengths instead of focusing on your weaknesses.

RECOGNIZING AND COPING WITH STRONG EMOTIONS

How are you feeling right now?

Are you interested in what I've been sharing?

Are you hopeful that you'll get to know who you are?

Are you happy because it's a school project you enjoy or bored because this is something you must do for school and you don't really enjoy it?

Something else may distract you, such as getting excited about your weekend plans or being sad because you just broke up with someone.

According to *KidsHealth Behavioral Health* experts, these feelings are normal for people. They inform us of what we are going through and assist us in determining how to respond.

The ability to recognize what we're feeling and put it into words rather than just reacting in a childlike manner is known as *emotional awareness*. Emotional awareness is simply recognizing, valuing, and accepting your emotions as they arise. We become better at understanding why and what we are feeling with practice and time.

Before you can cope with or control your emotions, you need to recognize them first.

SO, HOW DO YOU RECOGNIZE YOUR EMOTIONS?

#1 - IDENTIFY AND ADMIT THE EMOTION

Identifying your current emotion is the first step. It takes practice to learn to notice and identify your emotions. But it's possible. So here's what you can do:

✓ Pick just one emotion if you're feeling more than one.

✓ Sit down for a moment and pay attention to your thoughts and physical sensations if you are having trouble identifying the emotion.

✓ Try to give an emotion you're experiencing a name (such as sadness, rage, or shame) if you can. For instance:

> I'm so *mad* at that Jeff in my study group!

> I feel *scared* every time I'm called to give a presentation.

✓ Make a note of the emotion on a slip of paper once you have given it a name.

✓ Don't conceal/suppress your feelings from yourself.

✓ Know the reasons behind your emotions. Determine what caused you to feel the way you do. For instance:

> Jeff always gets credit for other people's efforts.

✓ Don't blame anyone for your emotions once you've recognized them.

✓ Don't judge yourself for feeling the way you do. Consider it a normal thing. Acknowledging how you feel can help you move on. So, don't be hard on yourself.

#2 - ACT!

You can decide whether you need to express your feelings after you've identified them. Acknowledging them could be enough at times, but at other times, acting could make you feel better.

✓ How best can you express what you feel? Do you need to gently confront someone who infuriated you? Or discuss your feelings with a friend? Or go for a run to get rid of the emotion? Thinking this through makes you a master over your emotions. That's the essence of this skill.

✓ Find a way to alter your mood. You will need to learn how to transform your negative mood into a positive one at some point. Otherwise, your thoughts might become stuck on how bad things are, which could make you feel worse.

✓ Consciously develop positive feelings. Focus regularly on the good things in your life, even the little things. Being mindful of what's good about a situation switches your mood from negativity to positivity—pessimism to optimism.

✓ Talk to someone about how you feel.

✓ Exercise is helpful, too. Physical exercises release stress and help the brain to produce chemicals that promote a positive mood.

#3 - AVOID TRIGGERS

Triggers are things that others say or do to influence us and draw a reaction from us. You might know or have people like that around you. They're just good at saying or doing things to manipulate or disorient you until they get a furious response from you.

They usually strike you in sensitive areas on purpose to incite you to rage. Such action makes you vulnerable to them. What do you do?

- ✓ Resolve that no one has the right to determine how you feel, regardless of what they say or do to you. When you grant them that right, they will believe they control you and will make you dance to their music.

- ✓ Forgive yourself. Some people might be using something in your past to incite you to anger. When you forgive yourself and start living in the moment, such talks will not hold any weight against you.

- ✓ Rely on your judgment, not other people's judgment of things.

- ✓ Avoid blaming yourself. You're not to blame for someone else's inability to take responsibility for their lives. Don't let anyone make you feel guilty.

- ✓ Such people are toxic; avoid them. Draw a boundary to keep them away. Stay away from people who project their negative experiences on you. They're toxic people.

#4 - DON'T ISOLATE YOURSELF

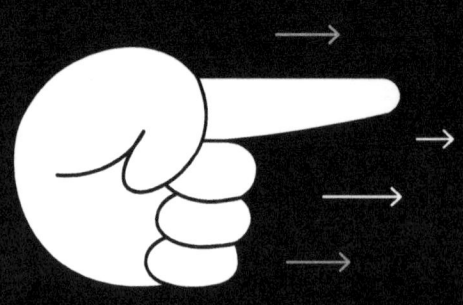

Negative thoughts thrive the most when we're alone. And once you open your mind to a single thread of thought, it begins to grow until you're compelled to act on it. Those thoughts result in difficult emotions that persist for days and become difficult to shake off no matter what you do.

In this instance,

- ✓ Defy shame and open up to a friend, a family member, or your teacher, as the case may be.

- ✓ Instead of opting to act on the emotions, step out of your cocoon and seek help from an older person you can trust or a specialist.

SIX MOST USEFUL EMOTION REGULATION SKILLS YOU SHOULD MASTER

I mentioned those skills while introducing this DBT technique. Let's begin to talk about them one after the other here:

STOP

Greene (2020) refers to this as an "emergency mindfulness skill." Just imagine what the STOP traffic sign on our roads does to drivers. It's a regulatory sign that brings them to a complete halt, right? They're not to proceed until the intersection is clear of vehicles.

The STOP traffic sign has been adapted as an essential DBT skill to regulate your emotions.

S – Stop!

Simply stop! Whenever you think your feelings are in charge, stop! Don't respond. Simply freeze, particularly the mouth muscles. You can avoid doing what your emotions want you to do (act without thinking) by temporarily not drawing any conclusions until you have gathered enough facts to guide your decision.

P – Proceed mindfully

This is the part where you get to act based on the facts you've gathered on the issue. At this point, you would have thought through the best outcome in that situation. Then you act on it.

OPPOSITE ACTION

This skill teaches you to do the exact opposite of your emotion. Sounds difficult? Yeah, I know, but it's also practicable. Here's the trick:

✓ Instead of getting *angry*, show kindness, concern or just walk away

✓ Instead of feeling *ashamed*, raise your head high and your shoulders back and advance

✓ Instead of being *afraid*, muster courage within, match forward, and remain involved.

However, don't do the exact opposite when you're faced with danger. Fear grips you when you're faced with danger. It's wise to respond to the flight mode and save yourself from harm.

ABC

This skill teaches you to

> **A** – Accumulate positive emotions by engaging in activities that give you positive emotions.

> **B** – Build mastery by engaging in activities that you enjoy. It could be domestic skills or games.

> **C** – Cope ahead by preparing for those things that make you anxious or fidget. Prepare for that class presentation, test, or exam ahead.

PLEASE

According to Dr. Paul Greene (cited by Rigby, n. d.), although it may seem counterintuitive, some of the best things we can do to control our emotions take place well before they occur. This especially has to do with how we take care of our bodies.

Hence, to learn this skill, you need to remember that your mind affects your body and vice versa.

Dr. Greene cautions ahead that these skills might look simple, but we've often neglected at least one of them when our emotions get the best of us.

PL – Physical illness. There's a link between your physical and mental health. Emotional regulation becomes difficult if you're not physically sound. Take care of your physical health, and you will have also taken care of your mind.

E – Eat a healthy, balanced diet regularly. Skipping meals can affect your mental health.

A – Avoid drugs or substances that alter your mood.

S – Sleep well every night. It's essential to your health and well-being.

E – Exercising your body for about 20 minutes daily is good for your mental and physical fitness.

If you want to opt for this skill, ask yourself, "How well have I been faring with these practices?"

BUILD MASTERY

Just as in ABC skills, engage in an activity that gives you pleasure.

✓ Devote time to learn as much as you can on that thing.

✓ Talk about what you're learning with someone else, perhaps someone who knows it better.

✓ Practice, practice, and practice some more till you feel competent.

You can as well:

✓ Try something new

✓ Practice until you gain some level of competence

✓ Don't hesitate to give yourself credit for each progress you make

AFFIRMATIVE SELF-TALK

PsychCentral suggests five ways you can practice affirmative self-talk:

1. Pay attention to what your inner critic is saying about you to you.

2. Create a psychological distance from yourself.

3. If the conversation isn't lifting you, change the conversation to agree with your worth, essence, and youSpeak compassionately to yourself as you would to a friend.

4. Instead of saying "I Can't" to resist the urge to express a negative emotion, say "I Don't." For instance:

    "I can't miss my homework" against "I don't miss my homework."

    "I can't get angry" against "I don't get angry."

    "I can't hit a colleague" against "I don't hit a colleague."

According to Vanessa Patrick (cited by PsychCentral, 2015), saying "I don't" puts you in charge of your emotions.r goals. You shouldn't be talking down yourself.

WHAT IS EMOTIONAL REGULATION DISORDER?

We wouldn't need to regulate our emotions if there hadn't been a form of dysregulation. Did you catch my drift?

So let's talk about emotional regulation disorder, but you can also call it emotional dysregulation.

Cuncic (2022) described emotional dysregulation as a poorly regulated emotional response that falls outside a range of commonly accepted emotional responses. This could be significant mood swings, mood changes, or lability. Examples of dysregulation include sadness, rage, irritability, and frustration.

Teens with emotional dysregulation experience volatile, uncontrollable, and explosive feelings, which is one of the most impairing symptoms of ADHD.

DO YOU STILL REMEMBER SOMETHING ABOUT THE PECULIARITIES OF YOUR AGE?

Those are the years full of a never-ending series of highs and lows. It's usually a rapid, difficult, and frequent transition between euphoria and misery, jealousy and generosity, irritability and vulnerability. These transitions hit differently for teenagers who suffer from ADHD. It's also associated with emotional dysregulation.

EMOTIONAL DYSREGULATION AND SOCIAL MEDIA

Did you know that emotional dysregulation affects every aspect of your adolescent life? That includes your friendships, romantic relationships, academic performance, and even the use of social media. That's a whole lot of stress to deal with.

Even though social media is a cool place to be and meet new people who are netizens, *The Wall Street Journal* reported that the use of social media, specifically Instagram, was linked to poor mental health outcomes for teen girls, who cited body image issues and even suicidal thoughts in a 2021 research study. This is particularly troubling.

Social media could also have a real negative effect on teens' mental health. Are you aware of issues like cyberbullying, extremism, sexual and financial manipulation, and addiction resulting from an excessive reliance on online relationships?

Teens with emotional dysregulation may be particularly vulnerable to these risks and effects of social media use because they are already more sensitive to peer rejection and acceptance than their neurotypical peers.

WHAT CAUSES IT?

There might be numerous answers to this, but according to Cuncic (2022), one of the clear ones is the one that comes from an early psychological trauma inflicted by a caregiver's abuse or neglect. And it could lead to a condition known as "reactive attachment disorder."

Another probable cause is when one is raised by a parent with emotional dysregulation.

WHAT ARE ITS SYMPTOMS?

Emotional dysregulation can manifest in adolescents with ADHD in the following ways:

- ✓ Impulsivity in emotions
- ✓ Low tolerance for frustration
- ✓ Quick to get angry
- ✓ Inability to cope with stress
- ✓ Avoidance of difficult circumstances
- ✓ Overwhelmed by emotions
- ✓ Mood swings
- ✓ Defensiveness
- ✓ Verbal and physical violence
- ✓ Anxiety
- ✓ Depression
- ✓ Intense emotions

WHAT ARE THE EFFECTS OF EMOTIONAL DYSREGULATION FOR A TEEN SUFFERING FROM ADHD?

The following outcomes may occur:

- ✓ Likely to be defiant

- ✓ Issues with complying with requests from teachers or parents

- ✓ Sensitivity to depression

- ✓ Explosive relationships with family and peers

- ✓ Issues with making and maintaining friends

- ✓ Limited focus on tasks

- ✓ Risky sexual behavior

- ✓ Self-harm

HOW TO MANAGE EMOTIONS WHEN YOU HAVE ADHD

The answer to this is the emotional regulation skills I shared with you in this chapter. I recommend you go over them again and start practicing with anyone appropriate for you. That's how to manage your emotions as a teen with ADHD.

Remember, you're the boss of your emotions. Take charge with these skills.

Let's do a quick recap - this chapter made having healthy relationships look possible despite your emotional instability and outbursts. With the different tools and practical tools shared in this chapter like STOP, ABC, and PLEASE, you can regulate your emotions.

It's important for you also to remember that emotions are neither good nor bad; your response to how you feel labels the emotion good or bad. You can regulate your emotions without hurting anyone, or yourself, using the skills listed in this chapter.

> What are the causes of emotional dysregulation you know?

> What are the things that trigger emotional outburst in you?

> Which emotional regulation skill works best for you?

CHAPTER 6: MANAGING INTENSE AND RAGING EMOTIONS WITH DBT

> 66 Anger is just anger. It isn't good. It isn't bad. It just is. What you do with it is what matters. It's like anything else. You can use it to build or to destroy. You just have to make the choice. 99
>
> — Jim Butcher

Saline (2021) once shared the case of a frantic parent who reported that her 15-year-old teenage son's anger frightened her. She said her son used to take Focalin XR since he had been diagnosed with ADHD. Whenever they disagreed about his social life, he got angry. He has gotten enraged to the extent of kicking a hole in his bedroom door. She said whenever they argue, he verbally abuses her by calling her X-rated names. She solicited help because, obviously, she had lost it with the kid.

Can I ask you this?

"How intense are your emotions?"

"Do you get so angry that your parents become afraid of you?"

"How bad does it get?"

Now, I didn't ask those questions to make you feel bad. It's just a simple way of diagnosing your situation. You don't have to judge yourself because I'm not sitting in the judgment seat either. So, attempt those questions again.

While she was trying to respond to the frantic parent's concern, Saline (2021) stated that teens with ADHD can become enraged due to fluctuating hormone levels and poor working memory, and parents frequently bear the brunt of this. Knowing this may not make dealing with your teen's raging outbursts any easier.

Wexelblatt (2022) also shared the story of another teenager with an intense anger issue. The teenage boy was called Daniel. He was a landmine because he was silent and alone until a family member stepped in the wrong direction. He immediately explodes at that point. The most horrifying error made by Daniel's parents was denying him unlimited screen time. 14-year-old Daniel would scream at his parents and younger siblings when they restricted his video game play. Additionally, he would move toward his parents as if he were going to hit them and make suicidal threats.

Daniel was unable to alter his behavior despite seeing several therapists. It got worse in middle school.

INTRODUCTION: THE CONNECTION BETWEEN ANGER AND ADHD

Don't you want to know the mystery behind your intense rage? Let's start with that.

Ohwovoriole (2021) described anger as that intense emotion when something goes wrong or someone wrongs you. Typically, it's characterized by feelings of stress, annoyance, and resentment.

Before going further, it's crucial to inform you that we all get angry occasionally. It's a perfectly normal reaction to difficult or frustrating circumstances. However, it becomes a problem when expressed excessively and it affects your day-to-day activities and interpersonal relationships.

Anger can be anything from mild irritation to rage. It may occasionally be unreasonable or excessive. When it gets to this point, it could be difficult to control your emotions. You could act widely in a way you wouldn't do normally.

Turner (2022) said that although anger is not always associated with ADHD, the two conditions have a significant connection. Stanborough (2021) also said that anger was once included in the definition of ADHD. For instance, ADHD was referred to as a "disorder of anger and aggression" in the United Kingdom. Although anger is no longer one of the criteria used to diagnose ADHD, many medical professionals know it can hinder your ability to function well at home, in school, and your social life.

SO, WHAT'S THE CONNECTION?

ADHD symptoms could make you appear more aggressive. But it might not necessarily be motivated by malicious intent, as is typically the case with proactive, aggressive behavior.

Emotions are frequently felt more strongly by people with ADHD than by those without it. This is also known as emotional dysregulation. If you didn't skip the previous chapter, you would have learned about emotional dysregulation. Some characteristics that accompany this intense emotion are:

- ✓ Outbursts of explosive anger
- ✓ Overreactions to minor stressors
- ✓ Intense emotions
- ✓ Difficulty expressing anger verbally
- ✓ Persistent irritability
- ✓ Increased impatience when stressed

WHAT ARE THE THINGS THAT TRIGGER THESE INTENSE EMOTIONS IN TEENS WITH ADHD?

IMPULSIVITY

Impulsivity is one of the symptoms of ADHD. An inability to concentrate and maintain behavior control is frequently the root cause of impulsivity. Because of their impulsive nature, people with ADHD express their anger immediately. This is more apparent with adolescents.

Saylor and Amann (cited by Low, 2022) stated that impulsive aggression, also known as *affective aggression*, is experienced by more than 50% of preadolescents with ADHD. Impulsive aggression is characterized by strong, unplanned emotions, typically anger, often expressed in the heat of the moment.

 **LOW SELF-ESTEEM**

Low self-esteem is common for people with ADHD, regardless of their age group. Adolescents who suffer from ADHD may have difficulty achieving academic success. In addition, it makes it harder for them to make and keep friends, which can cause them to feel alone and lower their self-esteem.

Anger can also result from this—low self-esteem—and anxiety about a situation they have no control over.

DISRESPECT AND HUMILIATION

Every teenager wants to be treated with respect. In their adolescence, they believe they deserve some level of respect. When they're denied that or humiliated before their peers, family, or in a public space, they go into a rage.

FRUSTRATION

Challenges that get in the way of achieving goals are what cause frustration. Frustration tolerance is the capacity to handle frustration. One of the symptoms of ADHD is a low frustration tolerance. When frustrated, a teenager with ADHD can have an angry outburst.

VIOLATION OF RIGHTS

Just as in the story in my introduction to this chapter, Daniel felt it was his right to have an Xbox. Every time he was denied that right, he exploded. Anytime teens with ADHD are denied what they think they have the right to enjoy, they react intensely with rage.

HYPERACTIVITY

Hyperactivity, or excess energy, can manifest as excessive physical and/or verbal activity. The energy and fretfulness that show up with ADHD might be an excessive amount to bear now and again until it at long last spills over into furious words or actual responses.

UNDERSTANDING THE LEVELS OF EMOTIONAL RAGE

To deal with emotional rage, you need to understand how it builds up and is expressed. In other words, you don't just express emotional rage; there's a process to it. To understand this process is to know how it works and, thus, curb it before it overwhelms you.

Parvez (2022) highlighted stages of emotional rage. Let me walk you through those stages:

THE TRIGGER

There is always a cause of anger, whether internal or external. Life events, negative comments from others, and other things can act as external triggers. Anger can be sparked internally by thoughts and emotions.

When a primary emotion like anxiety is triggered, anger can arise as a secondary emotion as a reaction to your anxiety.

But basically, any information that makes you feel threatened is a trigger for anger. You can still reevaluate the situation at this stage since you're not yet completely engulfed in anger.

THE BUILD UP

A step further from the trigger will bring you to the point where your mind begins to tell you a story about why your anger is justified. This story could be about something that happened recently. This begins to stir fury in you.

At this stage, you can still curb the emotions rising within. You can still shift gears and check to see if the story is true at this point. The rage you're already feeling within will continue to build up if you believe your anger story is legitimate.

GETTING READY TO ACT

Your body begins to prepare you for action once your anger reaches a certain point.

At this point, you'll notice that:

✓ Your body tightens up to get ready for action.

✓ Your pupils dilate to get a better look at your foe.

✓ Your nostrils flare to let in more air.

✓ Your breathing rate rises to get more oxygen.

✓ Your heart rate rises to get more oxygen and energy.

Your body is ready to act. At this point, it will be hard to reconsider the situation and let go of your anger. However, with enough mental effort, it is still doable.

THE INTENSE URGE TO ACT

The next step is for your body to push you to take action now that it has prepared you for it. The feeling of this "push" is an urge to act, scream, punch, etc.

THE ACT

It's hard to resist an impulse. The accumulated energy wants to be released quickly.

When you're just mildly irritated, you can fix your anger with little effort if the leak isn't that bad. However, repairing a pipe that leaks like a firehose requires more effort. A firehose that is difficult to close is opened when you act on your anger. You say and do mean things out of hostility in minutes.

Your fight-or-flight survival instinct is in charge at this point. You are unable to reason.

THE RELIEF

Once you explode and release the energy you've accumulated in a short time, how do you feel next? Relieved. It looks like you've just taken off a heavy load. This relief is transient, though.

THE RECOVERY

During the recovery phase, your anger has completely subsided, and you begin to calm down. It's like you've been restored to normalcy, and your senses are back after a temporary moment of madness has passed.

What usually follows afterward are feelings of guilt, shame, regret, or even depression.

I can also tell that at this phase, it looks like we were being possessed by a force higher than us that just used us for its destructive deed and left us to sulk. At least we're able to think straight again.

THE REPAIR

At this final stage, you might want to consider apologizing for your destructive attitude. But it's not always the case with most teens with ADHD. They might feel sober temporarily and try to act differently. Most times, expressing how sorry they are is difficult. They usually feel too ashamed to utter the word.

However, this is the point of repentance, at least until the next trigger comes.

How right is Parvez with his analogy? So, right!

But if this is the case, how do we control it?

HOW TO CONTROL EMOTIONAL RAGE WITH DBT

Do you remember that I spoke extensively about DBT—Dialectical Behavior Therapy—in the first chapter of this book?

Now let's see its application to treating an intense emotion like anger.

When Ciesinski et al. (2022) conducted research on the efficacy of DBT to treat anger and aggressive behavior, they found that DBT significantly reduced anger, though it required longer treatment to get this result. They also discovered that DBT effectively reduced dysregulated anger across different mental disorders.

With this finding, we can go on to apply DBT to treating anger. However, we can't use all the skills you've learned at once. Of the three, let's pick just one.

Which one did you choose? Okay, I'll use emotional regulation here; yay! But if that's not what you picked, it's OK; you can still go on to apply the skill you chose to control emotional rage.

OK, so, let's say you've responded to the trigger, and you're beginning to sense something strong stirring up within you, just before you act on it,

STOP!

Yes! You read that correctly; simply freeze! Let me ask you, who's in charge of you? You or your feelings? Can you see the sign on the road? You're about to rush into another vehicle (or person) at an intersection. If you don't halt immediately, the impact will be disastrous. Do you want that? I doubt it.

So, stop!

Muster all the strength within you to step on the brake pedals immediately. Stop!

Yea, that's right. You just saved yourself from another disastrous event. The last anger you vented that caused a lot of havoc should be your last. Just bring yourself to a halt.

Wondering if it's that easy? Have you tried it? It'll be easier if you do this next thing.

AFFIRMATIVE SELF-TALK

Talk yourself persistently into stopping until you stop. Don't say, "I can't get angry," say, "I don't get angry."

In my observation, if you want this self-talk to be effective, don't think it in your head; say it out loud with your mouth. This is how it works. Your mind is already fired up to act negatively. It's getting ready to throw a hard punch. When you speak loudly with your mouth to counter the signal your mind is about to send into your hand, it freezes it for a moment. When you persist, a counteraction is likely to take place.

So don't just think it; say it. Tell yourself, "No! I don't act brashly." "No! I don't obey my impulses."

Self-talk will also enable you to reframe the situation. You could pause and consider the reasons for your behavior rather than succumbing to anger. Irritation can be turned into curiosity and compassion. That's reframing.

A potent strategy for turning around negative emotions is reframing. Situations have many sides to them. We neutralize an emotional overreaction and instead connect with others by pausing and refocusing instead of acting on our initial emotion.

NOW TAKE A STEP BACK

By now, you should be calm. Now, you can step back from the whole situation and reevaluate what triggered your initial rage.

This can be done mentally or physically by taking a step back. You can use this to free yourself from the strong urge to react.

Take note of your breathing once you've stepped back. You might be breathing slowly or holding your breath. Make an effort to take a few deep, slow breaths.

Give yourself some time to sort through things. Remember that while your feelings may be strong, you are ultimately responsible for your actions.

OBSERVE WHAT'S GOING ON AROUND YOU

Take stock of the things you're going through. What might an outsider say about the situation? Try to notice what's going on without being critical.

Additionally, pay attention to your own mind and body. Are you experiencing muscle tension? Where? Are you weeping profusely on your face? How do they feel when you touch them? Do you clench your jaw? Are you having second thoughts? Which ideas are coming to mind? Is it just one or two of the same? Which is more relevant, the past or the present? Explore your inner and outer experiences with curiosity.

PROCEED MINDFULLY

You've eased some emotion by completing this DBT STOP skill step. Try to think of a wise answer by considering what you would like to happen in the current situation. Which outcome would be in line with your values, wants, and needs? Which outcome will give you the most satisfaction tomorrow or next week? Make an effort to proceed in accordance with these factors.

CHOOSE AN OPPOSITE ACTION

Practicing this technique now is easier because you won't have to apply it when the emotion is still intense.

Now you can easily transform unpleasant emotions into pleasant ones. You can choose a different line of action. The idea behind the opposite action is that taking a positive rather than a negative action can help you deal with negative emotions. By doing this, you avoid doing something harmful and counteract the suffering you might otherwise experience due to the distressing emotion.

In this instance, you're enraged, and there are numerous means by which you could have expressed your anger. But if the action you take is the opposite of how you feel, like walking away from that angry situation or doing something nice to distract yourself, you will have invested your energy in something that will eventually make you feel better. You not only reversed your behavior by walking away rather than yelling at someone, but you also started to change how you felt angry. Instead of escalating or intensifying your feelings, you did something that made them less intense by substituting something positive for them.

It's essential to understand that practicing this skill does not entail controlling your emotions. You are taking a different course of action by making use of your anger. This will cause your feelings to shift over time.

Wow! It's been a tremendous adventure with you up until this point. We've covered two parts of this book already. Can you take stock now? What have you learned so far?

Did you remember what you documented on that plain sheet of paper at the beginning of this adventure? Can you check it again to confirm if you're still on point?

In this chapter, I tried to strip off anger to show you the likely things that cause anger and how anger builds up. There's a point in the build-up of anger where you still have control over it. You'll lose the rein when it exceeds that point. I also showed you how emotional regulation skills can be adopted to control an aggressive emotional outburst. In other words, DBT skills are capable of helping you manage emotional rage. You can respond to things.

> What triggers anger in you?

> Which DBT skills do you think can work best for you to manage anger?

CHAPTER 7: INTERPERSONAL EFFECTIVENESS SKILLS: A REALISTIC WAY TO IMPROVE YOUR RELATIONSHIPS

> 66 The key to healthy communication is having a willingness to lay aside our defensive tendencies and accept responsibility for our part of the relationship 99

— *Asa Don Brown*

Are you ready to learn the fourth DBT skill?

Just to clarify, these DBT skills are not independent of one another. You could use two different skills for one issue. This depends on:

1. How well you've practiced and mastered the skills

2. The situation at hand is also a factor.

In the previous chapter, I used only STOP as an example to resolve an anger issue. There could be moments when you'll have to mix it with another skill. The goal isn't to see what skill you used. It's about which one you find most useful for you. The overall goal is your emotional well-being.

Now, about interpersonal effectiveness, let me introduce you to Stet from the 2014 Hollywood preteen movie, *Boychoir*. Stet is one of the lead characters in this movie. He was raised by a single mother who numbs her pain with drugs. And his father hasn't contacted him for 12 years. Stet isn't a privileged young boy. Well, maybe he has every right to be angry at everyone and everything.

Stet is known for his unruly behavior in school. Everywhere he goes, at least one kid irritates him to the point of rage. He doesn't respect teachers. He's always being grounded for one offense or another. This implies that it's hard for Stet to have friends.

Despite his gifted voice and ear for music, Stet will have been a waste, except for his principal, who is ready to overlook his misconduct and give him a chance to harness his gifts.

Dear young reader, relationships are essential to whatever you'll become during your time on Earth. Stet has someone who believes in him. You might think you don't, but there are people who do if you look well. Well, I'm one of those people. And I believe in what you can become. However, when you burn the bridges connecting you with those people, it'll be difficult for them to help you.

Those burned bridges are what the interpersonal effectiveness skill is designed to help you fix and rebuild.

INTRODUCTION TO INTERPERSONAL EFFECTIVENESS SKILLS

Which skill do you consider most valuable?

In the world we live in today, you need to have skills for virtually everything. If you don't have it, you acquire it, or else you'll lose relevance. Our skill set can be expanded, enhanced, and improved in many ways. To improve our lives by developing a specific skill or set of skills, there are thousands of courses, millions of books and articles, and countless tips and suggestions.

But which of those skills is the most significant?

That question may not have a definitive answer, but I believe one of the most common responses would be interpersonal or communication skills.

Do you know how many people you've met in your time on this planet? Countless, I bet. And you'll still meet more people. Without doubt, you'll come into contact with thousands, if not tens of thousands, of people during your lifetime. But you can't impress everyone you meet—that's not possible anyway—and you need to get along with the people around you well enough to survive.

I'm certain about what you just read above. I'm more certain that getting along with other people is a fact that applies to teens with ADHD as well. I know this could be difficult. However, it's not impossible. I'm here to make it possible for you.

WHAT MORE DO YOU NEED TO KNOW ABOUT INTERPERSONAL EFFECTIVENESS SKILLS?

Interpersonal effectiveness is a set of DBT skills that help you establish and maintain healthy relationships with yourself and others. Simply put, it means the capacity to interact with other people.

Mairanz (2019) also added that learning to balance demands and priorities—the things you want and need in your life—is central to the interpersonal effectiveness model in DBT. These skills can be used to navigate relationships with other people and figure out how to get what you need.

Vivyan (2015) suggested four basic things this skill will help you achieve:

✓ It'll empower you to take care of your relationships.

✓ You'll be able to find a balance between what you want and what others want.

✓ You'll be able to find a balance between your "shoulds" and "wants."

✓ You'll develop mastery and respect for yourself.

This is getting more interesting, isn't it?

Overall, the interpersonal effectiveness skills are aimed at three things. This should be your guiding star as you learn and practice these skills. *DBT Self-Help* neatly groups these goals:

✓ Objective Effectiveness – achieve something you want

✓ Relationship Effectiveness – improve or maintain a relationship

✓ Self-Respect Effectiveness – maintain self-respect

A SHORT EXERCISE:

Here's a little exercise I want you to try. Can you try to reflect on your most recent interactions? These are the things you'll consider during your reflection:

✓ How often did I meet all three goals?

✓ Is there any aspect of this framework that I find difficult?

Try to give it some thought and pinpoint the source of the discomfort. Do you have no idea what you want? Do you know how to talk to people in the right way? Are you uncomfortable asking for things?

The purpose of this exercise isn't to judge you. That is not consistent with the ethics of DBT skills. It's not about answering these questions correctly. However, to work toward moving forward, it's essential to investigate the source of our unease.

WHY'S THIS SO IMPORTANT?

You might be curious to know why interpersonal effectiveness warrants this much attention. Well, I've already started talking about the importance of communication earlier. Dr. Linehan (cited by Ackerman, 2017) also believed that these skills were crucial because how we communicate with others significantly impacts the quality of our relationships and the outcomes of those relationships.

In essence, your well-being, self-esteem, confidence, and understanding of who you are become significantly influenced by the quality of your relationships and interactions.

Whew! That is a significant impact that effective communication has on your life.

OK, SO WHAT ARE THE INTERPERSONAL EFFECTIVENESS SKILLS?

These skills are easy to remember with their acronyms:

- ✓ THINK
- ✓ FAST
- ✓ GIVE
- ✓ DEAR MAN

THINK

This skill is sort of new in the interpersonal effectiveness skill set. Here's what it means and how it's used:

T – Think

Consider the situation from the other person's point of view. Are they also enraged? Are they judging you as unreasonable in the same way that you judge them?

H – Have empathy

Think about what it's like to be someone else. Give yourself a moment to feel their emotions.

I – Interpretations

Consider the potential causes of their irrational behavior. To get your mind thinking, start with crazy reasons and work your way up to more plausible ones.

N – Notice

Take note of the other party. Pay attention when they try to be nicer and make the relationship better. You might think otherwise but notice how scared they look. You don't have to do anything right now. Just pay attention.

K – Kind

In your response, be kind. This does not necessitate immediate forgiveness and forgetting. You might say, "I hope we can fix this in the future, and what you said hurts." That's kinder than yelling and calling people names.

FAST

FAST assists you in maintaining self-respect during disagreements or discussions. The acronym consists of four skills that teach you how to behave in an argument to achieve your goal at the highest possible level without compromising your own values.

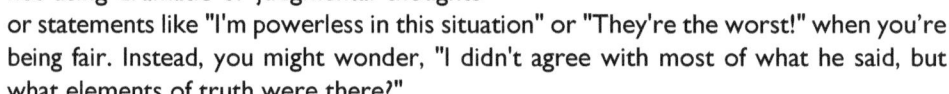

F – be Fair

Be fair to others and yourself. Ensure you're not using dramatic or judgmental thoughts or statements like "I'm powerless in this situation" or "They're the worst!" when you're being fair. Instead, you might wonder, "I didn't agree with most of what he said, but what elements of truth were there?"

A – no Apologies

This doesn't imply that you'll never apologize. Apologizing is really effective in relationships. However, you owe no one an apology if you've done nothing wrong. You shouldn't be sorry for being alive or making a request. You shouldn't apologize for disagreeing or having an opinion, either.

S - Stick to values

Your values are one of your greatest assets, don't sell them out. Don't ever do it for whatever reason. Stick to your guns and be crystal clear about what you consider the moral or valued way of thinking and acting.

T – be Truthful

Never lie. It doesn't suit you. When you are in control, don't act helpless. Do not exaggerate or invent justifications.

THINK AND FAST are two important skills that can help you handle relationship conflicts.

GIVE

GIVE is especially crucial for effective communication to build and keep relationships healthy.

G – be Gentle

Be polite and considerate in your approach. Threats, manipulation, and verbal or physical attacks should be avoided. Avoid all forms of harassment. Avoid making threats with your words. Gentleness demonstrates an awareness of the other person's feelings. The person you're communicating with will be able to feel loved rather than attacked due to this. When no one is defensive, communication is always better.

I – act Interested

Listen to the other person. Pay attention to their viewpoint. Turn to the person, keep eye contact, and instead of leaning away, lean toward them. By maintaining eye contact, actually listening to what is being said, and making a facial expression, you can use body language to show interest.

V – Validate

Show that you comprehend the other person's perspective on the situation. See things from their perspective and say or do what you see. This is like being empathic. You could say, "I know how hard this is for you, and I also see you are busy."

E – Easy manner

Wear a smile. Introduce some light humor. Sweet-talk. Don't bring your attitude with you. Throughout the conversation, project an air of ease and relaxation. You'll be easier to talk to.

DEAR MAN

The DEARMAN skill aims to help us develop healthy relationships with other people and meet our needs through effective interpersonal communication. It's used to effectively and respectfully ask for something that builds and maintains a relationship, regardless of whether you actually get what you ask for.

D – Describe

Describe the situation in a straightforward way. Follow the facts. Describe your exact reaction to the other person.

E – Express

Express your thoughts and feelings regarding the situation. Don't assume the other person understands your feelings.

A – Assert yourself

Clearly and politely ask for what you want or say no to make yourself heard. If you don't ask, don't assume other people will do what you want. Verify that you're assertive without being passive or aggressive.

R – Reinforce

It's more effective to politely tell the other person the importance of what you're requesting and what you might lose if you don't get what you're asking for. This is better than forcing a request. Do you think the other person will gain anything from that, too? Let them know.

M – stay Mindful

Stay focused on your goal, and don't get distracted. Don't be defensive or hostile if the other person starts to do so. Neglect attacks. Ignore the threats, comments, or attempts to divert the conversation if the other person attacks, threatens, or attempts to change the subject. You could practice mindfulness to deal with any overwhelming feelings that may arise.

A – Appear confident

Look competent, confident, and effective. Use your body language and voice to convey confidence. Maintain good eye contact. No muttering, whispering, glancing at the ground or retreating. Don't expect anyone to take your request seriously if you don't take yourself seriously.

N – Negotiate

Recognize that others have limitations of their own. Hence, don't be imposing. Be willing to make some concessions if the need arises. Be reasonable and considerate with your request. You could ask, "What do you think we should do?" or "How can this work?"

You could also make an offer and request additional solutions to the issue. However, be realistic.

10 WAYS TO IMPROVE INTERPERSONAL SKILLS

Consider this a plus in this book. Do you know why? Beyond treating ADHD, this skill will position you for great opportunities in your career. This implies that the earlier you start practicing these skills, the better.

Just like every other soft skill, interpersonal skills can be learned. Sounds great, right?

Here are 10 proven ways you can improve your interpersonal skills:

1. BE A GOOD LISTENER AND A BAD INTERRUPTER

You're accustomed to expressing your opinions, aren't you? The first step in building healthy relationships through this skill is to be a good listener. Give people space and listen to what they have to say. Listening attentively indicates you value what the other person is saying.

It'll also help you understand the message better. Your response will be more precise than when you speak without listening.

Refrain from interrupting people's train of thought or cutting in when they're trying to make their points. Some people are turned off when they're interrupted.

2. BE A GOOD PROCESSOR

As you listen to what the other person is saying and observe the communication trend, patiently process all you hear to give a reasonable and positive response.

3. ACCEPT THE OTHER PERSON

Accept others for who they are because not everyone is like you. You will gain a valuable perspective that will help you deal with them. Don't be judgmental of the other person before or during the conversation. Treat the other person with kindness. It'll create a positive environment for the other person to express their thoughts freely.

4. RESPECT THEIR VIEWS

Respect for oneself is crucial. Respect for other people is crucial in conversations, however. Don't stop at accepting them; respect their views as well. Remember that, even if you disagree with what they're saying, the other person has the right to their own opinion. Wait until they finish speaking before expressing your thoughts on the subject in a non-confrontational manner. Don't pounce on them immediately because they don't share your view. Disagree softly. You could further make them see things from your perspective, but not by yelling.

5. POSITIVE BODY LANGUAGE

Body language is using your voice tone, gestures, gaze, and various postures to convey your intended idea to the person you are communicating with. Ensure your body language doesn't send the wrong signals to the other person.

6. PUT AWAY DISTRACTORS

Do you want to have good communication? Then put away anything that could distract you during the conversation, especially when the other person is talking. You can't tell me you're listening to me when your fingers are dancing on your smartphone's keypad.

Phones are major distractors during conversations today. Teens and young adults are actually fond of this habit. There's always something to check on the phone. But do you know what? Even if you feel compelled to use your phone, resist the urge. Your phone will still be there after the conversation. The other person won't feel valued when you're pressing your phone during a conversation.

7. BE CLEAR

You can't just give your listeners only half-baked information and leave them hanging. Always ensure that you provide all the available information, even if there are still details to follow. It goes without saying that using words that are easy to understand is important to avoid confusion.

8. BE STRAIGHTFORWARD

Be direct and straightforward whenever there is a concern or issue so that people will understand what you want and what needs to be done. It will be difficult for others to take you seriously if you avoid the conversation or postpone making your point.

9. CHOOSE A GOOD PACE

You don't have to speak too quickly or too slowly to get your point across effectively. Know when to deliberately slow down, when to pause for emphasis, and when to speed up. The listening experience of your audience can be impacted by speed. You need to ensure that you are speaking at the appropriate pace if you want your listener to comprehend your message effectively.

10. MAINTAIN EYE CONTACT

Although it can be challenging, truly looking someone in the eye is a necessary part of having meaningful conversations. The person you speak with feels validated and understood when you maintain eye contact.

This nonverbal cue also informs the other person that you're paying attention to what they're saying. Don't even try looking at the floor or outside the window. It indicates you're not interested in what the other person is saying.

SEVEN SELF-EVALUATION PHRASES FOR INTERPERSONAL EFFECTIVENESS SKILLS

Let's take a quick assessment of your current level of interpersonal skills now that you've learned how to improve them. The result will let you know which areas to focus on while improving this skill.

I'll list seven areas here. Rate yourself on a scale of 1 to 10.

- ✓ Shows the ability to actively listen to other people's conversations without interrupting them.
- ✓ Communicates clearly and concisely, making it simple for others to comprehend what is being communicated.
- ✓ Disagrees with grace and respect when the other person doesn't share my view.
- ✓ Communicate with a positive attitude always.

✓ Assertive and demonstrates self-respect and comprehensible communication

✓ Have an awkward sense of humor and am always pissing others off.

✓ Difficult to approach me or begin a conversation with me.

What's your current state?

There's always room for improvement. Don't stop practicing.

GAMES & ACTIVITIES FOR GROUPS TO DEVELOP EFFECTIVE INTERPERSONAL SKILLS

Let's try to introduce some fun activities to spice up these practices. You can play these games to develop and improve your interpersonal skills. Of course, you can't play these games alone. You need a partner or more. Your partner or co-player could be from your family, a peer, or a neighbor.

Try this,

 ### CAN YOU HEAR ME NOW?

"Can you hear me now?" is one of the simplest games involving virtual communication. Participants need paper and pens to play the game. Each round, one player describes an object for the other players to draw one line or shape at a time, for instance, a cat, a stoplight, the sun, or a tree. The game requires the players to attempt to guess the object before the drawing is finished.

The game demonstrates how simple statements can have unexpected interpretations and stresses the significance of clear instructions. Additionally, it's entertaining to observe the finished drawings.

 ### YES?

"Yes?" is one of the communication games with the most energy. The activity's most crucial form of communication is eye contact. Form a circle. Then the participant whose turn it is looks across the circle at a teammate and inquires, "Yes?" which the teammate states is "Yes." The players then switch positions. Players can create new chains as the game progresses, allowing multiple players to speak or move simultaneously. The more active the chains, the more difficult it is for players to focus and respond. In a busy environment, this game teaches players to remain alert and multitask.

3.

BLINDFOLD STROLL

To play this game, here is what you need to do:

- ✓ Set up an obstacle course with one player blindfolded.
- ✓ Have other players shout instructions to the blindfolded player as they move through the course.

You can time course completion or introduce penalties and traps to make the game more fun and exciting. Regardless of how you play it, this activity emphasizes the importance of giving precise instructions and gives teammates a chance to practice giving each other directions.

4.

ANOTHER WAY TO SAY

The game, Another Way to Say, requires players to come up with alternative phrases and synonyms. The round begins with a single player saying a phrase. The other players come up with similar sayings until they run out of options.

The exercise can be a last-man-standing competition in which the player with the most contributions wins the round, or it can be a collaborative effort to generate phrases. The game's goal is to demonstrate how many different ways a thought can be expressed.

Players are encouraged to try to develop new phrases and use descriptive language, but the group can also challenge creative responses.

There are many other games you can play to practice your interpersonal skills. You can look them up on the internet.

SOME WAYS TO IMPROVE YOUR INTERPERSONAL EFFECTIVENESS AT SCHOOL AND HOME

This aspect of learning isn't restricted to teens with ADHD alone. I recommend that teachers and parents encourage these skills in their teens. Hence, while your teenage child or student is learning this, be around to encourage them.

GOOD COMMUNICATION BEGINS AT HOME

Most teens spend most of their early years of development at home with their family. Hence, any habit or culture they grow up with starts at home.

As ADHD teens learn to improve their communication skills, they need to practice with those they spend time with the most—family. Therefore, parents must encourage their teens to build confidence and support healthy communication.

PRACTICE FRIENDLINESS

Being friendly to other people is another way to improve your ability to interact with other people. Smiling and saying "hi" to everyone you see is all it takes to accomplish this. Parents and teachers should learn how to engage teens who struggle with ADHD. Basically, they should ask them how they spent their day.

Learn to engage in eye contact with everyone you meet throughout the day. Always smile. Don't fake the smile. It could seem weird and maybe difficult but keep practicing.

BUILD POSITIVE SELF-TALKS

Instead of telling yourself that no one wants to talk to you because you used to yell at people, try to replace it with positive self-talk. No one will know you've started working on becoming a better communicator until you try engaging people.

Push yourself to step out through a series of positive self-talks:

- ✓ I'm a good listener
- ✓ I don't yell at people
- ✓ I'm calm
- ✓ I'm a good friend
- ✓ I'm at ease around others
- ✓ I'm a team player

You could try this and many more to get yourself going and never relent.

This chapter introduced you to another crucial DBT skill. And like every other skill you've learned so far in this book, interpersonal skills require lots of practice. You must be consistent to get the required result. This chapter emphasized the importance of communication in having good relationships. If you're poor at communicating, you'll lose many friends and have no one to help you when you need them.

This chapter also offered hope for restoring and rebuilding bridges in relationships through practicable skills.

Just before you think you can't do it, step out first. I believe you can do this. Don't relent after a few difficult attempts. Push past that level. You're doing just fine.

Which relationship will you like to restore?

What will you do differently now that you know about this skill?

CHAPTER 8: THE PATH TO POSITIVE EMOTIONS AND IMPROVING YOUR MOOD

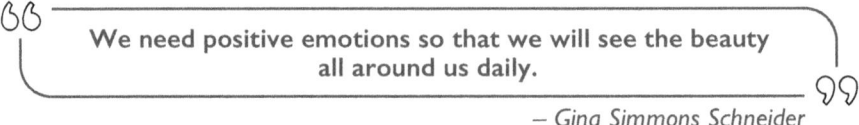

> We need positive emotions so that we will see the beauty all around us daily.

— Gina Simmons Schneider

Hannah had been anxious all her life; at 13, it became too much to contain. She was certain that her friends no longer liked her, and she was terrified of failing in school. She constantly fought with her mother and lashed out at her friends. She would scream and cry at the smallest things. Out of concern, Jill, her mother, finally took steps to help Hannah.

Finally, Hannah learned how to control her emotions and develop a sense of self-assurance and positivity due to her participation in dialectical behavioral therapy. She asserted that she was a hundred percent happier. She became a better student, friend, daughter, sister—everything.

In this book's final part, I'll show you the power that lies in building positive emotions. In the opening part of this chapter, Hannah turns out to be a better human by exuding positive emotions.

Just so you know, emotions let out a powerful, invisible scent. It could alter the state of an environment. It's difficult for anyone to laugh where people gather to mourn. It's difficult for anyone to make a joke when someone is letting out intense rage.

As our journey together in this book winds down, I want to give you something like a prelude to my final words.

Dear young friend, emotions are powerful—positive or negative—and could alter your destiny. According to psychologist and expert on emotional wellness at the University of North Carolina, Chapel Hill, Dr. Barbara L. Fredrickson (cited by the NIH, 2015), having a positive outlook doesn't mean you'll never experience negative emotions like sadness or anger.

In the right circumstances, any emotion, positive or negative, can change. It would appear that striking a balance between the two is the key. Fredrickson explains that while positive emotions expand our awareness and expose us to novel concepts, allowing us to develop and enhance our survival arsenal, negative emotions are necessary for people to cope with difficult circumstances and act appropriately in the short term. However, negative emotions that are unrelated to what is actually taking place in the moment and are based on excessive pondering about the past or worrying about the future can lead to problems.

Wouldn't it be wise to settle for positive emotions? To create a life worth living, increasing positive emotions is essential.

THE POWER OF POSITIVE EMOTIONS

Have you ever been told that all you have to do to make things work out is "stay positive"? Having optimism is a wonderful quality, but it takes more than just hoping for the best to cultivate it. Like I've been emphasizing from the beginning of this adventure, it will require an ongoing routine of practices to cultivate positive emotions throughout your life.

You wouldn't hit the gym for a few days to quit when you've not built enough muscle, would you?

Positive feelings are more than just "a nice feeling." Positive emotions have been shown by science to have a hidden value that directly affects (and improves) your day-to-day well-being.

In an interview with *BeWell*, Barbara Fredrickson said that positive emotions are like nutrients. In more ways than ever, science is demonstrating that, despite the fact that moments of happiness, gratitude, or serenity may appear fleeting and insignificant, they have a significant impact on the way our brains function. According to Fredrickson, such fleeting moments can have the following effects on us:

- ✓ Allow our mindsets to become more expansive and adaptable.

- ✓ Our resilience and resourcefulness become heightened.

That's what Fredrickson said gave birth to the broaden-and-build theory of positive emotions.

Isn't it amazing how small moments of joy add up to help us become better versions of ourselves?

TeensHealth specifically noted that positive emotions influence our brains in ways that improve our awareness, attention, and memory. They assist us in taking in more information, remembering multiple concepts at once, and comprehending how concepts relate to one another.

We can learn and improve our skills better when we experience positive emotions that open our minds to new possibilities. As a result, you'll do better on tests and tasks.

Positive emotions make you happier, healthier, and more able to learn and get along with others. That's just how Hannah felt.

DBT ENHANCES POSITIVE EMOTIONS

The essence of this book is to emphasize how you can build positive emotions using DBT skills. Hannah in our opening story and other examples in previous chapters, especially those with ADHD, could translate negativity into positivity using DBT. Don't forget this.

You could achieve positive emotions through different means; however, DBT skills are one of the few proven ways you could apply and practice to achieve such a level of positivity.

I must remind you why DBT is effective in this regard:

✓ DBT teaches you how to deal with negative feelings and encourages you to keep positive ones in your collection. That's part of what you learned on emotional regulation skills, right?

✓ It teaches you how to control your emotions instead of letting them control you.

✓ DBT makes you less likely to experience negative emotions and helps you to build more positive emotional experiences.

✓ DBT teaches that having a bank of positive emotions can assist you in preventing the outburst or persistence of negative emotions.

✓ Most importantly, DBT doesn't deny the existence of negative emotions. Increasing your positive emotions doesn't negate your negative feelings. It's a way to broaden your horizons and offer other options during trying times.

STILL STRUGGLING WITH SYMPTOMS OF ADHD AS A TEEN?

Let me emphasize to you again. You might have had it rough and difficult trying to cope with those outbursts of anger. You might struggle to build healthy relationships with others, especially your family, but don't quit trying.

A neurodevelopmental disorder like ADHD can be corrected through the consistent practice of behavioral reordering skills like DBT.

To quit trying is to allow negativism to overwhelm you. It's a positive attitude that will make you keep on practicing the skills you've been exposed to in this book.

WHAT ARE POSITIVE AND NEGATIVE EMOTIONS?

Fredrickson already stated the place of positive and negative emotions and their presence in some situations we face.

Let's say you begin making a list of all the feelings you've ever felt. Try it right now, just for fun.

What did you come up with? I bet such expressions like happy, sad, excited, ashamed, angry, depressed, fearful, grateful, proud, scared, confused, stressed, relaxed, etc., would come up naturally.

You will notice that these emotions are not one-sided. A careful observation will reveal that there are emotions that are positive and others that are negative.

Now, being human necessitates the ability to experience both positive and negative emotions. Although we may use the term "negative" to describe more difficult feelings, this doesn't imply that they are undesirable or that we shouldn't experience them.

However, most people would probably rather experience a positive emotion than a negative one. You'd probably prefer to be happy rather than sad or confident rather than insecure.

TeensHealth said that the amount of each type of emotion, whether positive or negative, that we experience is what matters. This is how our emotions are balanced.

DOES THAT MEAN WE NEED BOTH?

If you took a look at every negative emotion you've ever felt, do you ever wish to experience any of those feelings? You probably don't—just what I thought—because no one ever wishes for such feelings. There's literally nothing good about having any of those negative feelings.

How about the positive emotions? Of course! Everyone wants always to have a pleasant and loving feeling. No one ever thinks to themselves and says, "Oh, I wish I wasn't experiencing this emotion."

You don't need negative emotions to thrive, grow, and/or be effective in different contexts of function. But Fredrickson said negative feelings—at least moderately—also have their place.

What! What would you do with negative emotions?

NEGATIVE EMOTIONS?

Yeah, Ackerman (2019) stated that positive psychology isn't all about positive emotions alone. According to Ackerman, we must experience negative emotions to live a full and rewarding life. They're an inevitable part of life.

Perhaps if you pay a little more attention to the effects of negative feelings, you'll realize their purpose. For instance, usually, preparation is compelled by stress. You can protect yourself by being angry. You can accept an apology and make amends with guilt. Those are subtle ways negative emotions could serve a good purpose.

There are other ways negative emotions could be purposeful in your life:

✓ They alert us to potential dangers or difficulties that we need to face. Fear, for instance, can make us aware of potential danger. It suggests that we might need to safeguard ourselves.

✓ We can tell when someone is behaving inappropriately, crossing a line, or betraying our trust by feeling angry. Anger can indicate that we may need to take action on our own.

326

✓ They assist us in narrowing down an issue so we can address it.

✓ Anxiety could help us to prepare and plan for what's to come.

✓ Disgust could make us reject what we feel isn't healthy for us.

However, just like Fredrickson stated, experiencing excessive negative emotions can lead to feelings of overwhelm, anxiety, exhaustion, and stress. Problems might appear to be too big to handle when negative emotions are out of balance.

The more we dwell on negative emotions, the more negative we become. Concentrating on the negative only makes it worse.

HOW ABOUT POSITIVE EMOTIONS?

I've shared some basic things about positive emotions with you in the previous session and some previous chapters. However, you need to know that the field of positive psychology believes that learning how to adapt to negative emotions and effectively deal with them is just as important as learning how to boost our positive emotions and take advantage of the opportunities they present.

Ackerman (2019) also stated that we give ourselves the best chance of living a balanced and meaningful life when we can accept, embrace, and take advantage of both our positive and negative emotions. Because of this, the discipline of positive psychology is wary of emphasizing positive feelings too much; it's just as essential to comprehend how to transform negative feelings into positive experiences as it is to take advantage of our positive feelings.

So, the question again is, "Do you need both?" Yes! However, don't dwell excessively on the negatives. It could be harmful.

Here's how I believe you can balance the two emotions:

✓ Build your positive emotions to outweigh the negative ones.

✓ Every day, try to be positive.

Did you grasp that?

BENEFITS OF POSITIVE EMOTIONS

The "broaden-and-build" theory of positive emotions helps you understand how having positive emotions is essential for thriving in daily life and fostering mental wellness. Emotions of positivity assist you in expanding your experience and perspective. They can also develop crucial relationships and skills essential to maximizing performance.

Further studies show that positive emotions shape our lives. Rather than being limited to a single aspect of life, these effects pervade every nook and cranny of the human experience. They help with personal growth and fulfillment as well as improve relationships in the workplace, classrooms, and with families.

Gordon (n.d.) stated that a positive attitude is more than just a nice way to live. It's the right way to live.

Here are other benefits of positive emotions:

GREATER RESILIENCE

A study found that emotional regulation, which helps people recover from stressful situations and find meaning in them, was significantly impacted by increased resilience. Higher rates of empathy, cooperation, assertiveness, and self-control were found in students who participated in a program aimed at boosting resilience in schoolchildren.

Positive emotions can also help people learn how to deal with difficult situations.

Overall, you can remain more resilient in the face of challenges if you find ways to experience a little positive emotion each day. To effectively deal with adversity, it's helpful to consume a healthy diet rich in positive emotions to reduce stress.

IMPROVED OUTCOMES RELATED TO PERFORMANCE

You can become more creative when you feel positive emotions. Positive emotions can encourage you to think more creatively about solving a problem if you've been stuck trying to solve it for a long time. Positive emotions also make you more receptive to new concepts, challenges, and opportunities. Throughout the process of learning something new or mastering a new skill, you frequently experience these feelings.

Positive emotions can lead to improvements in academics, physical and mental health, social relationships, community involvement, and more. That's what gives you a life worth living.

MAKE NEW CONNECTIONS

Have you ever entered a room where everyone was having a good time laughing, and you couldn't help but join in, even though you didn't know what the other people were laughing about? Positive feelings spread like wildfire. They promote social interaction. Positive emotions not only make you more receptive to other people, but they also help other people become more receptive to you.

AID IN YOUR RELAXATION AND RESET

Do you remember the last time you were really angry? What happened? Did you remember that your heart rate accelerated, you felt agitated, or maybe you sweated? The benefit of positive emotion in that context is that, after experiencing the physical effects of negative emotions, positive emotions can assist you in quicker body recovery. Emotional well-being is essential for reviving and maintaining energy.

In addition, you must know that positive emotions don't grow out of the blues. For instance, in the academic context, positive emotions are facilitated by levels of self-motivation and contentment with learning materials. According to some studies, this indicates positive emotions facilitate learning and contribute to academic achievement.

NEGATIVITY BIAS

Now, if I ask you, "Would you always like to have positive emotions?" I know you won't say no. But I've found out that, although many people, especially teens with neurodevelopmental disorders, wish to always express positive emotions, they find it difficult to do so. The question then is, "Why?"

Why is it difficult to build or express positive emotions regularly?

It's because of something called "negative bias."

OK. SO WHAT DOES THAT MEAN?

Frothingham (2019) stated that negative bias tends to work this way, focusing on negative experiences and considering them to be more important to us—humans—than positive or neutral experiences. Even when those negative experiences are insignificant or unimportant, we frequently focus on them.

Consider the following scenario: you are on vacation with your family and have decided to stay in a nice hotel. Then, at night, you saw a large spider in the sink when you entered the bathroom. Which do you believe will be remembered more clearly: the room's beautiful decor and fine furnishings or the spider you encountered?

The spider experience will linger longer.

According to *Human Performance Resources,* you can successfully navigate a dangerous world because the human brain has evolved to recognize threats and obstacles. Warfighters, their families, and teammates all benefit from this ability by keeping an eye out for danger. However, it can also lead to a negative outlook on life.

We don't know how or when this happened, but it appears that our brain is programmed to prioritize, seek out, and latch onto negative information. This hardwired tendency is what is known as "negativity bias." Negative experiences are more likely to be absorbed by your brain than positive ones.

SHOULDN'T WE JUST QUIT TRYING TO BUILD POSITIVITY SINCE WE'VE BEEN WIRED TO LATCH ONTO NEGATIVES?

No! I don't think so.

Our brains can be reprogrammed to embrace positivity. We can overwrite that negative coding in our brains.

HOW CAN WE OVERRIDE A "DEFAULT" BIAS PROGRAM IN THE BRAIN?

✓ Focus on valuing and appreciating the positive aspects of your life.

✓ Practice mindfulness. Be mindful of what is and isn't important to you.

✓ Break the pattern of negative reactions.

✓ Allow positive experiences to deeply register in your consciousness.

✓ Create a portfolio of positive emotions.

✓ Engage in uplifting conversation with others.

Before you quit trying, practice these few tips to overwrite the default negative coding in your brain.

New habits, reactions, and emotions can be formed. Nothing can stand between you and your resolve to be a better young adult gunning for a life worth living.

In this final chapter, you've learned the positive and negative sides of emotions. Both are important; you simply need to have fewer negative emotions. You need more positive emotions. And this comes with lots of benefits, as you've learned here.

What positive emotions will you like to cultivate?

How often do you need to practice cultivating that emotion?

If faced with challenges while cultivating this positive emotion, what will you do?

FINAL NOTE

I'm glad you stuck through to the end of this adventure. But this is how far we can go together, for now.

This is just the end of a phase of this journey. It's the beginning of a new phase of adventure for you, dear reader. You've learned so much and experienced a lot of mind shifts in the course of this adventure; now it's time to experience much more.

It's time for applications. It's time to practice those new models I shared with you in this book, acquire new skills in DBT, and go on to live a happy and fulfilling life.

Let me remind you of a few important points.

✓ DBT isn't just for adults; preteens and adolescents, including you, can benefit greatly from it as well.

✓ DBT isn't a quick-fix scheme. It's a therapeutic program that could serve as a life tool. You could take it anywhere because emotions can be expressed anywhere, at any time.

✓ You begin to experience transformation when you accept your reality. Don't deny the fact that you have a behavioral disorder that has cost you a lot. In DBT, change only begins to occur after acceptance.

✓ ADHD is a disorder that can be corrected. It's not a hopeless situation. Don't conclude on your situation based on the intensity of your negative emotions. DBT skills offer you a way out.

✓ You can choose to re-order this behavioral disorder through DBT skills.

✓ Mindfulness is a DBT skill that helps to free your mind of the anxiety of the past and fear of the future to begin to live in the moment.

✓ Detailed appreciation for life and everything that makes your life worth living is a crucial practice that makes you mindful of the present moment.

✓ You're unique. Your situation is peculiar to you. There's a unique DBT skill for you. Find it and start practicing it. You're not meant to practice all the skills. Discover the one that suits you and your situation. Then start applying and practicing it.

✓ The best way to get the best from all you've learned in this book is through consistent practice. Don't quit when the results aren't trickling in. Channel your energy into some more practice. While you're at it, you begin to notice your changes in bits.

I'd like to give you this final piece as a gift to light up your path for the next phase of your journey.

The greatest and most positive emotion you can ever express is love. This isn't just that mushy feeling you have for your lover. Although love is many things to different people, it has different definitions and is expressed by different people in different ways.

However, one paramount thing about *love* is that it makes you consider others before you carry out any action or react in certain ways. You'll be careful to act rashly against anyone you love because you won't want to hurt them. Love also makes you a force of light that people will gravitate toward. Love conquers negativism and compels you to commit yourself to becoming a better version of yourself.

In my view, love is the foundation of all positive emotions. Cultivate a life of love, and you're headed towards a peaceful and happy life.

Keep living right. I'm rooting for you!

If this book has helped you or someone you recommended it to, I look forward to hearing from you. Leave a note for me on Amazon.

Cheers!

GET THIS EXCLUSIVE

5-minute Audio Guided Meditation

*To help safely **MANAGE YOUR TEEN'S** sudden emotional meltdown.*

and more mindfulness resources...

JOURNALS & SELF-CARE PLANERS

COLORING BOOKS

SCAN QR CODE TO GET YOUR COPY

MESSAGE FROM THE AUTHOR

I truly hope you found this book enjoyable and gained valuable insights from its contents.

If you could spare a moment to share your honest feedback or leave a star-rating on Amazon, I would greatly appreciate it.

(Rating only takes a few clicks).

Your review can guide other young adults to explore this book and potentially aid them on their personal journeys. Plus, it might just bring some good karma your way.

SCAN QR CODE TO GET YOUR COPY

DBT - ANGER MANAGEMENT & MINDFULNESS
REFERENCES

Ambrose. (2022, June 1). No one heals himself by wounding another [Quote]. Wisdom Quotes. https://wisdomquotes.com/anger-quotes/

American Psychology Association. (n.d.) Anger. https://www.apa.org/topics/anger#:~:text=Anger%20is%20an%20emotion%20characterized

American Psychology Association. (2011). Strategies for controlling your anger: Keeping anger in check. https://www.apa.org/topics/anger/strategies-controlling

Andrews, M. (n.d.). 10 types of anger: What's your anger style? Life Supports. https://lifesupportscounselling.com.au/resources/blogs/10-types-of-anger-what-s-your-anger-style/

Anwar, B. (2022, April 27). 4 DBT therapy techniques. Talkspace. https://www.talkspace.com/blog/dbt-therapy-techniques/

Attai, K. (2020, December 1). DBT: The emotional mind, the rational mind, and the wise mind. Living Well Counseling Services. https://livingwellcounselling.ca/dbt-emotional-mind-rational-mind-wise-mind/

Babauta, L. (n.d.). Learn to respond, not react. Zen Habits. https://zenhabits.net/respond/

Bajori, A. (2019, April 20). 8 types of anger: What they mean and what to do about them. Verv. https://verv.com/8-types-of-anger/

Balancing emotional urges. (n.d.). Dialectical Behavior Therapy. https://dialecticalbehaviortherapy.com/emotion-regulation/balancing-emotional-urges/

ABelcher, M. (2016, January 13). DBT skills: Moving through shame. Sunrise Residential Treatment Center. https://sunrisertc.com/dbt-skills-moving-through-shame/

BetterHelp Editorial Team. (2022, December 8). An overview of anger as an emotion. BetterHelp. https://www.betterhelp.com/advice/anger/what-is-anger-definition-psychology-behind-this-emotion/

Brach, T. (2019, February 7). Feeling overwhelmed? Remember RAIN. Mindful. https://www.mindful.org/tara-brach-rain-mindfulness-practice/

Bray, S. (2012, September 24). Managing your emotions through dialectical behavior therapy. GoodTherapy. https://www.goodtherapy.org/blog/managing-emotions-through-dialectical-behavior-therapy-0924124

Buddha. (n.d.-a). Holding on to anger is like grasping a hot coal with the intent of throwing it on someone else; you are the one who gets burned [Quote]. OutofStress. https://www.outofstress.com/calming-quotes-for-anger/

Buddha. (n.d.-b). Words have the power to both destroy and heal [Quote]. Tumblr. https://inspiredbywisdom.tumblr.com/post/181916778092/words-have-the-power-to-both-destroy-and-heal

Butler, L. (n.d.). 4 steps from DBT that can boost your self esteem. Bay Area Mental Health. https://support.bayareamentalhealth.com/kb/en/article/4-steps-from-dbt-that-can-boost-your-self-esteem

Camacho, N. A. (2021, December 23). Reacting and responding are different—And experts say one is much better for relationship health. Well+Good. https://www.wellandgood.com/reacting-versus-responding/

Cherry, K. (2022, September 2). Benefits of mindfulness. Verywell Mind. https://www.verywellmind.com/the-benefits-of-mindfulness-5205137

Cheung, L. (n.d.). Mindfully recognizing being overwhelmed already reduces the feeling of being overwhelmed [Pin]. Pinterest. https://za.pinterest.com/pin/327355466639072069/

Clear Concept. (2020, November 16). What does it mean to respond instead of react? Clear Concept Inc. https://clearconceptinc.ca/what-does-it-mean-to-respond-instead-of-react/

Cleveland Clinic. (n.d.). Dialectical behavior therapy (DBT). https://my.clevelandclinic.org/health/treatments/22838-dialectical-behavior-therapy-dbt

The costs and pay-offs of anger. (n.d.). Mainstream Corporate Training. https://mainstreamcorporatetraining.com/the-costs-and-pay-offs-of-anger/

The cycle of anger. (n.d.). The Wellness Corner. https://www.thewellnesscorner.com/blog/the-cycle-of-anger

Dialectical behaviour therapy (DBT). (n.d.). Centre for Addiction and Mental Health. https://www.camh.ca/en/health-info/mental-illness-and-addiction-index/dialectical-behaviour-therapy

Distract with wise mind ACCEPTS. (n.d.). DBT Self-Help. https://dbtselfhelp.com/dbt-skills-list/distress-tolerance/accepts/

Dorter, G. (n.d.). DBT Skills: Wise mind, emotional mind and reasonable mind. Greg Dorter Counselling and Therapy. https://www.guelphtherapist.ca/blog/dbt-skills-wise-mind-emotional-mind-and-reasonable-mind/

Do you recognize the 10 types of anger? (n.d.). Montreal CBT Psychologist. https://www.montrealcbtpsychologist.com/blog/122622-do-you-recognize-the-10-types-of-anger_8

Eddins, R. (2020, April 1). Grounding techniques & Self soothing for emotional regulation. Eddins Counseling Group. https://eddinscounseling.com/grounding-techniques-self-soothing-emotional-regulation/

8 ways to deal with anger. (n.d.). ReachOut. https://au.reachout.com/articles/8-ways-to-deal-with-anger

Elliott, C. H., Smith, L. L., & Gentry, W. D. (2016, March 26). The costs and benefits of your anger. Dummies. https://www.dummies.com/article/body-mind-spirit/emotional-health-psychology/emotional-health/anger-management/the-costs-and-benefits-of-your-anger-141936/

Greene, P. (2020, August 3). The DBT STOP skill: How to not make a bad situation worse. Manhattan Center for Cognitive Behavioral Therapy. https://www.manhattancbt.com/archives/1723/dbt-stop-skill/

Holland, K. (2019, January 29). How to control anger: 25 tips to help you stay calm. Healthline. https://www.healthline.com/health/mental-health/how-to-control-anger

Holmes, O. W. (n.d.). The great thing in this world is not so much where you stand as what direction you are moving [Quote]. Landmark Recovery. https://landmarkrecovery.com/addiction-recovery-quotes/

Imagine Boise. (2022, March 11). How can DBT help my teen? Imagine Boise. https://www.boiseimagine.com/mental-health-blog/how-can-dbt-help-my-teen/

Kriegler, S. (2020, December 1). Dialectical behaviour therapy: Reasonable mind, emotion mind & wise mind. Dr Susan Kriegler. https://www.susankriegler.com/post/cbt-reasonable-mind-emotion-mind-wise-mind

Lifford, T. (n.d.). When you know yourself you are empowered. When you accept yourself you are invincible [Quote]. Quotesgram. https://quotesgram.com/you-know-who-you-are-quotes/

Linehan, M. (n.d.). STOP skill. DBT Tools. https://dbt.tools/emotional_regulation/stop.php

Mind. (2018, July). How to manage angry outbursts. https://www.mind.org.uk/information-support/types-of-mental-health-problems/anger/managing-outbursts/

Mind. (2020, December). Dialectical behaviour therapy. https://www.mind.org.uk/information-support/drugs-and-treatments/talking-therap y-and-counselling/dialectical-behaviour-therapy-dbt/

mindfulness. (n.d.). Opposite to emotion Action: A DBT skill to reduce problem behaviors. Mindfulness Therapy Associates. https://mindfulnesstherapy.org/opposite-to-emotion-action/

Mitts, C. (2018, February 5). Understanding anger triggers. Ipseity Counseling Clinic. https://ipseitycounselingclinic.com/2018/02/05/understanding-anger-triggers/

Moore, M. (2022, July 7). 4 DBT skills for everyday challenges. Psych Central. https://psychcentral.com/health/dbt-skills-therapy-techniques

Nelson, S. (2021, June 18). 8 ways to help maintain emotional balance. Rest Less. https://restless.co.uk/health/healthy-mind/8-ways-to-help-maintain-emotional-balance/

Newport Academy. (2022, June 24). What is DBT for teens and how does it work? https://www.newportacademy.com/resources/mental-health/what-is-dbt/#:~:text= DBT%20teaches%20teens%20how%20choosing

O'Brien, M. (n.d.). R.A.I.N: A four-step process for using mindfulness in difficult times. Melli O'Brien. https://melliobrien.com/r-n-four-step-process-using-mindfulness-difficult-times/

Ohwovoriole, T. (2021, May 28). What is anger? Verywell Mind. https://www.verywellmind.com/what-is-anger-5120208

Out of Home Care Toolbox. (n.d.). Understand and recognise triggers. https://www.oohctoolbox.org.au/understand-and-recognise-triggers

Peterson, T. J. (2022, November 25). Meditation for anger: How it works & tips for getting started. Choosing Therapy. https://www.choosingtherapy.com/meditation-for-anger/

Physiology of anger. (n.d.). MentalHelp.net. https://www.mentalhelp.net/anger/physiology/

Pickford, M. (n.d.). The past cannot be changed. The future is yet in your power [Quote]. Goodreads. https://www.goodreads.com/quotes/44866-the-past-cannot-be-changed-the-future -is-yet-in

Pieper, J. (2022, November 24). DBT for teens: How it works, examples & effectiveness. Choosing Therapy. https://www.choosingtherapy.com/dbt-for-teens/

Promises Behavioral Health. (2022, August 22). Physical signs of anger. https://www.promises.com/addiction-blog/physical-signs-of-anger/

Radical acceptance & turning the mind. (n.d.). DBT Self-Help.
https://dbtselfhelp.com/dbt-skills-list/distress-tolerance/radical-acceptance/

Raypole, C. (2020, April 28). How to become the boss of your emotions.
Healthline. https://www.healthline.com/health/how-to-control-your-emotions

Recognizing anger signs. (n.d.). MentalHelp.net.
https://www.mentalhelp.net/anger/recognizing-signs/

Rista, M. (2021, February 20). Mindfulness of current emotions. The Behavioral
Therapy Collective.
https://thebehavioraltherapycollective.com/blog/2021/2/20/mindfulness-of-current-
emotions

Schenck, L. K. (n.d.). What is "wise mind?" Mindfulness Muse.
https://www.mindfulnessmuse.com/dialectical-behavior-therapy/what-is-wise-mind

Shenoy, S. (2018, June 1). How to find balance when you're emotionally triggered.
The Dream Catcher.
https://thedreamcatch.com/find-balance-when-youre-emotionally-triggered/

A simple formula for responding not reacting. (n.d.). The Growth Equation.
https://thegrowtheq.com/a-simple-formula-for-responding-not-reacting/#:~:text=R
eacting%20is%20quick

Skedel, R. (2022, November 28). 12 types of anger. Choosing Therapy.
https://www.choosingtherapy.com/types-of-anger/

Skyland Trail. (2019, October 28). Accepting reality using DBT skills.
https://www.skylandtrail.org/accepting-reality-using-dbt-skills/

Sukel, K. (2018, March 13). Beyond emotion: Understanding the amygdala's role in
memory. Dana Foundation.
https://dana.org/article/beyond-emotion-understanding-the-amygdalas-role-in-mem
ory/#:~:text=The%20amygdalae%2C%20a%20pair%20of

Sullivan, K. (2018, November 28). Mindfulness of current emotion. Accessible
DBT. https://accessibledbt.com/mindfulness-of-current-emotion/

sunriserTC. (2017a, August 18). DBT interpersonal effectiveness skills: The guide
to healthy relationships. Sunrise Residential Treatment Center.
https://sunrisertc.com/interpersonal-effectiveness/

sunriserTC. (2017b, September 13). DBT Distress tolerance skills: Your 6-skill
guide to navigate emotional crises. Sunrise Residential Treatment Center.
https://sunrisertc.com/distress-tolerance-skills/

Tayloe, D. (2022, April 26). 7 ways to unlearn bad habits that harm mental health.
Power of Positivity.
https://www.powerofpositivity.com/unlearn-bad-habits-that-harm-mental-health/

Tolle, E. (n.d.). Where there is anger, there is always pain underneath [Quote]. Quotefancy. https://quotefancy.com/anger-quotes

Vassar, G. (2011, March 1). Do you know your anger triggers? Lakeside. https://lakesidelink.com/blog/do-you-know-your-anger-triggers/

What is anger? (n.d.). Mentalhelp.net. https://www.mentalhelp.net/anger/what-is-it/
What is radical acceptance in DBT? (2021, September 29). Cyti Clinics. https://cyticlinics.com/what-is-radical-acceptance-in-dbt/

Winona State University. (2016, November 21). Grounding. https://www.winona.edu/resilience/Media/Grounding-Worksheet.pdf

IMAGE REFERENCES

Andrea Cassani. (2022, May 20). [Red image of woman grimacing] [Image]. Unsplash. https://unsplash.com/photos/0eekd4benvc

Andres Siimon. (2020, September 18). Man with magnifying glass [Image]. Unsplash. https://unsplash.com/photos/Oe3JidQ9UvU

Ása Steinarsdóttir. (2021, March 31). Erupting volcano in Iceland [Image]. Unsplash. https://unsplash.com/photos/_xmAPHUXXiU

Barry Weatherall. (2019, August 14). Waiting for the big show... [Image]. Unsplash. https://unsplash.com/photos/Hm_iFim94bw

Benjamin Wedemeyer. (2021, April 19). A young artist paints his dreams in his own world [Image]. Unsplash. https://unsplash.com/photos/hicQxC0SyVc

Ethan Rheams. (2018, August 28). [Trees beside body of water] [Image]. Unsplash. https://unsplash.com/photos/sSOYcNt3R54

Giulia Bertelli. (2016, May 20). Crossed hands [Image]. Unsplash. https://unsplash.com/photos/dvXGnwnYweM

Joshua Hoehne. (2019, November 1). [Selective photography of stop signage] [Image]. Unsplash. https://unsplash.com/photos/WPrTKRw8KRQ

Kelly Sikkema. (2020, January 16). Man handing a woman a heart shape [Image]. Unsplash. https://unsplash.com/photos/XX2WTbLr3r8

Lina Trochez. (2017, September 14). Brindar siempre lo mejor de ti [Image]. Unsplash. https://unsplash.com/photos/ktPKyUs3Qjs

Liz Weddon. (2018, March 16). [Gray empty locker room] [Image]. Unsplash. https://unsplash.com/photos/XrYS3pjzHhU

Markus Winkler. (2020, June 7). [Black flatscreen TV turned onto yellow emoji] [Image]. Unsplash. https://unsplash.com/photos/wpOa2i3MUrY

Michal Matlon. (2021, February 21). [White sheep on white surface] [Image]. Unsplash. https://unsplash.com/photos/4ApmfdVo32Q

Miguel Bandeira. (2020, November 1). [Persons hand on body of water] [Image]. Unsplash. https://unsplash.com/photos/6vHGBZ2A5Rc

Mike Enerio. (2016, April 28). [Ariel view of grass] [Image]. Unsplash. https://unsplash.com/photos/H58bnmnedTc

Natasha Connel. (2019, August 24). [Brain figurine] [Image]. Unsplash. https://unsplash.com/photos/byp5TTxUbL0

Sergei Wing. (2020, June 9). Lake in a volcano crater at the Azores islands [Image]. Unsplash. https://unsplash.com/photos/ZqZfY4IFqRl

Sydney Rae. (2017, October 10). [Brown dried leaves on sand]. [Image]. Unsplash. https://unsplash.com/photos/geM5lzDj4lw

Tingey Injury Law Firm. (2020, May 15). Lady Justice [Image]. Unsplash. https://unsplash.com/photos/L4YGuSg0fxs

Volkan Olmez. (2014, April 13). Female head from behind [Image]. Unsplash. https://unsplash.com/photos/wESKMSgZJDo

REFERENCES

Ackerman, C. (2017, January 18). *22 mindfulness exercises, techniques & activities for adults (+ PDF's)*. PositivePsychology.com. https://positivepsychology.com/mindfulness-exercises-techniques-activities/

Ackerman, C. E. (2019, July 10). *23 amazing health benefits of mindfulness for body and brain*. PositivePsychology.com. https://positivepsychology.com/benefits-of-mindfulness/

Behavioral Tech. (2016, September 1). *DBT's approach to treating individuals at high risk for suicide – behavioral tech*. Behavioral Tech. https://behavioraltech.org/dbt-approach-treating-individuals-high-risk-suicide/

Bray, S. (2013a, January 17). *Distress tolerance in dialectical behavior therapy*. GoodTherapy.org Therapy Blog. https://www.goodtherapy.org/blog/distress-tolerance-dialectical-behavior-therapy-0117134

Bray, S. (2013b, March 18). *Emotion regulation in dialectical behavior therapy*. GoodTherapy.org Therapy Blog. https://www.goodtherapy.org/blog/emotion-regulation-dialectical-behavior-therapy-dbt-0318135

Chapman, A. L. (2006). Dialectical behavior therapy: current indications and unique elements. *Psychiatry (Edgmont), 3*(9), 62–68. https://www.ncbi.nlm.nih.gov/pmc/articles/PMC2963469/

Cleveland Clinic. (2022, April 19). *Dialectical behavior therapy (DBT): what it is & purpose*. Cleveland Clinic. https://my.clevelandclinic.org/health/treatments/22838-dialectical-behavior-therapy-dbt

Davis, D. M., & Hayes, J. A. (2012, July). What are the benefits of mindfulness? *Https://Www.apa.org*. https://www.apa.org/monitor/2012/07-08/ce-corner

DBT distress tolerance skills (Worksheet). (n.d.). Therapist Aid. https://www.therapistaid.com/therapy-worksheet/dbt-distress-tolerance-skills

DBT emotion regulation skills (Worksheet). (n.d.). Therapist Aid. https://www.therapistaid.com/therapy-worksheet/dbt-emotion-regulation-skills

DBT skill: DEAR MAN (Worksheet). (n.d.). Therapist Aid. https://www.therapistaid.com/therapy-worksheet/dbt-dear-man

DBT tip: how can I skillfully maintain important relationships? (2022).
Eastbaybehaviortherapycenter. https://eastbaybehaviortherapycenter.com/dbt-tip-how-can-i-skillfully-maintain-important-relationships/

DeCaria, M. (2022, March 4). Part one: dovetailing emotional intelligence and dialectical behavior therapy (DBT). On Becoming a Person.
https://onbecomingaperson.com/2022/03/04/part-one-dovetailing-emotional-intelligence-and-dialectical-behavior-therapy-dbt/

Dialectical behavior therapy. (2018). Goodtherapy.org.
https://www.goodtherapy.org/learn-about-therapy/types/dialectical-behavioral-therapy

Dialectical behaviour therapy (DBT). (2021). Www.mind.org.uk.
https://www.mind.org.uk/information-support/drugs-and-treatments/talking-therapy-and-counselling/dialectical-behaviour-therapy-dbt/

Dialectical behavioural therapy. (2017). CAMH. https://www.camh.ca/en/health-info/mental-illness-and-addiction-index/dialectical-behaviour-therapy

4 DBT problem-solving options you can use to solve any problem. (2017, January 19). Bay Area DBT & Couples Counseling Center.
https://bayareadbtcc.com/dbt-problem-solving-options/

Gatewell Therapy Center. (2020, September 17). Wise mind: a balanced synthesis.
Gatewell Therapy Center | Miami FL.
https://gatewelltherapycenter.com/2020/09/17/wise-mind/

Gottlieb, A. (2018, January 17). DBT 101: what is mindfulness? Sheppard Pratt.
https://www.sheppardpratt.org/news-views/story/dbt-101-what-is-mindfulness/

Konen, J. (n.d.). A teacher's guide to helping students with anxiety. Education Degree.
https://www.educationdegree.com/articles/supporting-students-with-anxiety/

Levy, S. (2022, September). Overview of psychosocial problems in adolescents - Children's Health Issues. MSD Manual Consumer Version.
https://www.msdmanuals.com/home/children-s-health-issues/problems-in-adolescents/overview-of-psychosocial-problems-in-adolescents

Linehan, M. (2022). FAST skill. Dialectical Behavior Therapy (DBT) Tools.
https://dbt.tools/interpersonal_effectiveness/fast.php

Lorandini, J. (2021, August 8). 5 ways to apply DBT mindfulness skills in everyday Life.
Suffolk DBT. https://suffolkdbtjl.com/5-way-to-apply-dbt-mindfulness-skills-in-your-everyday-life/

Mairanz, A. (2019, December 19). *Using DBT skills to manage anxiety.* Www.intrepidmentalhealth.com. https://eymtherapy.com/blog/anxiety-relief-dbt-skills/

Mayo Clinic. (2020a, June 6). *Countdown to make anxiety blast off.* Mayo Clinic Health System. https://www.mayoclinichealthsystem.org/hometown-health/speaking-of-health/5-4-3-2-1-countdown-to-make-anxiety-blast-off

Mayo Clinic. (2020b, September 15). *Mindfulness exercises.* Mayo Clinic; Mayo Clinic. https://www.mayoclinic.org/healthy-lifestyle/consumer-health/in-depth/mindfulness-exercises/art-20046356

Medcalf, A. (2019, January 1). *The truth about setting relationship goals.* Abby Medcalf. https://abbymedcalf.com/the-truth-about-setting-relationship-goals/

Mercy, K. (2019, November 5). *Using DBT skills in addiction recovery.* Sandstone Care. https://www.sandstonecare.com/blog/dialectical-behavioral-therapy-in-drug-alcohol-addiction-recovery

Mindfulness from a DBT perspective. (n.d.). Cognitive Behavioral Therapy Los Angeles. https://cogbtherapy.com/cbt-blog/mindfulness-in-dbt

Motivation check your V.I.T.A.L.S. (n.d.). Dialectical Behavioral Training. https://peerguideddbtlessons.weebly.com/motivation-check-your-vitals.html

Novotney, A. (2019, May). The risks of social isolation. *American Psychological Association.* https://www.apa.org/monitor/2019/05/ce-corner-isolation

Parenting a child with intense emotions using dialectical behavior therapy (DBT) - Mental Help. (2019, March 19). MentalHelp.net. https://www.mentalhelp.net/parenting/dialectical-behavior-therapy-and-emotions

Parenting with DBT: A Series on Effective Parenting Strategies. (2019, May 26). Gatewell Therapy Center. https://gatewelltherapycenter.com/2019/05/26/parenting-dbt-series-effective-parenting-strategies/

Pieper, J. (2022, November 24). *DBT for teens: how it works, examples & effectiveness.* Choosing Therapy. https://www.choosingtherapy.com/dbt-for-teens/

Relationships and community: statistics. (n.d.). Www.mentalhealth.org.uk. https://www.mentalhealth.org.uk/explore-mental-health/statistics/relationships-community-statistics

Robinson, O. J., Vytal, K., Cornwell, B. R., & Grillon, C. (2013). *The impact of anxiety upon cognition: Perspectives from human threat of shock studies.* Frontiers in Human Neuroscience, 7(203). https://doi.org/10.3389/fnhum.2013.00203

Rudlin, K. (2019, October 9). *How therapy can help your teen.* Verywell Mind. https://www.verywellmind.com/choosing-a-therapist-to-help-your-troubled-teen-2610351

Schenck, L. (2011, October 19). *What is "wise mind?".* Mindfulness Muse. https://www.mindfulnessmuse.com/dialectical-behavior-therapy/what-is-wise-mind

Schimelpfening, N. (2022, July 22). *What to know about dialectical behavior therapy.* Verywell Mind. https://www.verywellmind.com/dialectical-behavior-therapy-1067402

Stevens, A. (2020, April 1). *DBT for addiction (dialectical behavior therapy).* The Heights. https://theheightstreatment.com/2020/04/01/dbt-for-addiction-dialectical-behavior-therapy/

Sunrisertc. (2017a, August 18). *DBT interpersonal effectiveness skills: the guide to healthy relationships.* Sunrise Residential Treatment Center. https://sunrisertc.com/interpersonal-effectiveness/

Sunrisertc. (2017b, September 13). *DBT distress tolerance skills: your 6-skill guide to navigate emotional crises.* Sunrise Residential Treatment Center. https://sunrisertc.com/distress-tolerance-skills/

Sunrisertc. (2017c, October 31). *Take control of your emotions using these 5 skills.* Sunrise Residential Treatment Center. https://sunrisertc.com/dbt-emotion-regulation-skills/

Surviving a crisis: dialectical behavior therapy (DBT) distress tolerance skills. (2019, March 13). MentalHelp.net. https://www.mentalhelp.net/dialectical-behavior-therapy/surviving-a-crisis/

Taylor, R. (2011, December 23). *Dialectical behavioral therapy.* WebMD. https://www.webmd.com/mental-health/dialectical-behavioral-therapy

3 quick DBT skills to help regulate anxiety that anyone can use!: Intrepid Mental Wellness, PLLC: Psychiatric Nurse Practitioners. (n.d.). Www.intrepidmentalhealth.com. https://www.intrepidmentalhealth.com/blog/3-quick-dbt-skills-to-help-regulate-anxiety-that-anyone-can-use

Tulane University. (2020, December 8). *Understanding the effects of social isolation on mental health.* Publichealth.tulane.edu; Tulane University. https://publichealth.tulane.edu/blog/effects-of-social-isolation-on-mental-health/

Tull, M. (2013, July 30). *Distress tolerance in post traumatic stress disorder.* Verywell Mind; Verywell Mind. https://www.verywellmind.com/distress-tolerance-2797294

Understanding anxiety | JED. (n.d.). The Jed Foundation.
https://jedfoundation.org/resource/understanding-anxious-feelings/

Using DBT therapy for anxiety: does it work? (2020, December 28). StoneRidge: Center for Brains. https://stoneridgecenters.com/dbt-therapy-for-anxiety/

Whyte, A. (2021, October 29). *DBT the gold standard for treating adolescent self-harm and Suicidal Ideation*. Evolve Treatment Centers.
https://evolvetreatment.com/blog/dbt-teen-self-harm-suicide/

World Health Organization. (2021, November 17). *Adolescent Mental Health*. World Health Organization; world health organization.
https://www.who.int/news-room/fact-sheets/detail/adolescent-mental-health

IMAGE REFERENCES

Askew, M. (2018, April 24). *Four girls in a wheatfield [Image]*. Unsplash.com.
https://unsplash.com/photos/tSlvoSZK77c

Bhutani, V. (2019, July 28). *Girl in yoga boat pose [Image]*. Unsplash.com.
https://unsplash.com/photos/NuFts2Ba4ro

Brown, A. (2016, April 21). *Woman and man talking outside the building [Image]*.
Unsplash.com; Unsplash. https://unsplash.com/photos/-Xv7k95vOFA

Brown, J. (2018, December 11). *Girl smiling in hail storm [Image]*. Unsplash.com.
https://unsplash.com/photos/wm4DuvlpLj8

Campbell, C. (2015, October 14). *Sad looking boy in white t-shirt [Image]*. Unsplash.com.
https://unsplash.com/photos/bNRPWgze3rA

Fernandez, O. (2020, August 24). *Girl in blue shirt holding hand out toward another girl [Image]*. Unsplash.com. https://unsplash.com/photos/0GFNAelMPZA

Ferrero, M. (2017, August 23). *Two happy girls [Image]*. Unsplash.com.
https://unsplash.com/photos/LlaLQ2SIQuk

Han, Y. (2017, April 17). *Stockholm man with headphones [Image]*. Unsplash.com.
https://unsplash.com/photos/lJrleCs3D4g

Jerabkova, K. (2020, June 23). *Girl meditating on wood flower [Image]*. Unsplash.com. https://unsplash.com/photos/6CLBoiWuzSU

Lopes, H. (2017, November 29). *Four friends outside on a sunny day [Image]*. Unsplash.com. https://unsplash.com/photos/e3OUQGT9bWU

Mossholder, T. (2019, September 27). *Friends at the beach [Image]*. Unsplash.com. https://unsplash.com/photos/UvMI5OF3vBc

Reyna, E. (2019, January 31). *Two girls and a guy outside [Image]*. Unsplash.com. https://unsplash.com/photos/5KrZ3UoDKC4

Rice, J. (2017, September 22). *A morning yoga session peering into the jungle in Ubud, Bali.* Unsplash.com. https://unsplash.com/photos/NTyBbu66_SI

Sikkema, K. (2019, February 18). *Man holding his hands and sitting on couch [Image]*. Unsplash.com. https://unsplash.com/photos/f_aHTIof44U

Sims, S. (2018, January 18). *Person holding white printer paper with a drawn smile [Image]*. Unsplash.com; Unsplash. https://unsplash.com/photos/fZ2hMpHIrbI

Singh, Y. (2021, June 1). *Guy screaming with broken glasses [Image]*. Unsplash.com. https://unsplash.com/photos/BxHnbYyNfTg

Tran, T. (2019, March 5). *Girl sitting outside with book over her face [Image]*. Unsplash.com. https://unsplash.com/photos/F8sCVSW4t4E

Vega, K. (2018, December 9). *Girl doing yoga by the sunrise [Image]*. Unsplash.com. https://unsplash.com/photos/F2qh3yjz6Jk

Villasmil, L. (2020, April 9). *Young man covered in sticky notes, work overload [Image]*. Unsplash.com. https://unsplash.com/photos/mlVbMbxfWI4

Wilkinson, S. (2021, May 3). *Mental health key words [Image]*. Unsplash.com. https://unsplash.com/photos/EDJKEXFbzHA

REFERENCES

5 Tips to Improve Your Self-Talk. (n.d.).

> 5 Tips to Improve Your Self-Talk. Retrieved February 2, 2023, from
> https://psychcentral.com/blog/5-tips-to-improve-your-self-talk

A. (2019, July 22).

> *14 Signs of ADHD: Does Your Child Have ADHD? - ADHD Ireland.* ADHD Ireland.
> Retrieved January 27, 2023, from
> https://adhdireland.ie/14-signs-of-adhd-does-your-child-have-adhd/

Ackerman, C. E. (2017, December 29).

> *Interpersonal Effectiveness: 9 Worksheets & Examples (+ PDF).*
> PositivePsychology.com. Retrieved February 7, 2023, from
> https://positivepsychology.com/interpersonal-effectiveness/

Ackerman, C. E. (2019, April 27).

> *What are Positive and Negative Emotions and Do We Need Both?*
> PositivePsychology.com. Retrieved February 7, 2023, from
> https://positivepsychology.com/positive-negative-emotions/

Badcock, P.B., Friston, K.J., & Ramstead, M.J.D. (2019).

> The hierarchically mechanistic mind: A free-energy formulation of the human
> psyche. Physics of Life Reviews. DOI: 10.1016/j.plrev.2018.10.002

Brillante, D. J. (2020, November 18).

> *Dialectical Behavior Therapy (DBT) for Teens Part I: What It Is and What it Helps With -*
> Expert CBT, DBT, and Testing for Children, Adolescents, and Families.
> Retrieved January 27, 2023, from
> https://centerforcbt.org/2020/11/18/dbt-for-teens-part-1/

Cheung, J. C., Chen, E. Y., McCloskey, M. S., (2022, July 1).

> *The effect of dialectical behavior therapy on anger and aggressive behavior: A systematic*
> *review with meta-analysis -* PubMed. PubMed. Retrieved February 2, 2023, from
> https://pubmed.ncbi.nlm.nih.gov/35609374/

Ciesinski, N. K., Sorgi-Wilson, K. M., *Emotion Regulation in Teens with ADHD*
- CHADD. (n.d.).

> CHADD. Retrieved February 2, 2023, from

https://chadd.org/adhd-news/adhd-news-caregivers/emotion-regulation-in-teens-with-adhd/

Compitus, D. K. (2020, October 1).

What Are Distress Tolerance Skills? The Ultimate DBT Toolkit. PositivePsychology.com. Retrieved February 2, 2023, from https://positivepsychology.com/distress-tolerance-skills/

Cuncic, A. (2022, November 14).

What Is Dysregulation? Verywell Mind. Retrieved February 2, 2023, from https://www.verywellmind.com/what-is-dysregulation-5073868

DBT for Attention Deficit Hyperactivity Disorder (ADHD); DBT Center of Marin. (n.d.).

DBT Center of Marin. Retrieved January 27, 2023, from https://dbtmarin.com/dbt-for-attention-deficit-hyperactivity-disorder

DBT Skills Group: Rules and Resources - Psychotherapy Academy. (n.d.).

Psychotherapy Academy. Retrieved January 27, 2023, from https://psychotherapyacademy.org/dbt/starting-a-dbt-skills-group/

DBT: What Is Dialectical Behavior Therapy? - Child Mind Institute. (n.d.).

Child Mind Institute. Retrieved January 27, 2023, from https://childmind.org/article/dbt-dialectical-behavior-therapy/

Dialectical Behavior Therapy: Children and Preadolescents - Child Mind Institute. (n.d.).

Child Mind Institute. Retrieved January 27, 2023, from https://childmind.org/care/areas-of-expertise/mood-disorders-center/dialectical-behavior-therapy-children-and-preadolescents/

Frothingham, S. (2019, December 16).

Do you have a negativity bias? What Is Negativity Bias? Retrieved February 7, 2023, from https://www.healthline.com/health/negativity-bias

Fung, T. T., Long, M. W., Hung, P., & Cheung, L. W. (2016, July).

An Expanded Model for Mindful Eating for Health Promotion and Sustainability: Issues and Challenges for Dietetics Practice. Journal of the Academy of Nutrition and Dietetics, 116(7), 1081–1086. https://doi.org/10.1016/j.jand.2016.03.013

Gordon. (n.d.).

  11 BENEFITS OF BEING POSITIVE. Retrieved February 7, 2023, from
  https://jongordon.com/positive-tip-11-benefits.html#:~:text=The%20research%20
  is%20clear.,It's%20the%20way%20to%20live

Greene, D. P. (2020, July 27).

  DBT: IMPROVE the Moment – How to Make Crises Bearable. Manhattan Center for
  Cognitive Behavioral Therapy. Retrieved February 2, 2023, from
  https://www.manhattancbt.com/archives/1699/dbt-improve-the-moment/

Greene, D. P. (2020, August 3).

  The DBT STOP Skill: How to Not Make a Bad Situation Worse. Manhattan Center for
  Cognitive Behavioral Therapy. Retrieved February 2, 2023, from
  https://www.manhattancbt.com/archives/1723/dbt-stop-skill/

Halmøy, A., Ring, A. E., Gjestad, R., Møller, M., Ubostad, B., Lien, T.,
Munkhaugen, E. K., & Fredriksen, M. (2022, November 28).

  *Dialectical behavioral therapy-based group treatment versus treatment as usual for
  adults with attention-deficit hyperactivity disorder: a multicenter randomized controlled
  trial - BMC Psychiatry*. BioMed Central. Retrieved January 27, 2023, from
  https://bmcpsychiatry.biomedcentral.com/articles/10.1186/s12888-022-04356-6

Hanh TN, Cheung L. Savor (2010)

  Mindful Eating, Mindful Life. HarperCollins Publishers.

History of DBT: Origins and Foundations - Psychotherapy Academy. (n.d.).

  Psychotherapy Academy. Retrieved January 27, 2023, from
  https://psychotherapyacademy.org/dbt/history-of-dialectical-behavioral-therapy-a-
  very-brief-introduction/

  How DBT Helped Me Cope With BPD | Real Stories. (n.d.).

  YoungMinds. Retrieved January 27, 2023, from
  https://www.youngminds.org.uk/young-person/blog/how-dbt-gave-me-freedom-fr
  om-borderline-personality-disorder/

  Interpersonal Effectiveness - DBT Self Help. (n.d.).

  DBT Self Help. Retrieved February 7, 2023, from
  https://dbtselfhelp.com/dbt-skills-list/interpersonal-effectiveness/

  Linehan, M. (n.d.).

  Emotional Regulation Skills - Dialectical Behavior Therapy (DBT) Tools. Dialectical
  Behavior Therapy (DBT) Tools. Retrieved February 2, 2023, from
  https://dbt.tools/emotional_regulation/index.php

Littman, E. (2022, July 11).

How Dysregulated Emotions Hijack the Teen ADHD Brain. ADDitude. Retrieved February 2, 2023, from https://www.additudemag.com/dysregulated-adhd-teens-relationships-social-media-support/

Low, K. (2022, December 22).

ADHD and Anger: How Are They Connected? Verywell Mind. Retrieved February 2, 2023, from https://www.verywellmind.com/understanding-adhd-children-and-anger-20540

Mairanz, A. (2019, December 6).

Interpersonal Effectiveness: Practicing a DBT Skill. DBT Therapist NYC. Empower Your Mind Therapy. Retrieved February 7, 2023, from https://eymtherapy.com/blog/practice-interpersonal-effectiveness-dbt-skill/

Ohwovoriole, T. (2021, May 28).

How to Manage Your Anger. Verywell Mind. Retrieved February 2, 2023, from https://www.verywellmind.com/what-is-anger-5120208

Partington, D. P. (2021, March 19).

Dbt Stories: Mindfulness Practice – Dialectical Behavior Therapy. Retrieved January 27, 2023, from https://dbtforlife.com/2021/03/19/dbt-stories-mindfulness-practice/

Parvez, H. (2022, February 9).

8 Stages of anger in psychology - PsychMechanics. PsychMechanics. Retrieved February 2, 2023, from https://www.psychmechanics.com/stages-of-anger/

Pierper, J. (2020, June 23).

DBT for Teens: How It Works, Examples, & Effectiveness. Retrieved from https://www.choosingtherapy.com/dbt-for-teens/

Positive Emotions and Your Health. (2017, May 4).

NIH News in Health. Retrieved February 7, 2023, from https://newsinhealth.nih.gov/2015/08/positive-emotions-your-health

Rigby, A. (n.d.).

12 Emotional Regulation Skills to Calm Inner Chaos. Retrieved February 2, 2023, from https://www.fingerprintforsuccess.com/blog/emotional-regulation-skills

S. (2021, July 28).

A Beginner's Guide to Distress Tolerance. Sokya Health. Retrieved February 2, 2023, from https://sokyahealthdev.wpengine.com/connection/tipp-a-beginners-guide-to-distress-tolerance/

Saline, S. (2020, February 14).

Q: My Teenage Son's Anger Is Frightening Me — Help! ADDitude. Retrieved

February 2, 2023, from
https://www.additudemag.com/dealing-with-anger-teen-adhd/

Schwartz, B. (2022, September 15).

Self-Soothing: What it is, Benefits, & Techniques to Get Started. Choose Therapy
https://www.choosingtherapy.com/self-soothing/

Stanborough, R. J. (2021, March 30).

ADHD and Anger: How They Are Connected. ADHD and Anger: How They Are
Connected. Retrieved February 2, 2023, from
https://www.healthline.com/health/adhd/adhd-and-anger

*The importance of positive emotions for performance optimization, mental health, and
strong relationships.* (2021, September 27).

HPRC. Retrieved February 7, 2023, from
https://www.hprc-online.org/social-fitness/relationship-building/importance-positi
ve-emotions-performance-optimization-mental

Turner, M. (2022, October 19).

ADHD & Anger: Connection & Treatments. Choosing Therapy.
https://www.choosingtherapy.com/adhd-anger/

Understanding Your Emotions (for Teens) - Nemours KidsHealth. (n.d.).

Understanding Your Emotions (for Teens) - Nemours KidsHealth. Retrieved
February 2, 2023, from https://kidshealth.org/en/teens/understand-emotions.html

Vivyan, C. (2015).

Interpersonal Effectiveness. Get.gg - Getselfhelp.co.uk. Retrieved February 7, 2023,
from https://www.getselfhelp.co.uk/interpersonal-effectiveness/

W. (2016, April 1).

The power of positive emotions - Stanford BeWell. Stanford BeWell. Retrieved
February 7, 2023, from
https://bewell.stanford.edu/the-power-of-positive-emotions/

Wexelblatt, R. (2020, December 29).

Q: My ADHD Teen Reacts Aggressively to Limits! ADDitude. Retrieved February 2,
2023, from
https://www.additudemag.com/anger-issues-teens-adhd-contain-behavior/

Smith, A. (2022, October 31).

DBT Success Stories; My Dialectical Life. DBT Success Stories; My Dialectical Life.
Retrieved January 27, 2023, from
https://www.mydialecticallife.com/dbt-success-stories

OTHER SOURCES

https://childmind.org/article/how-hannah-got-happy/

https://www.goodreads.com/quotes/tag/interpersonal-skills

https://www.goodreads.com/quotes/tag/positive-emotions

https://www.theminiadhdcoach.com/blog/adhd-teenager

https://www.chop.edu/stories/adhd-and-emotional-control-theos-story

https://www.goodreads.com/quotes/tag/distress

https://www.goodreads.com/quotes/tag/emotional-regulation

https://www.goodreads.com/quotes/tag/anger

https://newroadstreatment.org/annies-story-a-healing-journey-with-dbt/

https://www.therecoveryvillage.com/mental-health/stress/stress-statistics/#:~:text=America
n%20Institute%20of%20Stress%20Statistics&text=About%2033%20percent%20of%20people
,trouble%20sleeping%20because%20of%20stress

https://www.singlecare.com/blog/news/stress-statistics/

https://www.hopetherapyandwellness.com/blog/157559-what-is-mindfulness-and-how-does-
it-help-with-dbt

https://positivepsychology.com/mindfulness-quotes/

https://www.goodreads.com/quotes/tag/dbt#:~:text=Dialectical%20behavior%20therapy%20
depends%20on,%2C%20not%20acceptance%20or%20change.%E2%80%9D&text=%E2%80%
9CKeeping%20a%20stiff%20upper%20lip,does%20hurt%20to%20be%20invalidated.%E2%80
%9D

https://www.hopeforbpd.com/borderline-personality-disorder-treatment/quotes-about-dbt

https://researchoutreach.org/articles/explaining-mind-works-new-theory/#:~:text=Human%
20thoughts%2C%20feelings%2C%20and%20behaviours,and%20our%20relationships%20wit
h%20it.

https://www.hsph.harvard.edu/nutritionsource/mindful-eating/#:~:text=Mindful%20eating%2
0focuses%20on%20your,your%20responses%20to%20those%20cues.%20%5B

https://mindowl.org/the-purpose-of-mindfulness/

https://www.edgewoodhealthnetwork.com/resources/blog/the-seven-pillars-of-mindfulness/

https://calmind.com/what-is-the-purpose-of-mindfulness/

https://bmcpsychiatry.biomedcentral.com/articles/10.1186/s12888-022-04356-6#:~:text=In%
20line%20with%20this%2C%20a,ended%20group%20treatment%20%5B50%5D.

www.ingramcontent.com/pod-product-compliance
Lightning Source LLC
Chambersburg PA
CBHW051258120626
46547CB00015B/1989